RETURNING HOME

About the author

 Bernard Kelly is a Postdoctoral Research Fellow at the University of Edinburgh. Born in Dublin, he went to college at NUI Galway and the University of Edinburgh. He is working on a project with the Scottish Centre for Diaspora Studies.

RETURNING HOME

Irish Ex-Servicemen
after the Second
World War

BERNARD KELLY

MERRION

Dublin • Portland, Oregon

First published in 2012 by Merrion

an imprint of Irish Academic Press

2 Brookside	920 NE 58th Avenue, Suite 300
Dundrum Road,	Portland, Oregon,
Dublin 14, Ireland	97213-3786 USA

© 2012 Bernard Kelly

British Library Cataloguing in Publication Data
An entry can be found on request

ISBN 978-1-908928-04-7 (cloth)
ISBN 978-1-908928-00-9 (paper)

Library of Congress Cataloging-in-Publication Data
An entry can be found on request

Typeset by FiSH Books, Enfield, Middx.
Printed and bound by CPI Group (UK) Ltd, Croydon, CR0 4YY

Contents

Acknowledgements

Writing a book invariably means building up debts of gratitude which are impossible ever to repay. First and foremost, I would like to thank the men and women who kindly allowed me into their homes to interview them. Thanks are also due to the British Legion and Organisation of National Ex-Servicemen for providing lists of veterans to interview. I want to express my appreciation to Dr. John Cunningham for his continued assistance, Dr. Mel Sayers for reading over the manuscript, and to Professor Geoffrey Roberts for allowing me access to the Volunteers Archive at University College Cork. To Des Kenny go thanks for allowing me to turn his bookshop into an unofficial library, and to Tomás Kenny, whose knowledge, enthusiasm and occasional criticisms were invaluable. I am grateful for the assistance of my colleague Yvonne McEwan, who has allowed me access to her unpublished research. The Kelly and Brennan families also provided much-needed and much-appreciated help and assistance. To my wife Monica – without whose patience, tolerance and support none of this would be possible – I owe everything.

List of Illustrations

Introduction

My interest in the life of Irish ex-servicemen began when I heard the stories of two very different men who fought on opposite sides in the Second World War. One was an Irish recruit into the Royal Engineers; the other was a Luftwaffe technician. The first is Richard, who came from a large Catholic family in Belfast and joined the British army before war broke out. Recruitment into the British forces was always high in inner-city Belfast and, as part of the UK, Northern Ireland was expected to provide its fair share of recruits for the Crown forces. Richard fought his way through North Africa and was eventually transferred to Greece after the German surrender. While on guard duty one night, Richard opened fire and killed an intruder trying to break into his unit's camp. Upon discovering that the thief was actually a young Greek boy, Richard suffered a nervous breakdown and was invalided home to Belfast, where he remained in a psychiatric hospital for many years. He eventually moved home to his family and was awarded an army pension for the rest of his life.

The second man is Erich from Berlin, who joined the Luftwaffe as an engineer in 1935. Having fought in Italy and North Africa, his war ended when he was captured by the Red Army in Berlin in 1945. He spent three years in a POW camp near Moscow, before he was released in 1948. Erich returned to a city and a country which lay in ruins. Berlin had been reduced to rubble; first by heavy Allied bombing, and then again during the fighting in April – May 1945, when Soviet forces overran the capital. Like many Germans, his family life was fractured by the Cold War. When the division of Germany into east and west solidified in the 1950s, he was separated from members of his mother's family, who were now living in East Germany.

The paths of these two men diverged dramatically after the war. Richard, suffering the consequences of his tragic situation, had his medical care paid for and lived on an army pension for the rest of his days. Erich also underwent deeply traumatic experiences, but had no treatment afterwards; instead he spent years in a Soviet camp, saw his home taken away, his country divided and had to begin over again in a nation which had been destroyed. The basic difference between the two was that Richard returned to a country which had been victorious in the war, while Erich returned to one which had been totally defeated. War is forever divided into those who win and those who lose, and Richard and Erich's tales mirrored millions of others right across the world in 1945. But the stories of these two men raise an interesting question: what happened to those who took part in the Second World War, but then returned home to a country which had been neutral?

Precisely this situation faced thousands of Irish men and women once the war ended in 1945. It is estimated that 60,000 men and women from the twenty-six counties of independent Ireland joined the British armed forces between 1939 and 1945, despite the country being neutral in the war. Of these, somewhere in the region of 9,000 were killed and the majority of the survivors decided to remain in Britain after the war. However, British government sources at the time suggested that around 12,000 of these veterans elected to return to independent Ireland in 1945.[1] This book details their experiences once they did so.

Irish veterans of the Second World War found themselves slipping through the cracks between two extremes if they opted to return to Ireland after the war. Although they were the victors, once they crossed the Irish Sea they were cut off from the benefits and concessions put in place by a grateful British government for its servicemen and women. Irish ex-servicemen could not claim British unemployment benefits until 1947 and had limited access to subsidised medical care. What must have been particularly galling was the fact that their comrades who came back to Northern Ireland were first in the queue for jobs and housing, while those in Eire had to compete with men from the Irish Defence Forces in a limited employment market.

The Irish government was not eager to take responsibility for Irish war veterans. Dublin had already committed to taking care of ex-members of the Irish forces and put in place a wide-ranging system of concessions, offering sizable gratuities, jobs and, in some cases, access to houses. At the same time, the Fianna Fáil government, led by Eamon de Valera, was not overtly hostile towards ex-servicemen either. Although there were some who were suspicious of veterans, and particularly their organisations, there is no evidence that the government discriminated or targeted Irish ex-servicemen in any way. In fact, the archives suggest precisely the opposite: they gave them very little thought indeed. The only time they truly engaged with them was when ex-servicemen and government policy intersected, such as the public displaying of British symbols during commemoration services, wearing of British uniforms or deserters from the Irish forces. Certainly, de Valera and his colleagues did not accept responsibility for the veterans, but at the same time they did not actively single them out either.

The attitude of the Fianna Fáil government towards Irish ex-servicemen from 1945 onwards was rooted in two main factors. The first was how the Cumann na nGaedheal government had dealt with Irish veterans of the First World War. W.T. Cosgrave and his party had governed Ireland in the first decade of independence, from 1922 to 1932, after which it was ousted by Fianna Fáil. When the Irish Free State was founded in 1922, there were many thousands of Irish ex-servicemen in the country, veterans of the First World War who had come home and been caught up in the maelstrom of rebellion and civil war from 1919 to 1923. Leading a country which was deeply divided, Cosgrave trod warily between republicans and ex-servicemen. He refused to attend Armistice ceremonies (although he sporadically sent representatives to them), and shunted veteran's parades from Dublin city centre to Island-bridge, but on the other hand, resisted all calls to ban or suppress them. The restrictions which Cumann na nGaedheal placed on ex-service ceremonies, such as the ban on the use of military commands and the flying of British flags, were largely continued by Fianna Fáil in 1932 and after the war ended in 1945. For instance, the prohibition on the flying of British flags was continued right through from 1923 to 1948. Both Cosgrave and de Valera were leaders content to tolerate Irish veterans, while not attempting to engage with them publicly. The continuity of policy was also helped by the fact that the majority of civil servants had remained in place since the 1920s, assisting both Cosgrave and de Valera. As in the 1920s, ex-servicemen were expected to remain in the background. Even when they came to the government's notice, the reaction was fragmentary and ad-hoc. Issues such as the wearing of uniforms and the problem of Irish army deserters were addressed in 1945 using Emergency Powers orders, rather than ordinary legislation.

The second factor which conditioned de Valera's reaction to Irish ex-servicemen was Irish neutrality during the war. Although there was much secret and unofficial cooperation between the two countries, the public face of neutrality still had to be upheld. This meant that Dublin clamped down on the wearing of British uniforms in Ireland during and after the war. Irish ex-servicemen were affected by this, as many came home in uniform on leave, or kept their coats and boots once they were demobbed. Neutrality also meant that deserters from the Irish army would be on the government's radar once the war ended. An estimated 6,000 left their posts during the conflict, the majority of which went to the UK either to join the Crown forces or to work in the booming British war industries. There was simply no way that they were likely to escape unpunished; allowing thousands of the Defence Forces to don the uniform of a belligerent would have made a mockery of Irish claims to be non-aligned in the war.

But just because there was no government-inspired campaign against ex-servicemen does not conceal the fact that many had a difficult time once they returned home after the war. They had difficulty finding jobs; the Irish economy had suffered during the war and they had to compete against ex-members of the Irish forces. Even for those who returned to employment, there was the problem of the mental and physical scars from their service, which hampered their reintegration into civilian life. In addition, they faced a wall of apathy and indifference from the Irish public who viewed the war very differently than the veterans. By 1945,

Irish neutrality during the war had been firmly linked to partition, and the Irish tended to see the war through the prism of Irish history. Ex-servicemen were also sidelined because they unwittingly contradicted the version of Irish history which Fianna Fáil was eager to present. The enormous Easter Rising commemoration in 1941 illustrated the story which Fianna Fáil wanted to tell, but Irish veterans were not part of it. As we have seen above, deserters formed a specific sub-set of returnees who had more to fear than other ordinary veterans and many were anxious about their fate if they came back to Ireland. But there was one thing for which Irish ex-servicemen could be thankful: whereas Irish survivors of the First World War were often harassed, intimidated, assaulted and killed by the republican movement, veterans of the Second World War faced no such problems. Their difficulties after 1945 were of a far more safe and practical nature.

Ireland was the only neutral country in Europe to face the problem of a potential flood of returning war veterans in 1945. During the conflict, neutrals such as Belgium, Holland, Luxembourg, Norway, Yugoslavia and Greece were all invaded and overrun by Germany, while the Baltic States and Finland were attacked by Moscow (in Finland's case, pushing it into the German orbit). Fascist Italy voluntarily ended its neutrality and joined the war on 10 June 1940. Only Sweden, Switzerland, Turkey, Spain and Portugal joined independent Ireland in remaining outside the conflict. However, in none of the remaining neutrals was there an exodus to the forces of one of the belligerents as occurred in Ireland. In Sweden, around 8,000 volunteers fought against the USSR in Finland and some members of the SSS, a fascist party, also joined the Waffen SS during the war, but no evidence has surfaced of large numbers of Swedes choosing to join the forces of the Allies.[2] Franco's Spain sent almost 19,000 Spanish troops to the Eastern Front and even Switzerland dispatched a 67-strong medical team to the German forces fighting the Soviets.[3] However, none of the other neutrals were as geographically, diplomatically, culturally or economically close to Britain as independent Ireland was. Indeed, Sweden and Switzerland were completely hemmed in by German forces or German allies, while

Allied-leaning Portugal was mostly preoccupied with the pro-Axis activities of its Spanish neighbour.

Adding further to Ireland's exceptional position was the fact that although independent Ireland remained outside the conflict and Northern Ireland participated as part of the UK, every man and woman who joined the British forces from the island were volunteers. The British government, mindful of the probable reaction of the nationalist minority, and with de Valera's protests ringing in their ears, never introduced conscription into Northern Ireland. None of the other neutrals had such a complex relationship with one of the belligerents. Their citizens did not, or could not, join the Allied forces as easily as the Irish did; thus no other European neutral faced the post-war problem of dealing with returning ex-servicemen.

The actual figure for Irish enlistments in the British forces during the Second World War has never definitively been settled and the riddle may never be solved because contemporary records were so badly kept. In 1946, R.M. Smyllie, the editor of the *Irish Times*, suggested that the figure was 150,000, and this figure has remained in circulation ever since. It resurfaced recently in Cathy Molohan's *Germany and Ireland, 1945–1955: Two Nations Friendship* and in Clair Wills's excellent *That Neutral Island: A Cultural History of Ireland during the Second World War*. The figure the then Taoiseach John Bruton used when speaking at the Islandbridge memorial in 1995 was also 150,000.[4] The historical heavyweight F.S.L. Lyons preferred the rounded figure of 50,000[5] and this figure too has been quoted often since. Recent work by Yvonne McEwen at the University of Edinburgh, who worked with the Commonwealth War Graves Commission and the Army Roll of Honour, has suggested that the figure for independent Ireland was 50,644, with a further 49,302 joining from Northern Ireland.[6] British record keepers themselves admitted at the time that they had only the vaguest idea of how many Irish were in any of the services and that figures for the Royal Navy and Air Force were particularly incomplete.[7] Both the Irish military intelligence service, G2, and Britain's MI5 kept a very close eye on British recruitment in Eire. By intercepting mail to and from British recruiting centres in Northern Ireland, G2 suggested that at its height in 1943, 'it may be taken that approximately 200 men are enlisting every week.'[8] Both estimated that a figure of 10,000 Irish men and women left Ireland every year during the war to enlist in the British forces.[9] MI5 reckoned after the war that 45,450 men and women from Eire had joined the British forces: 'It is believed', the report said, 'that these are conservative figures.'[10] Recently, the historian Brian Girvin has suggested that a figure of 60,000 enlistments, a total which encompasses all three British services, is probably correct.[11] Given the paucity of records left, this is probably as accurate a figure as we are likely to get at the present time.

However, *returning* ex-servicemen are missing from the historiography of Ireland and the Second World War. Thanks to the work of writers such as Richard Doherty and Myles Dungan, we have a very clear picture of where and when Irish volunteers served in the war, and what they did. Robert Fisk, Geoffrey Roberts and Brian Girvin have presented persuasive arguments around the politics and diplomacy of neutrality, while Clair Wills has explored its cultural dimensions. But we know little about what happened to Irish veterans once they came back home. We cannot assume that they simply slipped back into their pre-war lives; how could they? They saw and did things which made lasting impressions on them. They suffered both psychological and physical wounds. Their minds were broadened and their personalities altered by their training, their travels and the whole experience of being part of the military machine. They came home profoundly changed and it would be foolish to think that they simply reverted to their pre-war existences. This book will illustrate that they did not.

The core of this work is interviews with surviving veterans, combined with oral testimony held in other places, such as the Volunteers Oral Archive at University College Cork, and the Sound Archives at the Imperial War Museum in London. They vary from a man who serviced RAF aircraft and never saw a shot fired in anger, to a woman who nursed malnourished and emaciated POWs in Burma, to a man who landed under fire at Anzio beach in 1944 and nearly died from multiple gunshot wounds. Their motivations for enlisting, their experiences during the war and their difficulties afterwards are all examined. Their stories are highly personal and, at times, very subjective. Oral history, like any other source, has its limitations. Memory can be erratic and is made even more unreliable by the passage of sixty years. Many of the veterans interviewed for this project were in their eighties or nineties. In addition, memories of a particularly emotive and striking period of a person's life – dubbed 'episodic memory' by some experts – can be complicated by the fact that the act of remembering is a form of re-living the recollections.[12]

In addition, when dealing with such a well-researched topic as the Second World War, veteran's testimony is often filtered through layers of secondary sources. The best example of this is John, a Kilkenny-born volunteer who joined the Irish Guards and who was nearly killed during the Anzio landing in 1944. During his interview, he gave his opinion that the initial landing failed because of the hesitancy of the American commander Lucas who, in John's view, 'could have taken Rome and everything' if he had pushed off the beach. However, British historian David Reynolds has pointed out that this assertion first appeared in Winston Churchill's memoirs and sprung from Churchill's frustration that the operation was not an immediate success. Indeed, Churchill's opinion was strongly opposed by the senior Allied commanders at the time. Field-Marshal Harold Alexander, for one, felt that Lucas's two divisions were too weak to take and hold Rome.[13] Churchill released his history of the war quickly after 1945 and it was his version of events which lodged in the public consciousness. John, in turn, digested this and repeated it in his interview, despite having seen the ferocity of German resistance on the beachhead itself. This is not to suggest that John was trying to mislead during his interview; far from it. But it does illustrate how hard it can be to shake long-held ideas and opinions. However, for all its flaws and inconsistencies, oral testimony is one of the most important resources available to the historian. It is particularly valuable nowadays, as there are so few veterans left. Experts such as Jarlath Dunford, who headed a project to interview all remaining war veterans in county Mayo, are to be commended for their work.

Because ex-servicemen were invariably changed by their experiences, the stories of their post-war lives are dominated by what they saw and did during their service. Their testimony lends colour to the story of the Second World War in a way that archives and government documents can never do. Their experiences, both during the war and after, are what drove this work on, first as a PhD dissertation and then as a book. I wish to thank them all: Albert, Hilda, Cathal, Irving, Kenneth, Joe, Jack, John, Geoffrey, Frank, Danny, Don and Thomas. Their assistance has been invaluable and I hope that I have done their incredible stories justice.

Note

The twenty-six counties of independent Ireland have been known by various names since the foundation of the state. From 1922 until 1937, they were officially known as the Irish Free State (in Irish, Saorstát Eireann). After Eamon de Valera introduced the new constitution in 1937, the name was altered to Éire and this remained so until 1949, when the state was renamed the Republic of Ireland. For the sake of clarity, this thesis will refer to the twenty-six counties as 'Ireland', 'Eire' or 'independent Ireland'.

In 1927, TD William Redmond said in the Dáil 'When I say British ex-Servicemen I mean Irishmen who have served in the British forces. There is no other means very well of expressing that position.' This book will adopt the same position; when the phrase 'ex-servicemen' is used, it refers to both Irish men and women from the twenty-six counties of independent Ireland who served in the British Armed Forces.

Unless otherwise referenced, quotations from veterans are from interviews conducted by the author.

Chapter one

Irish Ex-Servicemen, 1793-1945

It would seem that the ex-soldier must be with the I.R.A. or be regarded as an enemy

RIC report of the killing of an ex-serviceman

This Department is slow to arrive at a decision which might give offence to the large body of ex-servicemen in this country

Secretary of Justice to the Garda Commissioner, October 1933

The Irish ex-servicemen who came home after the Second World War were the latest in a long line of returning veterans to come back to Ireland into difficult circumstances. Right back to the eighteenth century, when large-scale Irish recruitment really began after legal restrictions were lifted, Irish veterans have had to adapt to trying situations when they returned from war. Fianna Fáil policy towards ex-servicemen after the Second World War was not conceived in a vacuum; it was based on that of Cumann na nGaedheal, which was, in turn, influenced by what had happened before independence came. All of this meant that after 1945 Irish ex-servicemen found themselves walking into a scene in which the script had largely been written many years before.

Ex-Servicemen 1793–1914

Irish ex-servicemen are difficult to trace through Irish history between 1793 and 1914. They rarely appear on-stage directly: they are invariably in the shadows, only rarely coming to the public's attention. The year 1793 is an important one in the study of Irish ex-servicemen. After the uprising and wars in Ireland from 1641 onwards, Catholics had been barred from joining the Crown forces by the Penal Laws, but Britain's imperial reach was growing and such was its need for soldiers that by the 1770s, even untrustworthy Irish Catholics were being covertly recruited. Irishmen joined the British forces overseas, and the army of the East India Company was a favoured destination for many. The recruiting trend continued into the 1780s, when Britain faced a world war against Spain, France and Holland, in addition to rebellious American colonists. The final straw came when Britain was drawn into the war against republican France in 1792 as part of a European coalition attempting to contain the revolutionary contagion which was threatening to topple monarchs all over the continent. London, in its desperation for military manpower, abolished most of the restrictions on Irish Catholic enlistment the following year,[1] although Catholics were not officially allowed to become officers until 1817.

Once the gates were opened, Irish Catholics flooded into the forces. Between 1793 and 1815, an estimated 159,000 Irishmen fought in the red coat of the King's army,[2] many under the command of Irish-born Arthur Wellesley, later Duke of Wellington, whose imposing monument still dominates the Phoenix Park in Dublin. (In 1927, an Irish Senator complained that it was a 'monstrosity', adding that 'There is not shelter on it for a sparrow.')[3] However, not all these enlistments were voluntary. Charles McGlinchy's memoirs tell the story of his grandfather who was kidnapped while out fishing and pressed into the Royal Navy in 1812, but who survived and returned home to Ireland with the princely sum of £20 in his pocket. By the mid-nineteenth century, whether through fair means or otherwise, the proportion of Irish recruits in the British forces was much greater than Ireland's percentage population of the UK: there were almost 41,000 Irishmen in the British forces in 1830, accounting for 42.2 per cent of the total, at a time when Ireland made up 33 per cent of the population of the British Isles.[4]

As the twentieth century dawned, the issue of Irish recruitment became a central topic for Irish nationalist groups. The Young Ireland movement had already moved against it in the mid-nineteenth century, and was among the first to publicly decry Irish enlistment during the early 1840s.[5] The heat generated by the campaign against Irish involvement in the Boer War of 1899–1902 made many Irish town streets unsafe for Irish soldiers or ex-servicemen to walk. Foreshadowing later events in the 1920s, Trinity College became the focus for clashes between soldiers and nationalists, and Dublin Castle advised uniformed soldiers to avoid the streets around the university itself and College Green,[6] sparking complaints from Edward Carson, the Dublin barrister and future Ulster Unionist leader.[7] When Joseph Chamberlain, the British Colonial Secretary, visited Dublin in December 1899, there was a riot in the city which was only stopped when the police charged the crowd with drawn swords,[8] but the anti-recruitment campaign had run out of steam by 1900.

As part of the nationalist offensive against Irish enlistment, ex-soldiers also found themselves under attack in subtle ways. Some nationalist-dominated local authorities attempted to block veterans' applications for poor relief and in February 1903 the nationalist newspaper *United Irishman* urged councils to ignore ex-servicemen's requests for employment. Leaflets were distributed in Longford town in 1905, urging the townspeople to boycott British officials and their families.[9] Ex-servicemen found themselves the uncomfortable focus of attention, not because of their service, but because the protesters saw attacking them as a way of stopping future recruitment.

The First World War

The Irish reaction to the First World War was unique in Irish history as men from both sides of the political and religious divide surged into the British forces once war broke out in August 1914. The competing paramilitary forces on the island, the Ulster Volunteer Force (established in 1912 to resist Home Rule) and the Irish Volunteers (founded in 1913 to support Home Rule) temporarily set aside their differences to follow their leaders and, by the war's end, over 200,000 Irishmen had volunteered for the British forces.[10] A small splinter-group of nationalists (around 2000 men led by Eoin MacNeill) refused to enlist and broke away, keeping the title of Irish Volunteers.[11] Sinn Féin pamphlets denouncing Irishmen marching to war as 'traitors' and 'Imperial mercenaries' had little effect as Irishmen joined in large numbers in 1914 and 1915.[12] However, this harsh attitude began to alter once news of the extraordinary casualties suffered by Irish units filtered back home.

The First World War had a huge impact on Europe and the wider world. Three enormous European empires – the Austro-Hungarian, the Russian and the German – were shattered, leaving violence and disorder in their wake. The Allies were victorious but exhausted as the war consumed vast quantities of lives and money; Britain, France and Italy faced the post-war world, suffering political and economic upheaval. The war also altered the course of Irish history profoundly. It provided the motive and opportunity for the 1916 Rising, an event that would detonate further seismic consequences in the years to come. The war also caused the destruction of the old Irish Parliamentary Party (IPP) which, once Home Rule had been placed on the statute books but suspended in 1914, found itself in limbo, a party waiting to govern. It eventually became little more than a recruiting agency for the British forces, offering nothing to the Irish public but a tired promise of Home Rule soon, and it was fatally tainted by the high casualty rates amongst Irish recruits. For instance, it has been estimated that of the 1,107 Galway men who enlisted during the war 755 were killed.[13] By the time of the 1918 general election, it had been overtaken by Sinn Féin as the voice of nationalist Ireland, retaining only six seats. To add insult to injury, John Dillon, who had succeeded John Redmond as party leader, also lost his seat.

Ex-Servicemen and the Irish Revolution

Once the war was ended and the Armistice came into force in November 1918, an estimated 98,600 veterans returned to Ireland.[14] They found themselves under pressure and being targeted from several quarters. The British government was suspicious of Irish ex-servicemen and they wondered where their loyalties lay in the fevered atmosphere of post-1918 Ireland. Ex-soldiers, radicalised by their war experiences, were at the forefront of the fascist movement in Italy and the Freikorps in Germany[15] and military discontent played a huge role in the Russian revolution in 1917. The German military collapse and revolution in 1918 was preceded by strikes and mutinies in the navy. All over Europe, soldiers and sailors turned their weapons on their former masters and London feared that the same would happen in the UK. In late 1918, a British veterans' organisation called the Soldiers, Sailors and Airmen's Union (SSAU) was discovered to have links with the 'Hands off Russia' movement, a leftist political grouping which aimed to end British intervention in the Russian civil war. The SSAU was also suspected of sparking dissent in the forces, and of causing riots in demobilisation centres in both Britain and France.[16] As a result the Home Office began to keep a discreet watch on ex-service organisations as a potential source of revolution and one official wryly observed that if anti-government violence erupted, 'for the first time in history, the rioters will be better armed than the troops.'[17]

They also kept a wary eye on events in Ireland. In 1917, two Irish soldiers were observed by British military intelligence at a reception for republican prisoners in Ennis and the Chief Secretary warned that 'it would be highly dangerous to have a large amount of men standing about idle.'[18] Fearful that Irish veterans would gravitate towards revolutionaries, bringing their military expertise and perhaps even their weapons as well, the British government ensured that there were no demobilisation centres in Ireland; Irish veterans were to be demobbed in Britain, where the authorities could be sure that their arms and equipment would not fall into the wrong hands. However, the European continent was awash with firearms in the wake of the war and London soon discovered that the IRA had turned to demobbed German soldiers in the Weimar Republic to purchase weapons.[19] There was no shortage of arms for sale in defeated Germany and the Weimar government estimated that there were almost 1.9 million rifles and over 8,400 machine guns being held illegally in 1920.[20]

In some ways, London was right to be fearful of its Irish ex-veterans. The true number is not known but historians estimate that several hundred joined the IRA after their demobilisation.[21] The best known example is Tom Barry, one of the best field commanders the IRA had during the war against the British, who joined the British army during the First World War and served with the Crown forces in Mesopotamia. Other famous British servicemen-turned-rebels included Erskine Childers and Emmet Dalton, amongst others, including William Kent, brother of the executed 1916 leader. In another example, a member of the Dublin Metropolitan Police (DMP) requested leave in 1925 because he was a Royal Navy reservist and wanted to go on annual training. An investigation of his background revealed that he had formerly been a full member of the Navy, then had joined the IRA and had been a section leader in Cork during the war of independence. He subsequently joined the Free State army in April 1922 and passed from there to the DMP.[22] In yet another case among many, during the war of independence, the secretary of the Longford ex-service association passed information to the IRA.[23]

In June 1922, British public opinion was outraged when Field Marshall Sir Henry Wilson was killed in London by two Irish ex-servicemen, Reggie Dunne and Joseph O'Sullivan. Not only were the two men ex-members of the British army, but Dunne's father had also been a soldier.[24] Even more strikingly, the revolvers and ammunition used by the two assassins were British military issue. Afterwards Dunne pointed out that he had been inspired by British propaganda about the rights of small countries, saying just before his execution that the 'same principle for which we shed blood on the battle-field of Europe led us to commit the act we are charged with.'[25] British military training, weapons and propaganda could be very dangerous when turned back on the authorities.

Irish veterans of the First World War were also under pressure from the IRA, but – perhaps surprisingly – the rebels did not target them simply because they had been in the British forces. Indeed, veterans brought much-needed experience to the untrained insurgents, and the IRA leadership was actually keen to enlist them.[26] However, ex-servicemen were often found in the categories of people the IRA classed as enemies and actively pursued during the conflict. The British forces were an obvious target, but the revolutionaries also sought out suspected informers and 'social undesirables': criminals, beggars or strangers.[27] It was the RIC which bore the brunt of the IRA campaign throughout the war of independence and many veterans were caught up in this. An unknown number of ex-servicemen exchanged the khaki uniform of the army for the green of the RIC and were consequently killed by the IRA as the rebellion unfolded. In addition, some Irish veterans also joined British paramilitary forces, the notorious Black and Tans and Auxiliaries. Between January 1920 and April 1921, 150 ex-soldiers were killed in Ireland; of those, 80 were members of the RIC and 30 were Auxiliaries which would have made them legitimate targets in the eyes of the insurgents regardless of their past service.[28]

Ex-servicemen also fell victim to republican violence in the IRA's war against informers. This was waged with varying degrees of severity by local commanders and whether or not ex-soldiers were singled out depended on the attitude of the individual IRA leader. Giving an account of the punishment meted out to an ex-serviceman from Bandon in Cork, the IRA officer in charge pointed out that 'My policy was that those who were not for us at the time were against us, and as I had been informed Fehilly [the ex-soldier] was in touch with the enemy, I naturally presumed he was hostile.'[29] It often took very little to persuade the rebels that ex-servicemen were actively working against them. When the tide of the war began to turn against them in Longford, the IRA took out its frustration on Irish veterans in 1921.[30] Historian Peter Hart estimated that of the 23 ex-servicemen shot in Cork by the IRA between 1919 and 1923, only four had actually given information to the authorities.[31] Bodies of the executed were sometimes found with notes attached to them, saying 'Convicted Spy', 'Spies and Informers-Beware IRA' or 'Getting them at last-Beware.'[32] Tom Barry describes informers in his memoirs as 'bloodhounds' and the felt that 'they were a menace to the very existence of the Army of the Republic.'[33] He relates in detail how he unsuccessfully pursued a postman who had given away the position of his unit to the authorities.[34] He also viewed ex-officers as a greater danger than enlisted men, claiming that retired army and naval officers in Cork were 'a prop on which British power rested'[35] and that they 'worked feverishly to destroy the IRA'.[36]

The battle for Ireland's morality also claimed some ex-servicemen's lives. The *United Irishman* railed against the British army as a purveyor of venereal disease and loose morals in Ireland in 1905[37] and a number of Sinn Féin speakers called for returning soldiers to be imprisoned and examined for VD.[38] The IRA in both Cork and Longford in 1920 tracked down criminals, beggars and adulterers,[39] while they also put a stop to illicit alcohol stills and detained thieves.[40] Some unfortunate ex-servicemen fell into poverty after the war and turned to begging: they were sometimes swept off the streets and harassed by IRA men. In addition, many IRA leaders were particularly mistrustful of unemployed ex-servicemen because they thought them more likely to become British informants for money.[41] They were an easy target because there were over 24,000 unemployed ex-servicemen in Ireland in 1921.[42] Unsurprisingly, the police wrongly felt that veterans were targets of a systematic campaign. As one RIC report on the killing of a one-armed veteran in Limerick surmised, 'it would seem that the ex-soldier must be with the I.R.A. or be regarded as an enemy.'[43]

Much like the IRA, Sinn Féin had no strategy to deal with ex-servicemen, but still victimised them in several ways. Their houses were attacked or destroyed or some GAA clubs were instructed not to admit them. Many Sinn Féin controlled councils refused them welfare; some hospitals declined to give them treatment (in 1920, the Clonmel Board of Guardians passed a resolution to refuse ex-servicemen admission to the hospital).[44] Rather than being a coherent party, Sinn Féin was in reality a large umbrella movement which encompassed a great number of competing ideas. It should come as no surprise that it had little to say in relation to ex-servicemen.

Finally, Irish veterans often found themselves the target of public jealousy and resentment in post-war Ireland. Their service entitled them to secure, pensionable government jobs: the postman-informer described in Tom Barry's memoirs is a good example. Social reformers after the First World War in Britain argued that the best way to cure the country's ills was to create a 'settled, healthy, content and loyal' class of small farmers.[45] This merged with Lloyd George's promise to create a 'Land Fit for Heroes' and land was offered to returning personnel to reward them for their service. In Ireland after the Great War, ex-servicemen were entitled to apply for subsidised housing or land, under the auspices of the Irish Soldiers and Sailors Land Trust. The British Treasury set out three main aims: to build houses, to employ ex-servicemen in the construction and to offer training and employment which 'must tend in the long run to increase the wealth of the nation generally'.[46] As Ireland lurched into political upheaval, recession and revolution after the war, many civilians were jealous of veterans who received jobs or land from the government. Disturbances over land distribution, such as occurred during the harsh winter of 1916–17 when land-hungry farmers in parts of Connacht and Clare drove livestock off large cattle farms,[47] was harnessed by Sinn Féin, who also opposed the building of veteran's houses claiming that the scheme was a way of 're-colonising' Ireland by stealth.[48]

Ex-Servicemen and the Irish Free State

After the chaos of 1919-1921, ex-servicemen played an important role in consolidating the Irish Free State, established by the Anglo-Irish Treaty and governed by the Cumann na nGaedheal party from 1922 to 1932. The IRA split over the Treaty and the anti-Treatyites (dubbed 'Irregulars' by the Free State authorities) began to sporadically attack the structures of the new government. With mounting disorder in the country and violence starting to spiral out of control, the government called for volunteers for the newly-established Free State army and around 1,000 recruits a day came forward.[49] The army swelled to enormous proportions and by 1923 had reached 50,000. This new force was recruited specifically to deal with the anti-Treaty IRA and little time or money was available for training. One contemporary account claims that the Free State troops which attacked the Four Courts in June 1922, after it had been occupied by IRA forces, had to be shown how to fire their rifles the night before the government recaptured the building.[50] Like the IRA between 1919 and 1921, ex-servicemen were particularly welcome in the Free State army for their skill at arms and previous combat experience, and many were appointed to important posts during the civil war.[51] Unemployment amongst Irish ex-servicemen was exceptionally high – the percentage of veterans unemployed in 1919 was 46 per cent, compared to 10 per cent in Britain – so many were glad to earn a steady wage and to put their training to good use.[52]

For the Cumann na nGaedheal government, employing Irish veterans not only brought much-needed experience into the army, but also provided a stability that many ex-IRA recruits could not provide. Michael Collins and Richard Mulcahy did not want to have to worry about the anti-Treaty IRA infiltrating the army. Collins himself is said to have approached ex-service organisations in Dublin to ask them for help in attracting veterans.[53] When the Free State government began to execute republican prisoners, the reliability of the army became paramount. An eyewitness account of the death of Erskine Childers mentioned that there were 'no Irishmen' in the firing squad: instead it was composed of 'Irishmen who were in the British Army'.[54] We should remember, of course, that Childers himself was a veteran of the Great War, and had been decorated for his service. So effective were Irish veterans in helping the Free State win the civil war that Liam Lynch, IRA chief of staff during the civil war, ordered the killing of ex-servicemen serving in the Free State army during November 1922.[55] One contemporary estimate suggested that of the 1,300 officers in the Free State army, 75 were non-IRA veterans.[56] The number of ex-servicemen in the army was one of the causes of the so-called Army Mutiny in 1924 in which ex-IRA men complained that the Free State government was retaining ex-British army men in the new force while discharging IRA veterans, many of whom faced unemployment and poverty.[57]

However, it would be wrong to think that once the civil war was over, Irish ex-servicemen faded into the background. They had a persistent and vocal champion in William Redmond, TD for Waterford and son of John Redmond, who had led the Irish Parliamentary Party from 1900 to until his death in 1918. When John Redmond called on Irishmen to enlist in the British forces in 1914, William joined the British army, fought on the western front, and eventually rose to the rank of captain. Already an MP in Tyrone, he resigned and successfully stood for election in his father's constituency of Waterford when the elder Redmond died. He was one of only six IPP members elected in 1918, as Sinn Féin dominated the election results in the south of the country. In 1926, he founded a new political party called the National League. If ex-servicemen were to have a political voice in post-1918 Ireland, the National League could be seen as their natural political home. Redmond was a distinguished veteran himself, and his party attracted the support of many ex-servicemen, unionists and former Home Rulers. Throughout the 1920s, he consistently challenged the government's policy towards ex-servicemen.

In April 1927, he sparred with Ernest Blythe, the Free State minister for Finance, asking if there was evidence of discrimination against veterans in the distribution of temporary positions in the civil service, to which Blythe replied that 'it is not proposed to make any exceptional arrangement in respect of temporary clerks who are British ex-servicemen,'[58] words which Séan Lemass would echo in 1945 when speaking about returning Irish veterans. In this debate, Redmond was supported by Bryan Cooper, independent TD for Dublin county, who had served with the Connaught Rangers during the First World War. Cooper and Redmond often argued in tandem for ex-servicemen's rights and a quick glance through the Dáil debates shows their names side by side on several occasions. Both Cooper and Redmond were particularly irritated by the fact that Irish veterans of British service were barred from applying for jobs which were reserved for IRA veterans, a policy which Blythe steadfastly refused to change. However, the two men were also just as likely to clash in the Dáil and alliances between them appear to have been short-lived affairs. Cooper, initially an independent TD, eventually joined Cumann na nGaedheal, and was elected as a member of the party in the September 1927 election.

One of the great triumphs of advocates on behalf of Irish veterans was the establishment of the Committee on claims of British ex-servicemen, the setting up of which the Dáil debated in November 1927. 'I make no apology to the House in bringing forward the motion', Redmond said in his speech to the chamber on the issue. 'I make no special claims on behalf of British ex-servicemen from the Irish Government. I want them to be regarded and recognised by the Irish Government of the day as Irishmen with equal rights of citizenship in this State. I ask no more and I claim no less.'[59] He also urged the government to look into the issue of reciprocity of unemployment insurance between the Free State and the UK, as veterans in independent Ireland were having trouble claiming back their contributions upon their return from the war. In 1945, the independent TD James Dillon would call on the Fianna Fáil government to do the same thing, and Sean Lemass, then Minister for Industry and Commerce, would pursue this vigorously.

In 1927, the Cumann na nGaedheal government was reluctant to establish the ex-service commission, as they were not keen on being publicly identified with them. W.T. Cosgrave, the President of the Executive Council of the Free State, queried if a commission was the best way forward. 'Is this the way to help them', he asked the chamber, 'or is this the way simply to score off politically – to put us in the position of being in the dock with the British Government? Is not that what is behind this motion?'[60] Bryan Cooper – who had become a Cumann na nGaedheal TD by this time – also opposed it and suggested that veterans make their grievances known through the British Legion or other organisations. Cosgrave publicly welcomed this proposal. However, he announced on 23 November 1927 that the government was forming the committee to look into the complaints of veterans, particularly that they were being discriminated against in the allocation of publicly-funded employment.

The Free State government had reason to be very pleased with the findings of the committee. Far from uncovering discrimination, the committee reported that there was little evidence of Irish ex-servicemen being targeted or victimised at all. Well-known organisations such as the

British Legion provided testimony before the committee, as did lesser-known associations such as the National Federation of British ex-servicemen in Cork, the Ex-Servicemen of Cavan Town and District, the Non-Permanent Government Clerks Association (British Ex-Servicemen Branch), the British Ex-Service Temporary Civil Servant Association and the Municipal Ex-Servicemen and Dependents Association (Dublin). Individual veterans also presented themselves to the committee, which held meetings in other major cities and towns outside Dublin. After looking at issues such as work preferences, land and housing grants, rents, war graves, pay, unemployment insurance and unemployment itself, the committee found that the problems faced by Irish ex-servicemen were no greater than those faced by other Free State citizens at the time. It reported, for instance, that the Cumann na nGaedheal government was well within its rights to reserve government employment for ex-Irish Army and IRA members, and that in the allocation of land by the Land Commission, ex-servicemen were fairly treated.[61]

Presenting the findings to the Dáil, Cosgrave pronounced himself satisfied with the committee's work. He laid emphasis on the fact that no discrimination was found and that 'in so far as British ex-Servicemen are also ex-National Army men, they share in the preferences accorded to that class.' He even found time to take a swipe at veterans who had become civil servants, who were complaining that they were lower paid than their colleagues in the UK: 'Before the change in Government it was the British practice to discharge civilian clerks and other subordinate employees to make room for ex-Servicemen', he said. '…no doubt some of the British ex-Servicemen who now complain of being discharged entered Government employment in such circumstances.'[62] Having listened to accusations of favouritism and discrimination, he was no doubt delighted to have the opportunity – and factual proof – to refute those claims publicly and on the record. The most surprising thing about the committee was that, despite continually bringing ex-servicemen's issues to the government, William Redmond refused to give evidence before it.

Ex-Servicemen and Fianna Fáil

Civil servants appointed by the Cumann na nGaedheal government feared that the election of de Valera in March 1932 would lead to a purge of government officials, as triumphant republicans took over the levers of power. Many thought that the new government would have revenge on its mind. Ex-servicemen also had reason to be wary of the new administration, as it contained many prominent pre-Treaty IRA and Sinn Féin figures. However, Fianna Fáil proved as willing as Cumann na nGaedheal to leave ex-servicemen to their own devices and did not embark on a root-and-branch reshuffle of civil servants. Fianna Fáil did not have a majority in the Dáil; it was instead supported by the Labour party, and it did not yet dominate Irish politics as it would in later years. Stability, rather than revolution, was the order of the day.

A major factor in ensuring that there was no radical policy towards ex-servicemen was the fact that Fianna Fáil retained so many of Cosgrave's civil servants. Officials such as Stephen Roche at Justice, Michael Beary at Defence, Michael McDunphy at the President's office (after 1937) and Joseph Walshe at External Affairs had all began their careers under the Irish Free State and continued right through de Valera's reign. Roche, for example, became assistant secretary of Justice in 1926; Beary had been the secretary of the Committee on Ex-Servicemen in 1927; McDunphy had served as assistant secretary to the Provisional Government and the Executive Council of the Free State; and Walshe remained at External Affairs from 1927 to 1946. They brought with them a thread of continuity from the Cumann na nGaedheal government, as they had previously advised Cosgrave in his dealings with veterans of the First World War. Walshe already had extensive experience with the difficulties of Irish participation in British Legion events: writing to Irish officials abroad during the 1920s and 1930s, he was very cautious about Irish attendance at Legion ceremonies, as long as it did not cause any controversy. For instance, in 1930, he advised the Irish representative in Paris against attending Legion dinner, particularly if there was a chance that there might have to be a speech.[63] Surrounded by officials who emphasised stability rather than rocking the boat, once he took office 1932, de Valera stuck resolutely to the constitutional route and began to dismantle the objectionable sections of the Anglo-Irish Treaty, as well as provoking a trade dispute with Britain, known as the Economic War.

In 1933, he abolished the oath of allegiance; in 1936 he removed the King from Irish politics; in 1937, he introduced a new constitution and the state was renamed Eire; in 1938, he negotiated the return of the so-called Treaty Ports, which allowed Eire to be neutral when the Second World War broke out in 1939. In addition, the de Valera government had its hands full with the Army Comrades Association (ACA), more commonly known as the Blueshirts. Originally formed as a welfare organisation to provide for ex-Irish army men, the Blueshirts developed into a semi-fascist organisation which clashed in the streets with the IRA and got involved with agrarian unrest during the Economic War. The movement faded away in the mid-1930s and enjoyed its final fling of publicity when Eoin O'Duffy led a remnant to fight for Franco and the Nationalists in the Spanish civil war. Irish veterans of the First World War and their problems were almost forgotten in the diplomatic, economic and constitutional turmoil of the 1930s. Almost, but not quite: in 1938, de Valera considered attending the Armistice ceremonies at Islandbridge, but later cancelled as European tensions mounted over the Sudetenland.

In the 1930s, it was the turn of the Fianna Fáil government to be closely questioned on ex-servicemen's rights. Both the issues on the agenda and the name of those asking remained the same as a decade before. In April 1936, Bridget Redmond − wife of William Redmond, who had successfully inherited her husband's seat in Waterford when he died in 1932 − challenged the government over the plight of Irish veterans who, because they were drawing a British military pension, were automatically disqualified from claiming unemployment insurance. In response, Sean Lemass rebuffed any suggestions of discrimination with the reasonable point that the affected men were over the government's income limit for claiming unemployment, and that all types of pensions were counted as income.[64] Although Redmond's National League party had been disbanded in 1931 after running out of funds, the interventions of Bridget Redmond show that Irish ex-servicemen still had a vocal advocate throughout the 1930s.

Conclusion

From the late eighteenth century onwards, the large-scale Irish recruitment into the British forces meant that the issue of ex-servicemen in Ireland would assume increasing importance. However, they remained on the fringe of events until the country plunged into revolution. Even then, they were not victimised because of their service, but because they fell into many of the categories that the IRA deliberately singled out during the war of independence. They played an important but understated and largely unacknowledged role in both the revolution and the civil war. Between the early 1920s and the outbreak of the Second World War, they retreated to the periphery of Irish history again, despite having forceful advocates such as William Redmond and Bryan Cooper. It was as the Second World War drew to a close that ex-servicemen in their own right became an issue for de Valera. He, however, did not chart a new course in government–veteran relations after 1945. As thousands of Irish ex-servicemen came home from the war, he was content to follow the path which had been set out by Cosgrave and Cumann na nGaedheal, which had been dealing with Irish ex-servicemen of another war, before de Valera had taken office.

Chapter two

Joining Up: Life in Uniform

Even if Eire is staying neutral, I am not
Dublin-born Romie Lambkin on why she joined the ATS

Are you goddamn mad or something?
US troops to Kilkenny native John in the Irish Guards

One of the most common reactions that Irish men and women in British uniform met with while on duty during the Second World War was incredulity. British, Commonwealth and American soldiers, most of whom had been conscripted, could scarcely believe that anyone would leave the safety and relative comfort of neutral Ireland and choose to go to war. Over and over again, Irish volunteers were confronted with disbelief and astonishment from their conscripted colleagues. Cathal, a Dublin-born RAF volunteer, was asked, when his comrades discovered what he had done, 'What sort of fucking eejits are you, that you joined up when you didn't have to?' Irish author Paddy Galvin, who left Cork to join the RAF, wrote in his memoirs that an English friend of his said to him 'I sometimes wonder why you joined this lot. Ireland is neutral, isn't it?…I wouldn't join my hands, let alone the Armed Forces.'[1] Albert, like Cathal, a native of Dublin and an RAF recruit, was confronted by his English friends, who asked him 'You must be mad, what are you doing? [volunteering for the RAF] We were *called* up.' Geoffrey, yet another Dublin-born RAF volunteer who enlisted in 1940, was asked by his conscripted pals 'What the hell are you doing here, you're a

Paddy!...We're conscripted, we stayed out as long as we could...We're trying to get out of it and here you come across volunteering!' John, who left Kilkenny before the war to join the Irish Guards in London, found himself sitting in a bar in Tunis after it had been liberated by the Allies in 1943. After a few drinks with American soldiers, one of them asked him where he was from. Upon hearing that he was Irish, the American exclaimed 'You guys are neutral, you're not in the war at all!' When John explained that he was a pre-war volunteer, the American asked him 'Are you goddamn mad or something?' It was a reasonable question. Why would thousands of Irish men and women leave a country which was neutral and voluntarily put themselves in danger?

There is no single explanation, and Irish volunteers often had multiple reasons for enlisting. The decision to join up was highly personal, sometimes emotional, other times highly rational. One of the dominant reasons, however, was very simple: the wish to see some action. '...to be in the war was the most glorious thing in the world' said Cathal. 'You had to get in; it was the biggest thing that was happening.' With war raging in Europe and across Asia, as well as above and below the Atlantic and Pacific Oceans, and with life in neutral Ireland largely following its slow peacetime rhythms, it is hardly surprising that young Irish men and women were attracted by the prospect of excitement and adventure. David Power, an apprentice panel beater from Clonmel who ran away from home to join the British Army, spoke in his memoirs of the

> lure of faraway places...the Coral Island, Tarzan of the Apes, Gungha Din and the North Western Frontier, all this excited young imagination. But the reality of Dag Long and Mick Roles, home on leave from the British Army in Shanghai; the beautiful clothes they wore, so different from the shapeless dark sombre of the hungry thirties, was what really changed imaginative longing into realisable adventure.[2]

Cathal also joined seeking adventure, excitement and to see exotic foreign places. He described himself as a 'foolish young man' who joined because he wanted to fly Spitfires and live the life of Paddy Finucane, the famous Irish RAF pilot. He was so eager to join, and so afraid that it would all be over before he could enlist, that he altered his baptismal certificate to state that he was eighteen, when he was actually sixteen. He was so young going to war that he had never shaved before. Don, who joined the Royal Engineers, said that, '...it was the *thing to do*. We didn't think about Hitler and the Nazis intellectually, no, no, it was going on; it was the thing to do.' Likewise, Albert felt that 'It got a bit boring in Ireland then. It's hard to describe it, as a young man, you know, you're dying to get stuck in.' Jack, in his memoirs, spoke about having 'little to do in a bleak and dreary Dublin', and being eager for some excitement.[3] Nor was thrill-seeking confined to Irish men: Hilda, who left Kildare to join the army nursing service, felt the pull of adventure when she signed up and Romie Lambkin, a young Dublin woman who joined the ATS in 1941, wrote in her diary that

> Even if Eire is staying neutral, I am not. I don't want to be left out of war shaking events – the Battle of Britain decided me on that – and I do want to be in uniform driving all sorts of exciting people about instead of being cooped up in a ghastly boring office behind the Four Courts.[4]

The parallels with stories of men who volunteered in 1914 are striking. One said afterwards that he and his friends were 'tired of landlords...of fathers, of advice from relatives...of our dull southern Irish town. Blow the lot...we got adventure. We enlisted.'[5]

Another powerful motivation to enlist was to continue a family tradition of British military service. The practice of family members following each other into the military is technically known as 'endo-recruitment' and, given Ireland's long connection with the British armed forces, it is not surprising that many Irish volunteers from 1939 onwards followed the family path to the recruiting office. Probably the greatest influence on them was the First World War. Over 200,000 Irishmen fought in the conflict;[6] an estimated 27,000 were killed and just under

100,000 returned to the country in 1918 after being demobbed.[7] This meant that the war touched almost every family in Ireland and thousands of homes had photos of fathers, brothers or uncles in British uniform on the mantelpiece. Geoffrey remembers following in his father's footsteps to enlist. (Interestingly, he did not follow his father into the infantry.) Jack also followed the example set by family members: his father was a veteran of the First World War, while his brothers had both joined the British Army. Jack remembered hearing about his father's war as he grew up: '…you'd be listening to your father telling stories about the war, about his own experiences.' Even after learning that his father was temporarily blinded in a gas attack at Ypres, Jack was not discouraged, and in 1937 he ran away from home in order to enlist. He recalled seeing 'buskers, amputees, from the First World War still busking in the streets in Dublin', a constant reminder of Ireland's connection to the war. Joe left Dublin in 1941 and joined his brother in the RAF. Kenneth, yet another Dublin-born volunteer, had a very long military lineage. His family connection to the British forces began in 1818, ran through the American Civil War (on the confederate side), the First and Second World Wars. It also continued after 1945, with his relative serving with the US Air Force in Vietnam.

However, just because there were family members in the British forces did not necessarily mean that younger siblings would inevitably follow the same path. While endo-recruitment was undoubtedly a potent reason to enlist, the example of Jack shows that it was not always followed. As already mentioned, he joined in the wake of his father and two brothers, Archie and Tom. The oldest brother, Jimmy, was an entirely different case: he was, in Jack's words, a 'red hot republican…we didn't know what police station to ring up at times' and he had been caught drilling on several occasions with the IRA. Not only that, Jack's uncle was also a republican and had been involved in '1916 and in the civil war'. One evening, Jimmy came home to find Tom's British Army tunic hanging on a chair in the kitchen. When Tom arrived back, he found Jimmy holding the tunic 'like a bit of dirt, on his finger' and a shouting match ensued between the two men. Even after the war, when Jack and

Ken as a Royal Artillery NCO.

Ken in 2011.

his brothers had arrived home safely, Jimmy listened to their war stories 'barely able to keep his republican views in check. He was passionate about Ireland and couldn't understand how three of his brothers could have joined the British Army.'[8] He was certainly glad to have his brothers back in one piece, but it shows that Irish family members could have very different trajectories. Similarly, Hilda was another whose family was militarily divided: she had relatives in the IRA and the Black and Tans, as well as the Blueshirts and the British forces.

Of course, one motivation to enlist which should never be underestimated was that the British forces offered relatively well paid employment, as well as a pension (for those who served long enough), allowances for families, accommodation, food, clothing and the possibility of learning a trade, or going to school. John joined the British Army at sixteen, and was put through school in Egypt. In his interview he spoke fondly of the prospect of a boy from Kilkenny going to school in the shadow of the pyramids. He recalled warmly being 'young lads, you know, and touring the museums, I spent my time touring the museums, down in the marketplaces in Cairo and everything. Do you know what it was, it was two years of tourism.' Even when he returned to London at eighteen to take up his army duties, his enjoyable life continued.

> You were fitted out with all this ceremonial uniform by civilian tailors in the Tower of London, there's central heat in part of the Tower of London, and I enjoyed life when I was there. Put on civilian clothes and go off out, go to the pictures. Molly and Eileen, two sisters of mine were in London at the time, we used to go out and have a meal and go to the pictures, the Victoria and all over the place. Then one day I was sent for and told that I was being sent to Regents Park barracks, a lovely barracks actually, which was the Brigade of Guards Headquarters, and I was sent there. Jesus, a more luxurious life. I didn't do anything! I dressed up in civilian clothes, go walking, go where I wanted, got paid for it…it was a lovely life.

All of this was a real contrast to life in his native Kilkenny at the time, and it was rudely interrupted when war came, much to John's annoyance. It was just as true for those who chose to join the Irish forces. Danny, who joined the Irish army in Athlone in November 1940, was an early school leaver and 'there was no work. There was no work around for people…there [w]as a scarcity of work, and you couldn't get any work anywhere. You might get an odd day here and there, there was no social welfare at that time, no social welfare, no handouts, if you weren't working, that was *it*.' When the woollen mills in Athlone burned down, Danny saw the army help tackle the blaze, and he decided that was where his future lay. He counted himself lucky. He had previously tried to join the British Army, but had been stopped by his parents. Two of his childhood friends joined the British forces around the same time, and both were killed in action.

Membership of the forces also meant access to a network of clubs and societies, both inside and outside the barracks. In the 1930s, Europe was in the grip of a deep depression. Ireland was not as badly affected as some countries, such as Germany, but still suffered from high levels of unemployment and stagnant economic growth. For some Irish men and women, the risks that a soldier's life entailed were far outweighed by the prospect of an exciting job, the duty of upholding family traditions and the possibility of a steady income. Donald left Dublin to join the Royal Artillery simply because he wanted to own his own pair of boots. Another Irish recruit, Patrick, was pleased that his mother was paid £2 a week while he was away[9] and George, who left Wicklow to join the Royal Navy, spoke about never having to spend his 34 shillings weekly wage, as the Navy took care of everything.[10] It was not like a normal job; it was far better.

Political volunteers were much rarer than those who enlisted for mundane reasons. Analysis of veterans' testimonies both in the Volunteer Archive at University College Cork and in the sound archives of the Imperial War Museum reveal that ideology played a small role in the decision to enlist. As Geoffrey said, he 'just joined up, we went away, that was it. We didn't start querying it, or why other people should be worried about it.' For many veterans, the reality of the Nazi regime was only revealed when they were confronted with the results of Nazi rule in Europe during 1944–45; few gave it much thought when they first joined. True, once the stories of the horrors of the concentration camps began to filter through, Irish volunteers were horrified. An Irish chaplain with the RAF observed that having seen the concentration camp at Belsen, he felt that the Irish population needed 'to be shaken badly. They don't understand the horror of this war because it has not been brought home to them.'[11] An Irish motorcycle courier with the RAF recalled that his feelings towards the enemy underwent a complete change when he saw the results of Nazi rule at the camp. Up to that point, he felt that the Germans had been 'a worthy foe' and that they had been an abstract, faceless enemy. He came to the swift conclusion that 'I'm on the winning side now' and that Nazism was inherently evil.[12] Despite this, there were few truly political recruits. Analysis of surviving veteran's testimony show that only a very small number joined because they wanted to fight Nazism; they joined for a myriad of personal and family reasons.

However, once they saw what they were fighting against, many certainly felt justified in their decision.

The fact that they were volunteers meant that they had certain leeway and more freedom of choice than their British counterparts who were conscripted. For instance, Albert initially enlisted in the Royal Artillery but his friends persuaded him to change his mind:

> 'What? You'll get killed! We've joined the Royal Air Force; you've a better chance of living. Go back and tell them you want a transfer!' And I said 'No, I cant, I've got a ticket here for the boat tomorrow to England.' 'No, you're a volunteer, go and tell them you want a transfer into the RAF.' So I went back in, very sheepishly, and saw this Sargent, and he was raging and he just tore the thing up, and said 'There's the RAF room over there' and that was it. I went in and I joined the RAF.

Not only that, but some decided to join under false names. Irish author Paddy Galvin provided a memorable description of the ease with which he enlisted under an assumed name:

> Stacked on the desk in front of me was a neat pile of Enlistment forms. The Sergeant asked me to fill one in and I listed my cousin's name, his superior education, his total lack of contagious diseases, and his ardent desire to fight for freedom anywhere in the world. I signed his name with a flourish and sat back, impressed.[13]

When the decision was made to join, the volunteers found that the Irish government did not put many obstacles in their way. Workers in essential industries were not allowed to emigrate, but for the most part, Dublin did not stop Irish men and women who chose to enlist in the British forces. As Cathal recalled, 'The one thing that was quite surprising was that there was no difficulty placed in your way if you *wanted* to join the British forces, I mean nobody sort of stopped you at the Border and said that you can't go up there if you're going to join the Army or the

RAF or the Navy.' Gerardine Cusack, a young Irishwoman who left for Britain in September 1939 recalled in her memoirs that the mailboat was crowded with Irishmen heading for war. 'They were noisy, calling out to each other, obviously eager and excited about the prospect of war. Nan and I sat in the corridor of the overcrowded London train that night listening to the Irish songs and stories and to arguments for war and peace.'[14]

Even when Irish citizens who were reserve members of the British forces were called up at the outbreak of war, de Valera refused to get involved. It has been estimated that over 20,000 Irishmen, from either side of the border, were reservists and were called up when Hitler invaded Poland in September 1939.[15] De Valera's office received several requests for information from reservists who had received their call-up papers. The line taken by Joseph Walshe, the secretary of the Department of External Affairs, was that the government would 'neither discourage nor help Reservists to break their contract, nor on the other hand should we force them to join their units if they do not want to.'[16] The only time that de Valera decisively acted to stop Irish enlistment was in the case of civil servants who wish to take a leave of absence to join up. Faced with a flood of requests for leave immediately before the outbreak of war, he issued instructions that 'no Irish Civil Servant should be allowed to contract new obligations inconsistent with his position as an Irish Civil Servant', except if the person in question was already a member of the British reserve forces, and if he or she was not needed for vital work in their department. Several British-born civil servants were allowed to go before the war broke out, but once de Valera had banned it, it was applied to all civil servants, regardless of nationality.[17]

Whatever their motivation to join, and however the government reacted to their decision, the war was the most important experience in the ex-servicemen's lives. Their attitudes, opinions and outlook on life were changed forever by their time in uniform. Time and again, veterans spoke of their service as being a formative experience in their lives; that they came back to Ireland very different than when they left. As Cathal, the 16 year-old Dublin RAF recruit, said 'I joined it as a youth and came out a man... any education I have, the education of the experience of life, came from being in the British Army, in the Royal Air Force.' Geoffrey, another RAF volunteer from Dublin, felt that the travel had expanded his view of the world. 'It broadened your mind', he remarked, 'when you travelled around and you met all classes and types of people.' RAF life meant living in close quarters with 'all sorts of nationalities, all sorts of religions' and he felt he was utterly transformed by it, even though he acknowledged that he saw little action. For many, it was a place where they encountered new and bewildering things: Romie Lambkin described in her diary a time when a lesbian made a pass at her and she had to ask her friends what had happened.[18] She had never encountered anything like it before.

Kenneth, too, felt that his outlook on life was changed by the sheer number of different nationalities he encountered in the Royal Artillery. 'I served with Mohammedans, Muslims, you name it, every kind of race out there, Jews, we had quite a number of Jews...Canadians, Norwegians, Danes, Poles, Czechs, all on the course together.' Jack, in particular, felt that the British Army had turned his life around. 'I lived wild until I was going away...' he said. But after his return, 'I was a much more mature person, a boy going away at 16, now I came back at 24, you know, I'm a man.' This, of course, was not just confined to Irish members of the Allied forces. Arthur Schlesinger, an historian who fought with the US forces in Europe during 1944–45, wrote that his service 'was a liberating experience, annulling routine expectations, providing new contexts and challenges, testing abilities, widening horizons and opportunities, nourishing honesty, individuality, complexity, irony, stoicism.'[19]

One point was repeated over and over again by Irish war veterans: the bonds of friendship, the feeling of solidarity and the sense of adventure generated by the war made a lasting impact on them. Irving fondly remembered a soldier he had never met before snapping a cigarette in half to share with him on duty. 'You'd never get anyone doing that in civilian life', he commented. Desmond, a Dublin man who joined the British Army in 1942, reminisced about the time he and his pals hijacked a captured German Tiger tank and drove around the northern

Italian town in which they were billeted as a Patrick's Day prank. 'Fortunately nobody was hurt and not much damage was done...' he remarked, wryly.[20] Kenneth was hugely enthusiastic about the African soldiers he served with, particularly their native home-brewed alcohol: when he sipped some gingerly, 'it nearly blew the wax out of my ears.' During the post-war riots in Calcutta, Kenneth and his mates delivered supplies to a beleaguered hotel in the centre of town, and were rewarded by being allowed to eat and drink their way through an expansive five-star menu. They had left 'the lorries outside the hotel with sentries on them, and we were so drunk when we came out, we'd have nearly handed them over...' he laughed in 2007. Albert, when asked for his autograph by grateful locals towards the end of the war in Europe, often signed himself 'Eamon de Valera' and chuckled at the thought that some villager in Holland imagines that he has a priceless autograph. Coincidentally, Myles Dungan in *Distant Drums* relates the story of an Irish volunteer who was confronted by a liberated, and very drunk, Frenchman after D-Day, who greeted him with cries of 'De Valera, Irlande'.[21] The remarkable type of connection the war forged between people was summed up by Joe: one of his good friends during his time in the RAF was a fellow pilot called Timolty, whom he called Timo. When he tried to find him after the war, he realised he had never known his proper name. 'I don't know his Christian name, all I knew was Timo. And I was beside him in a plane for six months.' Life in uniform introduced a whole new set of routines and values. In civilian life, not to know the full name of one of your best friends would be unthinkable.

However, it is easy to over-romanticise the war and its effect on people. The Second World War is particularly prone to mythologising: it is been packaged as a straightforward fight of good against evil. But history does not run on such clean lines. For the vast majority of people who were touched by the war, it was a time of death, deprivation, grief and misery and although many Irish ex-servicemen looked back on it with a sense of nostalgia, a sense of their difficulties also seeped through. Joe certainly did not enjoy contracting malaria and dengue fever or the cramped conditions on his troopship as he was being shipped to the Far

East. '…you were together more or less like bloody cattle. It was rough going, rough going', he said. He did realise that people tended to only recall the good days: 'It's like when you were a schoolboy, there was never a bad summer…It didn't rain during the summer at all. What a load of tripe!'

Kenneth grimaced when he recalled the poor rations he and his comrades received when in India, including 'weevily bread…it was full of weevils, and they used to bake the weevils in. We were really fussy at first, we used to pick the weevils out like that, and all you have left is the crust! So, we ate the bread, weevils and all.' Albert, as will be discussed later, was taken aback when his landlady deliberately kept food from him in order to make more profit from tourists in Blackpool, and John was left with a profound distaste for the military after his service. 'Quite frankly,' he said in his interview, 'if I was young again, a young lad, children, sons or something like that, I wouldn't have them join *any* army, because I think it's a notorious waste of human life… Jesus, it was a waste of young life, that's all, bloody wars.' Even those who had enlisted looking for adventure found that it was not all it had promised to be. 'I can't tell you how dull things were in Burma', Cathal recalled having been posted there in 1945. By the time he joined up, the war was grinding to a conclusion and he was disappointed. Romie Lambkin also recorded some downsides to her service, and was particularly shocked by the racism she encountered. 'To our utter disgust,' she wrote in her diary, 'the Ulster Hall has now put up a "No Coloured Troops" notice. We won't go there again, I can tell you.'[22]

'A Terrible Innocence'

One of the things that made the leap for soldier to civilian difficult for Irish ex-servicemen was the attitude of the public towards the war in Ireland. Coming home on leave during the war, Kenneth was struck by the bizarre atmosphere that existed in Dublin. The day before, he had been in uniform in Britain, a country in which food was strictly rationed, in which the blackout was enforced and life was geared to winning the war. He experienced a sense of culture-shock after stepping off the mail boat in Dun Laoghaire. In contrast to Britain, Kenneth found Ireland a 'country of steaks and cigarettes and wonderful lights and everything. I remember on leave here going down to the Dalkey tram, down past the German embassy, Northumberland road, and the Nazi flags out and the whole country lit up, lights and it was like a different world.'

Dublin-born volunteer Brian Inglis felt the same thing when he came back to Dublin on leave from the RAF. Writing about the city during the war, he recounted that it was full of 'drinking in the Hibernian buttery, eating steaks in Jammets or the Dolphin and dancing at the Gresham'.[23] For some, leave in Ireland was even better than the Forces. Albert was billeted in a guest house while training with the RAF in Blackpool and remembered

> Only for the fish & chip shops we'd have starved. They hadn't got room in the camp for us and they put us in houses along the front, what they called civvy billets, and it was rationing time and the RAF gave these people who were running these things our books, our ration books, but they starved us. What they were doing was saving up our points for the summer visitors, so they could give them lots of food that we should have had. I complained, I took my breakfast to the CO one day, it was a piece of cold toast and I said 'This is my breakfast today sir, in the billets, and I think it's disgusting.'

Jack also experienced difficulty dealing with the mental shift to a neutral country when he returned to Ireland after his recuperation in Britain, and he found himself ill at ease with many Irish civilians. Some were incredibly insensitive towards him and made fun of the fact that he had spent two years as a POW. One particularly thoughtless individual at the Guinness brewery taunted him that he had not been much of a soldier, since he had 'found a lovely warm prison camp to go into to get out of the war'. Later on, he often found himself introduced to people as a concentration camp survivor, and he would have to correct them, explaining that concentration camps had been for political opponents of Nazism, while he had been a Prisoner of War, an entirely different type of detainee. The distinction was very important. Life in a POW camp was hard, but there was none of the institutionalised brutality and murder that existed in concentration camps. Jack's rationale was that a lack of information available to the Irish during the war had lead to what he called 'a terrible innocence' among them regarding the Nazi regime. Simply put, Irish civilians, for the most part, simply did not understand what he had been through.

Jack's experience was not unique among Irish veterans. Many felt misunderstood by Irish civilian society. Although British ex-servicemen experienced difficulty in adjusting to peacetime, they had one crucial advantage over their Irish counterparts: British civilians had been involved in the war, while Irish civilians, by and large, had not. From 1939 onwards, British life was dominated by the conflict and civilians played a huge role in the war effort. They helped to rescue the British Expeditionary Force from the beaches of France in a flotilla of small boats; they toiled in factories to produce weapons and ammunition with which to wage the war; and they endured months of bombing in British cities from September 1940 to May 1941. Dunkirk, the battle of Britain and the Blitz formed the kernel of the 'People's War': the popular perception that British civilians had been in the frontline alongside soldiers, sailors and airmen.[24] The physical fabric of British society and civilian life was changed completely by bombing, by military camps springing up all over the country, and by the uprooting of millions; homeless refugees, evacuated children, conscripted servicemen and migrant workers were part of a human tide that ebbed and flowed over Britain as the war progressed. Britain was overrun with men and women in uniform from all over the world. This created a bond of common experience that helped British veterans reacclimatise themselves to post-war life, and made the transition from soldier to civilian less of a jolt. By contrast, despite the huge emigration to Britain and the large number of Irish people in the British forces, day-to-day life in Ireland remained generally tranquil.

Whereas everyday life for the British civilian between 1939 and 1945 was shaped and dominated by the war, that was not the case in neutral Ireland. Historian Clair Wills wrote that her mother's memories of the war were

> of shortages, particularly of sugar, tea and flour; of trains… running so slowly on inferior fuel that you could climb off and on them as they went uphill; of visits to a pair of relatively well-off elderly Protestant neighbours who owned a working radio… In many ways, the war years for my mother's family were a continuation of life in the 1930s, with its local focus, its seasonal liturgical ritual, as well as its economic privations. Frugality was the order of the day, and worries about the supply of day-to-day necessities took priority over the seemingly distant war…As a schoolgirl her day-to-day lessons, friendships and fraught relationships with the nuns were no doubt more present to her than the far-off events of the world war.[25]

The author Paddy Galvin recorded similar sentiments, recalling that in his home city of Cork they 'were more concerned with the horrors of rationing than with anything that was happening in Europe'.[26] A wide emotional gap was opened by neutrality between the people of independent Ireland and the UK. Sir John Maffey, the British wartime representative in Dublin, wrote in August 1945 that independent Ireland, after six years of neutrality, had effectively become a foreign country. 'An Englishman who did not know Ireland', he wrote, 'who studied in any country town the faces, the names over the shops, the procession to Mass on a Holy Day, would know at once he was in a foreign land.'[27]

Officially, neutral Ireland had experienced 'the Emergency' between 1939 and 1945. Even though hundreds of thousands of Irish citizens travelled to Britain during the war, the majority of them stayed there when peace came. Of those who remained at home, many *were* interested in the war. The Irish newspapers were full of details of the campaigns overseas, BBC radio was available and Allied newsreels were played in

Irish cinemas, albeit censored. The Irish population was well aware of the war, but for the most part, Irish civilians just were not as emotionally invested in the conflict as the British were. This caused great difficulty for some Irish ex-servicemen when they returned as they struggled to come to terms with a world that had not changed a great deal during the war. Cathal, the Dublin RAF veteran, found that the key factor that helped him to readjust was that he had married an English woman, who had lived through the war in Britain. Just being able to talk on equal terms with someone who had experienced the war greatly assisted him. He found that

> British civilians talked about their experiences in the war, Irish civilians had nothing like that to talk about, except the scarcities of the half ounce of tea and the Glimmer Man. They weren't able to talk about queues and rationing and the Blitz and bombers and the big one that fell on Kingdom Road and so on like that and air raid shelters and the life down in the Tube and so on. So that, this, to somebody like my wife, this was a different world. Dublin and Ireland was a different world in the war and after the war.

Kenneth also found it tricky to fit into a world that did not fully understand what he had been through. '…apart from your relations and other people whose family had served in the war, they didn't want to know. They just didn't want to know.' But he did understand their apathy. 'It was a lack of information', he said of his neighbours. 'They didn't realise what was going on. You got no recognition whatsoever, of war service.' Similarly, when George returned to Dublin from service with the Royal Navy in the Far East he felt 'it was as if you didn't exist. Nobody wanted us.'[28] Some were dumbfounded by the ignorance of the war in Ireland. William, who left Dublin to join the RAF, was told by his neighbours when he was home on leave that stories about German concentration camps were simply British propaganda, and were not to be believed. William, however, knew better because some of his comrades had been to Belsen.[29]

Larry, who left Wicklow to join the Royal Navy, was absolutely 'shattered' by people's attitudes when he returned home. He found that his fellow countrymen were interested only in 'drinking themselves into oblivion, not a single thought about what was going on beyond the horizon. And they didn't care a damn either.'[30] Hilda pointed out that the main thing which embittered veterans was that they had few people to share their experiences with and that there was little awareness in Ireland of the war, making it hard for ex-servicemen to express their feelings. She remembered that her family were not interested in her service and instead preferred to talk about 'horses and cards': 'You never spoke about any of that and they didn't ask you,' she said. Speaking about her husband, whom she married after the war, she said that 'he was like all the Irish; he didn't want to hear about the war.' Prior to meeting Hilda he had no family connections to the war; he had no stake in it and therefore had no interest. Hilda understood his indifference. 'It's a bit boring,' she said, '…talking about the war when you're not involved in it.' James Hickie, who had been a major in the British Army, made the interesting point that members of the Irish army 'would try and tell you tales of wonderful things that happened to them on exercises…They didn't ask one any questions as to what experiences one had.'[31] In other words, they equated their time on manoeuvres with his time in combat.

Added to this sense of disconnection and isolation were scattered incidents of animosity towards ex-servicemen. Many reported that they had been verbally abused, but none were physically attacked. A family friend of Albert gave him 'a right bollocking for joining up…[he said] that I shouldn't have been helping the British after what they'd done for [sic] Ireland' and that neighbours sometimes called his family 'Bloody West Brits'. Kenneth revealed that a few of his school friends, who 'were strongly republican elements…they gave me dirty looks, I'll put it that way.' Cathal was called a 'louser' by some of his contemporaries when he came back and he got the feeling that some people thought 'we soldiered at home…you buggered off and soldiered elsewhere.' Geoffrey too recalled some local people saying to him 'you bloody well served for the Brits', but he laughed it off. Among veteran's testimony in the Imperial

War Museum was one man who recalled that his uncle, a republican, told him sternly that 'I like a good Irishman and I like a good Englishman, but I don't like an Irishman who fights for England.'[32] His family were reluctant to acknowledge his service, despite the fact that he won the Military Medal during the war. These were isolated incidents. The dominant reaction to the returning ex-servicemen was neither positive nor negative; it was simply indifference.

Identity

Service in the Crown forces had other, more subtle, effects on Irish volunteer's minds. In many cases, how they viewed their surroundings and themselves was altered by their time in the military, because the war had interesting effects on the sense of identity held by both Irish civilians and Irish military volunteers. Neutrality, the experience of being thrown onto their own resources and of resisting Allied pressure to join the war gave a great stimulus to southern Irish nationalism. This, in turn, gave independent Ireland a new legitimacy and opened a deep emotional gap between neutral Ireland and belligerent UK. On the other hand, the Second World War gave Ulster loyalism a further boost and cemented Northern Ireland's place within the UK. Although Angus Calder dismissively pointed out that the province had 'a decidedly Irish sort of war',[33] the people of Northern Ireland and Britain shared a common war experience. Belfast was bombed by the Luftwaffe, although not as heavily as British mainland cities. An estimated 49,000 men and women from the six counties joined the British forces, of which over 2,000 died.[34]

The melting pot that was the British forces had an interesting effect on Irish volunteers. Rather than diluting their sense of Irish identity, service in British uniform tended to concentrate it. The clearest example of this is the Belfast native Sam McAughtry, who grew up in the staunchly Unionist Shankill and joined the RAF in 1941. He was astonished that upon enlisting he was instantly nicknamed Paddy. This shocked him because:

Round about where I came from, Paddies tended to be as rare as crucifixes at the Presbyterian General Assembly. Oddly, coming from a district which had provided so many men for the King's colours, nobody had ever mentioned the fact that in the armed forces all Irishmen were Paddies, all the way up to and including officers of Air rank.[35]

For McAughtry, it was like a rebirth and he embraced what he called the 'warm discovery of my Irishness': he felt as if he had been reborn. Revelling in his new-found identity, he would 'run down and corner the owner of every Irish accent, North or South, that stood out from the British. I would find out where in Ireland he came from and I would pull out the fags or buy beer and talk about home.' He even went so far as to draw the Red Hand of Ulster on his helmet and write 'Uladh' in Irish script underneath. Rather than using his Ulster heritage as a way of marking himself as British, McAughtry instead used it as a way of pointing out that he was Irish.[36] Other Ulstermen, however, were less pleased with being labelled 'Paddies'. Denis from Dublin, who joined the RAF in November 1941, remembers Northerners in his group being horrified at being called Paddy, protesting 'We're British subjects!'[37] Likewise, Gerardine Cusack, who left Mayo for the UK in September 1939, was told at the Government Employment Office that 'they had just the job for an Irish girl, and directed me to the Northern Ireland Office in Cockspur Street. I didn't remind them that there they claimed to be British', she wrote wryly in her unpublished memoirs.[38]

Brian Inglis also discovered that his time in the RAF had made him more Irish than he had been at home in Dublin. The 'intermittent mess ribaldry' kept his 'patriotism simmering' during the war.[39] He too noticed that his British comrades did not differentiate between what side of the Irish border you hailed from. 'The fact that many of them came from Northern Ireland was immaterial', he wrote, 'as to mess colleagues every Irishman was Paddy, whether he was from Bantry or Belfast, so long as he spoke with an Irish accent.'[40] By war's end he felt he was:

> ...more Irish – in the sense of thinking of myself as Irish – than when it began; too indignant with Churchill for his sneers at de Valera in his Victory broadcast to be appeased by his references to the Irish volunteers who had won V.C.s; and taking it for granted, when my demob number came up on New Year's Day 1946 that I would be returning to work on the *Irish Times* and to make Dublin my home.[41]

'Paddy' or 'Mick' became standard nickname for any Irish recruit, regardless of their religious or political background, or where they came from on the island. This extended to all nationalities: Geoffrey, another Dublin-born RAF recruit, remembered that 'you were never known as your Christian name, if you were Irish you were Paddy, Jock if from Scotland, Taffy for Wales.' There were other standard nicknames as well: Joe called to mind that 'if your name was Miller you were called Dusty Miller. If your name was Wilson you were called Tug Wilson. If your name was White you were called Chalky White. And if your name was Murphy, you were called Spud Murphy. I often wondered where all these came from, but that was, it was automatic.' Albert, who came from a strongly Unionist background in Dublin, was 'called Paddy from the time I opened my mouth in England'. He was introduced to his future wife at a dance in Copenhagen in 1945 as Paddy and had to tell her his birth name. Even after the war, when he joined the British police, he was again referred to as Paddy. He had considered himself to be both Irish and British before he left for war, and had even been named Albert after Queen Victoria's husband.

Don, another Dublin volunteer from a pro–British Dublin background, also enjoyed the new sense of Irishness. Having grown up with a 'Union Jack over my cot', he went so far as to alter his uniform: over the Royal Engineers flash, he sewed a label which said 'Southern Ireland'. This was so common that Dublin complained to the British Air Ministry in 1942 that an RAF squadron, training in the United States, was known as the 'Squadron of Eire' and had 'Eire' embroidered on their sleeves. The reports had been made by civilians in the US and gathered

Albert in RAF Uniform.   **Albert in 2011.**

by G2, Irish military intelligence. In August 1943, London issued a categorical denial, but it is fairly clear that both Frank Aiken, the wartime Minister for the Coordination of Defensive Measures and Peadar McMahon, the secretary of the Department of Defence, did not believe the explanation.[42] Kenneth also went out of his way to point out his Irishness. On one occasion, the unit was being given a lecture by a Protestant minister. When all other denominations had been marched away, the minister said to those who remained 'well now, I suppose, we're all Church of England. I put up my hand… "What are you?" he said. "Church of Ireland!" – I couldn't resist it!' Kenneth laughed. Romie Lambkin, wandering around the ruins of post-war Berlin, also deliberately advertised her nationality. Stopping and chatting to a German civilian, she was asked if she was from Ulster:

> 'Not at all', says I to him in my best idiomatic Irish, ''tis from the South I am, but I am in the British Army.' How is that? wondered he, all puzzled. 'Because I like England' says I, 'and auf

Wiedersehen to you.' I hope that wipes out whatever delusions he cherishes regarding Eire.[43]

Conclusion

Part of the reason for this unique sense of Irishness is that the British forces have a long tradition of tolerating diversity in its ranks and, in particular, has always contained Scottish, Welsh and Irish regiments. Irish soldiers in these regiments have long been called Paddy or Mick, regardless of which side of the border they came from. With their British comrades drawing no distinction between volunteers from north or south, it is no wonder that those volunteers did likewise and developed a distinctive Irish identity, one that did not correspond to the more schismatic one that the war generated at home.

For some, it was hard to comprehend the divisions of peacetime society. Sitting in his local Belfast bar after being demobbed, Sam McAughtry was accosted by a civilian handing out application forms. 'It was for the B Special Constabulary. "That's in case there's a real war," the man said.'[44] In a similar vein, Geoffrey remembered that his Catholic neighbours lined the streets of Sandy Cove for his father's funeral, but most refused to enter the Protestant church when the cortege reached it. Religion and politics may have been forgotten at the front, but were not neglected at home.

Irish ex-servicemen's lives were changed by their service; the person they returned as in 1945 was shaped by their wartime experiences. For each of them, enlisting in the forces, being trained in the UK, meeting new people, being shipped abroad, seeing exotic sights and being involved in combat, was an incredibly exciting and emotional time in their lives. Another challenge, however, lay ahead at the end of the war: how to rejoin civilian society once they returned to Ireland.

Chapter three

Diplomacy

It is fairly safe to say that between 150,000 and
180,000 young Irishmen served under the British flag
R.M. Smyllie, *Foreign Affairs*, 1946

There might be some advantage in taking informal
measures to deflate some of the exaggerated claims which
have been made by Eire's supporters
Eric Machtig, Dominions Office, February 1945

At the end of the Second World War, Ireland found itself in an uncomfortable and delicate position. Irish neutrality during the conflict had opened a wide diplomatic breach between Dublin, the UK and the USA. Strained relations with Britain, Ireland's closest neighbour and former colonial master, were problematic but fairly common. After all, de Valera's alterations of the Treaty and his pursuit of autarky in the 1930s had produced tensions between Dublin and London, but did not stop them cooperating on a whole range of issues. However, the frosty post-war relationship with America was a real predicament. The US was the pre-eminent power in the world at the end of the war – not a country to be at odds with. In addition, America contained millions of Irish and, probably most importantly of all, Dublin was interested in taking part in the Marshall Plan, the scheme to rebuild Europe which was being bankrolled by Washington. The evidence presently available suggests that Taoiseach Eamon de Valera was willing to accept a short-term rupture in relations with the Allies in order to demonstrate beyond doubt Ireland's independence from Britain.[1] At the same time, de Valera had one advantage: the presence of a large body of Irish ex-servicemen within the country after the end of the war proved that Ireland had made a sizeable contribution to Allied victory. During the war, de Valera was content to allow the media and government officials – sometimes even Irish cabinet ministers – to circulate high figures for Irish enlistment in the British forces, while not publicly acknowledging it himself. However, while attempting to exploit their achievements, the Irish government did not make any attempt to engage with the ex-servicemen themselves, despite the fact that many Irish veterans approved of Irish neutrality.

Irish–Allied Relations during the War

The Irish declaration of neutrality in September 1939 did not take the British political leaders by surprise, as neutrality had been on the Irish agenda as far back as 1921. Once he had taken the reins of power in Dublin, de Valera spoke openly of his intention to remain outside future European conflicts: in 1936 he said Ireland would 'strengthen ourselves so as to maintain our neutrality'.[2] De Valera himself, ever the pragmatist, was willing to countenance stretching Irish neutrality, and made many concessions towards the Allies during the war. Amongst many other things, weather reports were routinely passed on, military intelligence was regularly sent to London, crashed aircraft were sometimes returned to British hands and Allied aircraft were allowed to fly through certain corridors of Irish airspace. However, other leading Irish politicians were determined to preserve both the spirit and image of neutrality. Frank Aiken, the Minister for the Co-ordination of Defensive Measures, argued in the Dáil in 1945 that Ireland could not play 'Tadh a'dá thaobh ('Timothy two-sides')'[3] and it was under his watch that the oppressive censorship regime was implemented during the war.

Neutrality did, however, provoke some anger and frustration among the British public. As Dominions Secretary Christopher Addison wrote in September 1945, 'There is a strong if latent feeling of resentment in this country against Éire's attitude during the war. This may perhaps not be enduring, since it is not a British habit to bear undying grudges.'[4] Dublin-born RAF recruit Cathal felt that many people in the UK were of the opinion that Ireland 'should have been in the war...we were white and English-speaking; therefore we should have been in the bloody war.' (Interestingly, there was also a definite feeling of anger in Britain towards American neutrality as well.)[5] When Irish neutrality was declared, one of the few expressions of support came from the leader of the US communist party, Earl Browder, much to Dublin's embarrassment.[6] Anglo-Irish relations deteriorated sharply after the Germans overran western Europe in May and June 1940; with the European coastline in German hands from the northern tip of Norway to the Spanish frontier, British trans-Atlantic convoys were increasingly at risk from U-boats now able to operate from France. These convoys carried much-needed supplies for Ireland as well as Britain. Pressure mounted on Dublin to allow the RAF and Royal Navy to use Irish ports, and de Valera's stubborn refusal to even consider it caused understandable frustration in London. Even when tempted with offers of Irish unity in the summer of 1940, de Valera refused to budge. As a former First Lord of the Admiralty, Winston Churchill felt the loss of the ports keenly, and he raged against the 'so-called neutrality of the so-called Eire' early in the war.[7]

The traditional friendship with America was also under strain. A visit by Frank Aiken to Washington in April 1941 to secure much-needed weapons for the Irish forces resulted in little more than a heated exchange with Roosevelt. Legend has it that Roosevelt was so infuriated with the dour Aiken's stubborn attitude that at one point he pounded his fist on the table, sending his tea set into the air.[8] In a message to de Valera after the meeting, the President caustically commented that he considered Aiken's attitude to be 'one of blind hostility to the British Government and to the British people' and that American exports were reserved for countries that were resisting aggression. In his opinion Irish neutrality 'at least potentially affords real encouragement to the Government of Germany'.[9] Myron Taylor, the US representative to the Vatican, advised Roosevelt in 1941 to 'ignore de Valera, grant him no favours and treat him with contempt'.[10] The entry of the USA into the war in December 1941 did not improve matters. De Valera's attempts to clarify Ireland's position, describing Dublin's stance as 'friendly neutrality'[11] did not mollify Allied opinion, which was further irritated when de Valera complained about the stationing of American troops in Northern Ireland. In February 1942, Roosevelt urged Ireland not to stand aside from the war, but to join 'its traditional friends, and among them, the United States of America'.[12]

While top-tier relations between Ireland and the Allies were rocky, cooperation was relatively good at lower levels. The British intelligence agencies, although they ran agents inside Ireland during the war, was satisfied with the help it received from G2, the Irish military intelligence service. After the war, MI5 admitted freely that 'Eire's neutrality was a "friendly" neutrality' and that they were pleased at the level of cooperation, particularly their surveillance of 'enemy agents and their Eireann sympathisers'.[13] The Irish and British militaries also kept in close contact throughout the conflict. Generally the British service ministries in London had no problem with releasing experts from the British forces to bolster Irish defences. For example, in March 1941 Dublin secured the release of an Irish RAF officer to help organise Irish anti-aircraft defences[14] and in July 1941 secured the transfer of an Irish officer in the Royal Navy to come home and assist in the establishment of the fledgling Irish Naval Service.[15] Of course, it was not all plain sailing and there were rough patches along the way. In July 1943, when the British government were holding up the release of an Irish RAF officer for service in the Irish Defence Forces, de Valera angrily remarked that the RAF had 'thousands of Irish officers whom they might not have had if our Government adopted a similar non possumus attitude'.[16] However, the UK represent-ative in Ireland, Sir John Maffey, commented during the war that low-level cooperation was generally good with the Irish and that

> Whenever possible, *i.e.*, when the principle of neutrality is not publicly and violently outraged, the Éire authorities endeavour to solve the problems which the war brings in a manner favourable to us (stranded aircraft, deserters, &c.)[17]

As the war turned against the Axis in 1942–43, the importance of the Irish ports waned, particularly after the Allies began to master the U-boat campaign. However, Dublin moved to centre stage again in early 1944. The Allies were massing forces in the UK for the invasion of German-occupied France and, apparently convinced that Ireland was awash with enemy spies, Washington – supported by London – demanded in February 1944 that Dublin expel all Axis diplomats. There is also evidence that the demand was designed to get de Valera 'on the record' refusing to help the Allies, to put more pressure on Dublin. The request, which was dubbed the 'American note', created a heated controversy both inside and outside Ireland. De Valera predictably refused to comply, arguing that it would be an unneutral act. The press in Allied countries attacked Ireland, variously accusing it of being small-minded, pro-Axis or a combination of both. There is some evidence that the note was a part of a wider Allied crackdown on European neutrals: throughout the first six months of 1944, Washington and London pressured Sweden, Switzerland and Turkey to end or drastically curtail their economic relationships and exports to Germany.[18] During the crisis, Walshe met with David Gray, the US minister in Ireland, and complained that the American had 'misinformed his Government with regard to Irish policy…and was thereby primarily responsible for what might have been a serious rupture in the relations between Ireland and the United States.'[19] However, de Valera was unmoved, and even turned the situation to his advantage by calling a snap election and recapturing an overall majority in the Dáil in 1944. During the furore, de Valera toyed with the idea of attacking Washington head-on over its denunciation of Irish neutrality: one ill-tempered (and fortunately unsent) draft reply to the note stated that, although Ireland was being indicted for harming the Allied cause,

> by a similar reasoning process America herself could be accused of being responsible for the thousands of lives lost before her breach with Germany. The opportunities for espionage, especially in relation to shipping, must have been in proportion enormously

greater in the United States than in Ireland. Yet the American Government waited until an act of war had been committed against them before taking the final step.[20]

Throughout the war, the commitment to neutrality meant that the government was eager to keep Irish members of all belligerent forces at arm's length. The government received several requests from Irish citizens, both at home and abroad, requesting permission and asking for instructions to enlist in the Allied forces. In each case, the Department of External Affairs replied that it was not the business of the department to do either for potential volunteers. 'It would be awkward' wrote one official, 'to give formal consent to our citizens joining a belligerent army.'[21] In one case, an ex-IRA man from Waterford applied for permission to enlist in the German forces: he was told that the department would not authorise any citizens to travel to Europe 'save in cases of the most exceptional gravity and urgency'.[22] Predictably, they were less blunt when they received a request from a Protestant vicar to join the US Army chaplaincy service. Joseph Walshe wrote to him, pointing out that 'the permission of the Irish Government is not required' if he wished to enlist.[23]

The end of the war in 1945 saw Ireland's battered international reputation take a trio of blows. First, the ugly scenes in Dublin on VE Day, which will be detailed in Chapter 6, made headlines in Allied countries. Secondly, the Irish government's initial reaction to Irish army deserters, which will be examined in the last chapter, also caused some consternation. But it was de Valera's visit to the German Legation in May 1945 which caused the most damage. Diplomats, newspapers and the public all over the world were astonished to hear that on 2 May de Valera had personally gone to visit the German representative in Ireland, Eduard Hempel, to express his condolences at the death of Hitler. De Valera justified this as a matter of diplomatic protocol and said that it would have been discourteous to have done otherwise. He had something similar after US President Franklin D. Roosevelt had died in April 1945, giving a speech full of warm praise for Roosevelt and adjourning the Dáil as a mark of respect. However, personally expressing sorrow at the death of Hitler when images were filtering back of Dachau, Belsen and other camps – places where Irish servicemen were documenting and liberating – was spectacularly insensitive. What made the timing even worse was that Belsen had been liberated only a few days before; Dubliner Albert, as we shall see in the next chapter, was an early visitor to the camp. In addition, the visit came almost three months *after* the Soviets had arrived at Auschwitz and uncovered its horrors. The full details of the Final Solution were still sketchy, but it was becoming very clear that something terrible had happened in the forests of Poland. Nor could de Valera claim that he had no knowledge of what was going on: on 10 October 1944, the British government issued a warning to the Nazi government over BBC radio – freely available in Ireland – to halt the 'murderous acts' which were going on in Eastern Europe.[24]

Bearing all this in mind, it is no wonder that after the visit to Hempel, both of de Valera's offices were flooded with angry letters. One of them was from an Irishman in the British Army, who pointedly asked de Valera if it was fair that he and his Irish comrades 'be made isolationists and shown in a light of betrayel [sic] of the basic principles of democracy'.[25] Much to Dublin's discomfiture, the single expression of support for the visit came from the British Union of Fascists.[26] De Valera's actions also had repercussions far beyond Ireland and caused rancorous debates among Irish–Americans.[27] The reaction to his visit was so negative that he was undoubtedly glad to be able to seize the gift that was presented to him by Churchill, whose bad-tempered denunciation of Irish neutrality was broadcast on 13 May 1945. De Valera's measured response won back many Irish who were uncomfortable with his visit to Hempel. All of this meant that by 1945, Ireland and de Valera were far from popular amongst the Allies.

Attempts at Rehabilitation

One of the ways in which Dublin attempted to blunt Allied criticism during the war was to emphasise the number of Irish citizens participating in the Allied war effort, and as the war wore on de Valera began to allow international journalists to make the point for him. Early in the war, when the outcome was still in doubt and the Axis Powers were in the ascendant, the government made sure to conceal Ireland's connection to the Allies. For instance, in July 1940, an issue of the British magazine the *Picture Post* was banned in Ireland because it contained an article by a journalist named Tania Long, who suggested that Ireland's defences were dependant on the British military.[28] One of the contributors was Dorothy McArdle, who had written a brief history of Ireland in the magazine and whose pen had always been friendly to Ireland and de Valera. Aghast at the ban, she sent the Taoiseach a telegram to insist that there was nothing offensive in the magazine. Although the decision was re-examined by the Department of Justice (and was passed by Seán Lemass as well) the ban was not lifted.

Two years later, however, all such sensitivity had gone from Irish censorship. In 1942, *The Nation* magazine reported that 150,000 southern Irishmen, or 5 per cent of the population, had joined the British forces.[29] In mid-1943, *The Atlantic Monthly*, an American magazine, quoted the same figure, and pointedly questioned if 5 per cent of the US population would join a foreign army if Washington was neutral. No protest was made by the Dublin government. Around the same time, even cabinet members were openly talking up the Irish contribution: in 1943, the Minister for Supplies, Seán Lemass, spoke to British officials in Dublin and mentioned that there were at least 250,000 Irish in the British war effort.[30] De Valera was not above doing the same himself: in a conversation with Maffey in 1942, the Taoiseach 'pointed to the significance of the number of Irishmen who had gone over to the British Forces…he added that it was the policy of his Government to put no difficulty in the way of this recruitment.' Maffey later added that enlistment in Ireland 'for our armed forces and for our labour requirements is not hampered and, indeed, is largely facilitated'.[31]

When the tension between Ireland and the Allies was ratcheted up during the American note crisis, the Irish High Commissioner in London, John Dulanty, wrote a letter to the *Spectator* in which he claimed that 170,000 people from independent Ireland were helping the British war effort and that a number of them had 'outstanding achievements to their credit'.[32] Later, the government was questioned about the matter in the Dáil, and the Minister for Finance Sean T. O'Kelly replied that Irish diplomatic representatives, the Government Information Service and 'other such channels' were all vigorously defending the good name of Ireland. Officially, he said, Dublin did not engage in counter-propaganda.[33] The increasing circulation of pro-Irish enlistment figures caused some concern in London. Eric Machtig, the Permanent Under-Secretary in the Dominions Office, wrote to Maffey in February 1945, musing that

> there might be some advantage in taking informal measures to deflate some of the exaggerated claims which have been made by Eire's supporters and for this purpose, it would probably be possible to arrange that the Ministry of Information should give these figures, off the record, to selected press correspondents who would be able to put out a correcting story on some suitable occasion.[34]

De Valera, however, suspected that this had been the unofficial British policy throughout the war and protested to Maffey in July 1940 about 'press propaganda' against Dublin.[35]

Irish newspapers and international journals joined the debate as the war ended. On 13 May 1945, the *Irish Times* editorialised that 'No people whose sons have won seven Victoria Crosses have much reason to feel ashamed: scores of thousands of other Irishmen have made [a] proud contribution to all the fighting services.'[36] Five days later, it went even further and claimed that 100,000 'and probably more' Irish people joined the British armed forces and that their 'fighting record can bear proud comparison with that of the fighting men of any of the officially belligerent countries'. In July 1946, the newspaper's editorial declared that Ireland's admission into the United Nations was almost certain to be accepted because 'this little country, for all its neutrality, contributed more towards the winning of the war than almost any nation of its size in the world.'[37] Taking a similar line to the *Irish Times*, the *Longford Leader* declared in August 1945 that 'a greater proportion of young men from southern Ireland are fighting with the United Nations than from many portions of the British Commonwealth.'[38] In June 1945, the *British Legion Journal*'s Irish Supplement waxed lyrically about 'how distinguished was the part which the Volunteers from Éire played in saving the world from the lustful military domination of Germany', before lamenting the lack of accurate figures for Irish enlistment.[39]

However, the most striking example of this determination to stake a claim for Ireland in the war was the article written by R.M. Smyllie, then editor of the *Irish Times*, for the international journal *Foreign Affairs* in 1946. Titled 'Unneutral neutral Eire', the article was a comprehensive and unabashed attempt to repackage Irish neutrality as being a pro-Allied policy. Smyllie claimed that it was 'fairly safe to say that between 150,000 and 180,000 young Irishmen served under the British flag'. He also took a swipe at the Unionist regime in Belfast, declaring that 'the volunteers from Eire were not only greater in number than from Northern Ireland, which, forming an integral part of the United Kingdom, was a belligerent state, but also were larger in proportion to population.' Further Irish assistance came in the form of food exports and Smyllie even attempted to claim credit for Irish army deserters who enlisted in the British forces. 'Eire was a non-belligerent' he wrote, 'but she was never neutral in the accepted sense of the term.'[40] Dublin's evident satisfaction with the article can be judged by the fact that the Department of External Affairs kept copies of it on file, and sent them to people who wrote to enquire what the figures for Irish enlistment in the British forces were. For instance, in 1952 Seamus MacDea, de Valera's private secretary, sent a copy to an Irish migrant in Australia, who had requested Irish enlistment figures having read Nicholas Monsarrat's novel *The Cruel Sea* which had severely criticised neutrality. MacDea admitted in his reply that he did not know the true figure for Irish volunteers.[41]

The United States was also partially and unwillingly drawn into the numbers debate. Future American president John F. Kennedy, in Dublin in July 1945 during a European tour, noted in his diary that the figure for Irish volunteers was as low as 30,000, and that Ireland 'kept strict neutrality even towards the simplest United States demand'.[42] The accuracy of the diary is open to question: Roger Casement is named as the leader of the 1916 rebels at one point. Kennedy's information came from David Gray, whom he called on during his visit. Gray was an outspoken critic both of Irish neutrality and of de Valera. A contemporary US intelligence report stated bluntly that Gray 'distrusts de Valera profoundly' and stated that he was in touch with James Dillon, the former Fine Gael TD and opponent of neutrality.[43]

Gray denied that Irish enlistment was anywhere near what Dublin was claiming, and even got into an argument with Sir Hubert Gough, who had a long connection with Ireland. He had been one of the ringleaders of the so-called Curragh Mutiny in 1914, had commanded Irish troops in the First World War and was President of the Commonwealth Association in Ireland. He had also campaigned for ex-servicemen's rights after the First World War. Using the next-of-kin details provided by recruits, Gough publicly claimed that 165,000 men from Ireland had joined the British forces during the Second World War. In a letter to Gough in January 1946, Gray openly questioned this and said that his own investigation had revealed only 30,000 enlistments from the south, a figure which he obviously then passed to the young Kennedy. He also pointed out that Irish-American leaders were openly quoting wildly inflated figures of up to 425,000, and that they were doing so to pressure Washington into forcing Britain to end partition. He left Gough in no doubt as to his true feelings on the matter. He wrote

> I do feel that if only 50,000, 40,000 or 30,000 Irishmen from Éire volunteered, not only without compulsion but in spite of difficulties and discouragements, Ireland had saved her soul and made a priceless contribution to our cause; but I feel it to be indecent that propaganda aimed at disparaging the Six Counties which gave us invaluable bases and moral support should be used by a faction in the United States for political ends inimical to

friendly Anglo–American relations…the truth must be established at some time, and I can see no reason for delay in publishing it now.[44]

Kennedy was told by Irish sources (which he did not identify) that the amount was much higher, somewhere in the region of 250,000.[45] The figure of a quarter of a million was, interestingly, the one that the Irish government had settled on and which both de Valera and Lemass had used when speaking about the issue. Perhaps Kennedy had been in conversation with Irish officials, but there is no record of it.

At the same time, Ireland was not totally friendless. During a speech to parliament in June 1946, the prime minister of South Africa, Jan Smuts, declared that 'in spite of Ireland's formal neutrality, she had through her voluntary manpower made a greater contribution than in any previous war.'[46] In broad terms, the British Dominions were relatively well-disposed towards Ireland and its right to be neutral. In October 1939, Anthony Eden, Dominions Secretary at the time, had warned Churchill that any move to seize the Treaty Ports by force would be opposed by the Dominions.[47] In September 1945, the post-war Dominions Secretary, Christopher Addison, pointed out that in the other Dominions there was a 'certain sympathy with the Eire point of view and the right to be neutral, and nationalist opinion, therefore, in the Dominions is inclined to support Eire's independent stand'. This meant, however, that Britain had to be careful in how it handled Ireland. There was a chance that Ireland might 'encourage the growth of a similar spirit in other parts of the Commonwealth'.[48] Aware that they also contained large communities of emigrant-Irish, the other Dominions urged London to take a moderate stance towards Ireland after the war.

Belfast and Dublin

The hugely inflated figures for Irish enlistment being bandied around were a hot and much-debated topic between the two Irish capitals. It would be a huge embarrassment to the unionist administration in Belfast if it was established that neutral Éire provided more manpower for the British forces than loyal Ulster. Northern Irish Prime Minister Basil Brooke bombarded London with requests for accurate figures of Irish recruitment and, in public, dismissed the contribution from south of the border. 'I have heard it said in a boasting manner that Eire men went forward to war,' he said. 'Of course, they did, but they were our men, they were our people who thought as we did.'[49] Similarly, Edmund Warnock, Northern Irish Minister for Home Affairs, told the Stormont chamber in October 1945 that those Irish workers from the south 'came to the Six Counties during the war…not for our good, but their own.'[50] However, London was unable to provide the figures Brooke desperately wanted, because British officials simply had no idea how many southern Irish were enlisting. Records were poorly kept, and the problem was exacerbated by the fact that many Irish volunteers enlisted under a false name or, because they joined in Belfast, were counted as Northern Irish volunteers. As we have seen, the author Paddy Galvin enlisted under his cousin's name.

British record keepers themselves admitted at the time that they could only estimate the true number of Irish enlistments and that figures for the Royal Navy and RAF were particularly patchy. They suggested a rough estimate of 40,000 but again said that they had no real idea as to the true figure.[51] As a result, official estimates from London varied widely. In 1942, the British War Office estimated that there were 28,549 southern Irish volunteers[52] and another investigation by the Dominions Office in 1944 concluded that a 'very approximate' figure of 40-70,000 was probably correct. London's inability to provide accurate numbers gave de Valera the public space to stake a claim for a high level of Irish participation in the war. Belfast remained extremely worried that enlistment figures would reflect badly on Northern Ireland's place within the United Kingdom. The issue was also a potentially embarrassing one for London. The British government was determined that de Valera would not be allowed to 'get away' with being neutral during the war by claiming a contribution to Allied victory and they were also concerned that if Irish figures were allowed to stand unchallenged, this would diminish the contribution from other British Dominions, all of which had joined the war.

Ex-servicemen and the Debate

Those who knew best about the Irish contribution to the war and whether Ireland should have been neutral or not were never asked their opinion. Many ex-servicemen had strong feelings over whether Ireland should have joined the war, and how many had enlisted. Some supported neutrality; others opposed it; a few more were too excited by the thrill of enlisting to give it any thought. Albert, the RAF recruit from Dublin, was an advocate of neutrality, because he did not 'want to see Dublin smashed by bombs'; the destruction he saw on the continent as he followed Allied ground troops strengthened his conviction. 'It was pathetic really to see all these lovely little villages smashed to pieces, it was terrible,' he said afterwards. Hilda was also fearful of the damage that Ireland would suffer if de Valera joined the Allies. Even when neutral, Éire had a minor taste of aerial bombing and was attacked several times during the war. Between August and December 1940, when the Luftwaffe campaign against Britain was at its height, Ireland was bombed six times. Three people were killed when a creamery in Campile, County Wexford, was hit in August 1940.[53] In January 1941 bombs fell near the town of Drogheda.[54] The worst attack of the war came in May 1941 when twenty-eight people were killed when unidentified aircraft attacked the North Stand area of Dublin city.[55] The West German government admitted responsibility for the bombing in 1958 and paid £327,000 in compensation.[56] In another example of what might happen, Belfast was twice raided by the Luftwaffe in 1941, killing 900 people and making thousands more homeless.[57] Belfast, although at war as part of the UK, was relatively unprepared for air attack; Dublin was even less defended. This is what many Irish volunteers feared would happen if Ireland entered the war.

Irving, who joined the Royal Artillery after leaving Dublin, strongly felt that de Valera should have joined the Allies, or at least opened the ports for British use. '…it was a stupid thing to do,' he said. '…not having those ports cost an awful lot of British lives.' Joe too felt that the de Valera should have allowed the Royal Navy to use Irish facilities, and saw no contradiction in fighting for Ireland in British uniform. When challenged on the issue, he replied '…we were *there*, that was it. That was the answer we have.' Another veteran felt that he was clearly fighting for Irish neutrality in British uniform. The Germans dropped bombs on Ireland during the war: 'No one fired on him, no one took him down. But we took him down and we fired on him.'[58] Other veterans had mixed feelings. Kenneth feared the result of a Luftwaffe attack on his native Dublin, but also regretted that so many merchant seamen had died bringing supplies to Ireland. Jack felt that Éire, despite being a young nation, still had an obligation to help the British. Cathal, on the other hand never gave it a second thought, nor did Geoffrey, until he realised that the British forces might actually invade Ireland; in which case, he and his cousin decided that he would refuse to obey his orders. Similarly, a Dublin man who joined the British Army in 1943 decided that if he heard of an Allied invasion of Ireland, he and his comrades were going to steal as many weapons as possible, flee to the hills in Asia and join the Indian National Army to fight against the Allies.[59] His remarkable testimony is preserved in the University College Cork Volunteer Archive. Of the fifty-five veteran interviews studied in UCC, twenty-two agreed with neutrality, thirteen disagreed and a further sixteen had no opinion.

They may have had contrasting views on neutrality, but they were certain that Ireland had made a significant contribution to the Allied victory. Albert recalled that in his training camp in Northern Ireland 'there was nothing else but Southern people… I was amazed; they were all over, County Cork and everywhere.' Kenneth reckoned the number could not have been less than 100,000 and that there was a great deal of unofficial Anglo-Irish cooperation which people never knew about. Most of them had stories of meeting up with other Irish in the most incongruous of places. For Joe, it was meeting a young Irishman who would sing rebel songs in the barracks mess at night; for Hilda, it was

Joe in 1942.

Joe in 2011.

encountering an Irishman in a crowded and noisy post office in Rawalpindi when an Indian postmaster was insisting that he had never heard of any such country as Ireland; for John, it was being rescued by a medic from Kerry while bleeding to death on the beach at Anzio in 1944. They left Ireland to fight abroad, but kept running into fellow Irish men and women.

Conclusion

De Valera's attempt to deflect Allied criticism of Irish neutrality both during and after the war had little effect. The Allies were frustrated and irritated by the Irish government's and people's attitude – an examination of Irish neutrality in 1945 described the Irish as 'profoundly and incorrigibly self-centred and provincial'[60] – and were not going to forgive Dublin for not joining the war simply because Irish citizens had flooded into the British forces. Ireland's tactic of highlighting the number of Irish recruits simply annoyed London and Belfast, while Washington cared little. Instead, Washington hoped to use Ireland's difficult economic and diplomatic position to its own advantage. In essence, the State Department wanted to help the Irish agricultural market recover from the wartime slump, which would, in turn, increase exports to the UK, thus helping the British economy to recover and reducing London's dependence on American aid.[61] As one historian has succinctly put it, Ireland was seen as 'a branch of the British economy'.[62] Ireland eventually received Marshall Aid loans, but the effect of Irish neutrality is debatable. Perhaps Washington may have given Dublin grants, rather than loans, but there is no compelling evidence either way. The relative importance that Washington placed on Ireland can be seen by the fact that Dublin received Marshall Aid while Spain, which was also struggling economically but was identified as being strongly pro-Axis, did not.[63]

It was not a priority matter for de Valera either, as he was far more concerned with demonstrating Ireland's independence from Britain, both during and after the war. The actions which shocked the Allied nations the most, particularly the visit to Hempel in May 1945, amply illustrated Ireland's freedom from London, but left behind a feeling of disgust that even full Irish participation in the war would not have dispelled. As for the ex-servicemen themselves, they were not asked to contribute either to the debate on Irish enlistment or about the pros and cons of Irish neutrality, despite the fact that they were uniquely qualified to speak about both. Instead, they focused on more pressing issues once they returned to Ireland – the first and most important of which was how to readjust to civilian life after years of being in uniform.

Chapter four

Health

You never knew which day was going to be your last

Irving, veteran of the Royal Artillery

Post Traumatic Stress?…I think everybody suffers from that

John, veteran of the Irish Guards

In late 1943, a young Dubliner, Jack, found himself at the sharp end of the Second World War. He was among the British forces which stormed ashore on the Dodecanese Islands, just off the coast of Turkey, soon after Italy surrendered in September 1943. Churchill had ordered the taking of the islands against American advice and Washington refused to support Britain in its Mediterranean adventure. For a month, the British troops endured exceptionally heavy German air-raids and Jack, stationed on the island of Leros, vividly remembered 'swarm after swarm of Stuka 87 and 88 fighter-bombers…strafing and bombing incessantly.'[1] For some, the strain was too much and their nerves gave way under the constant pressure. Faced with yet another bombing raid, some men 'curl up, shaking, unable to take any more'[2] but their ordeal was not over yet. On 12 November 1943, German troops landed on Leros and, after heavy fighting, overran the exhausted British garrison, which was short of food, water and ammunition. Jack found himself a prisoner of war and was transported by boat and by train across Europe to a POW camp in Germany. Daily life was harsh in the camps, although he noticed that other nationalities were treated far worse, particularly the Russians. Lack of food, grinding cold, extreme boredom and the dispiriting experience of being a prisoner took its toll on Jack. By the time he returned to Britain, he was suffering from malnutrition, anaemia, dysentery, abdominal problems and weakened eyes. He was treated with great care in a Cambridge hospital for five weeks, before returning to Ireland to a rapturous reception from his family, and with a job in the Guinness brewery and marriage on the horizon.

However, it did not take long for the war to seep back into Jack's peacetime life. Watching a newsreel in a Dublin cinema, he walked out when images of German concentration camps were shown, as they reminded him too much of his own experiences. Even worse, not long after beginning work at Guinness, he noticed something strange happening to him in the mornings before he went to work. 'My hands start[ed] to lock,' he said afterwards. 'I'd have to walk for ages…then [my] hands would start to come right.' He knew what the problem was even before he was diagnosed by the Guinness medical team: he was, as he described it himself, 'Bomb Happy, from the Stuka bombs, the dive bombers.' If he was diagnosed today, the condition would probably be described as Post Traumatic Stress Disorder. Luckily, the Guinness medical doctors were familiar with the problem – Guinness employed many ex-servicemen from both world wars – and Jack was gradually cured with drugs such as Librium and Phenobarbital.

Prisoners of War

Jack was just one of an estimated 1,000 Irish volunteers who had been captured and held as a POW during the Second World War,[3] many of whom returned home mentally and physically scarred by their experiences. All of these veterans were offered the chance to avail of the Civil Resettlement Scheme, a program established by the British government to help former POWs adjust to civilian life. Large houses in the British countryside, called Civil Resettlement Units, were taken over, each of which catered for up to 250 ex-prisoners. Psychiatrists were on hand, group therapy sessions were held and there was even table service at mealtimes, as it was found that having to queue for food sparked unease among the veterans.[4] Eventually 15,000 ex-servicemen passed through these centres.[5] In December 1945 the Irish High Commission in London was approached by representatives of the scheme, who wanted to extend it to Ireland as well. To make sure that no Irish POWs had returned home without being screened by resettlement officials, medical examination boards were established in independent Ireland. They consisted of one Ministry of Pensions official and two local Irish doctors. De Valera himself, through Joseph Walshe, authorised the setting up of these boards.[6]

One Irishman who went through this process was Larry, who hailed from Cork and joined the Royal Navy. He had several horrific experiences, the worst of which was when he was fighting in Norway in April 1940. Trying to dislodge the enemy from the strategically important port of Narvik, British troops landed at Namsos and Åndalsnes in an attempt to out-flank the Germans, supported by the Royal Navy. However, British air cover was weak and the Luftwaffe pounded the expeditionary force. Larry's ship was hit during an air raid and began to sink rapidly. Although Larry managed to scramble overboard and escape, the men in the forward compartments were not so fortunate. 'There they were inside,' he said. 'Their faces out through the portholes, screaming, hoping for help. But there was nothing we could do. And it took them twelve minutes to die.' When he returned to Britain, the first thing he did was go out and get drunk, which did not take long as he had never touched alcohol before. He was then posted to the Far East and was eventually captured by the Japanese and held in a POW camp outside Nagasaki, where he saw the mushroom cloud from the atomic bomb that destroyed the city on 9 August 1945. Larry developed a cynical sense of humour as a way of coping with his traumatic experiences. 'Wherever I seemed to be,' he said afterwards, 'there seemed to be an awful lot of Germans about the place and latterly there seemed to be an awful lot of Japanese.' His release and return to Ireland was a blur, as he spent much of his new-found freedom drunk, trying to come to terms with what he had seen. He was eventually assessed and sent to a psychiatric hospital in Derry, where he was distinctly unimpressed with the treatment he received. He was told to simply forget the war and to find himself a nice girl to settle down with.[7] Ex-prisoners were advised not to talk about their feelings to civilians once they returned home; the accepted wisdom was that society would have limited sympathy for a soldier who had surrendered rather than fight.[8]

The scale of the problem faced by returning POWs in trying to adapt to normal conditions was huge. Quite apart from psychological damage suffered as a result of their imprisonment, what had become normal behaviour in the camp was outrageous by normal standards. One witness to this was Hilda, who had left Dublin to join the Queen Alexandra's Imperial Nursing Service (QAIMNS) and spent the war working in India and Burma. Returning to Europe aboard a troop ship in late 1945, her duty was to care for 120 recently released POWs. Their behaviour shocked her:

> Young men, all middle-aged, they'd had such a time, they used to snatch and bury their food in the bed, even after those months…Every day they'd go down to the NAAFI and take as much as they could get and stack it up. They'd never eat it, they couldn't eat it. They never offered you a thing. We were rattled about that, because we were dying for a bit of chocolate. All that chocolate, we weren't allowed to get it, and they could and they'd have it, stacked on their locker. They couldn't clutch in enough. But you see, that was the way. They'd never be right.

Emotional Demobilisation

Former POWs were in a minority among returning Irish veterans. The problem faced by the vast majority of Irish ex-servicemen was the phenomenon of 'emotional demobilisation': after the stress, exhilaration and danger of life in uniform, the transition to civilian life was very difficult indeed. Many found themselves very unsettled and unable to readjust for a long time. In modern terms, it is known as 'fox-hole-to-front-porch' syndrome.[9] Life in the military was ordered, regimented and punctuated with bouts of frantic activity: as Stephen, a RAF volunteer from Cork put it, '…most of the time you're bored stiff, and the rest of the time you're frightened out of your life.'[10] By contrast civilian life had far less rules, but had very different habits and routines. Irving, for example, had an extremely eventful war. His transition from military civilian life was particularly jarring; having served in Northern Ireland, North Africa and Italy for over five years as both an anti-aircraft gunner and infantryman, when he came home he had to move back in with his retired parents. The difficulty of adjusting from life at war to his suburban home in Dublin was intense. His parents treated him as if he was still the young man that had left, not the combat veteran who had returned. When he was going out, they wanted to know where he was going and if he was late back they would sit up and wait for his return. 'I suppose they were so glad to have you home that they didn't realise I had grown up a bit,' he said afterwards. His situation was further complicated by the fact that he was not given his regular job back by the Royal Bank when he returned. He was instead listed as temporary staff, which meant that he could be shifted from branch to branch with little or no notice. This uncertainty, coupled with his parents' inability to see that he had matured during his time abroad, made life 'very trying' for him. 'It was difficult; it was totally different, real life,' he said. 'Going to a job, nine to five, and then coming home.' It was very different from life in uniform.

This was similar to many other veterans. George, who was a Royal Navy volunteer from Wicklow, found it very difficult to sit in an office after the war, despite the fact that he had seen very little combat. Nevertheless, his transition from sailor to civilian was extremely difficult for him and after his return, he would abruptly leave his desk to wander about Dublin, in an attempt to find peace of mind. He was lucky: like Jack in the Guinness brewery, his employer was sympathetic and never made a fuss when he went missing for an afternoon.[11] Cathal tried to go back to college upon his return, but found it extremely difficult because

Irving in 1943.   **Irving in 2011.**

he felt that he had 'lost the ability to learn things'. While some ex-servicemen, such as Irving, were distressed because their families did not recognise that they had changed during their time away, others felt disjointed because their world had changed so much in their absence. Royal Artillery volunteer and Dubliner Kenneth said of his return 'we found the attitude completely changed. Naturally, in four and a half years, old friends had got married, old girlfriends had gotten new boyfriends.'

Traumatic Experiences

The difficulty experienced by many Irish ex-servicemen in adapting to civilian life was exacerbated by the fact that many had suffered severely traumatic experiences during the war. These things were not easily forgotten. Working as ground staff for the RAF, and following the Canadian forces as they advanced through Germany, Dubliner Albert arrived at Bergen-Belsen concentration camp, not long after it had been liberated in April 1945. As the war drew to a close, the camp had been flooded with prisoners as camps near the front lines were evacuated and as the inmate population swelled, conditions deteriorated rapidly. Allied troops who liberated the camp discovered 10,000 unburied corpses and a further 40,000 dead buried in mass graves. Of the surviving 40,000 inmates, many were so emaciated that they could not be saved and it is estimated that 28,000 died after the Allies arrived.[12] The camp was over-crowded, ridden with disease, and the inmates were malnourished. The sight that confronted Albert and his friend when they walked through the gates was something that he would never forget.

> I was with an Irishman actually, and he said, do you know what he said, 'Belsen is up this way, lets go have a look at it.' So we did. We went and had a look at Belsen, and it hadn't long been liberated. The British Army had set fire to most of the huts they were in because they were so stinking rotten that they had burnt them down and they arrested all the guards and they…the people who were strong enough, who had only recently gone there, they had put them in the huts the guards were using, beautiful huts with all conveniences. But when they saw me, the women came around, they tried to talk, they hadn't much English, and they were pulling up their sleeves showing their…everyone had their number tattooed on their arm, and they were lucky to be alive, but the ones that had gone there previously, they had just starved to death, they weren't gassed there, they were just ignored, it was a terrible, terrible state of affairs. They were sleeping like animals in long huts with beds all close together and just left. They were ruined for life, really, some of them was half mad. It's very sad; it brought it home to you. And that Irishman, I forget his name now, he came from Dublin, he said 'If we ever needed a reason for joining up, this was it. This is what we joined up for.' I'll never forget that.

Frank, a Grenadier Guardsman, also saw the terrible scenes at Belsen. He and his comrades came across a railway car carrying prisoners to the

Frank in 2011.
(Frank did not keep any photos from his time in uniform.)

camp:'…we opened the door [of the train carriage] and Jesus, we were stopped dead. Don't want to remember it; want to forget about it, not worth thinking about.' He was also unfortunate enough to see the concentration camp at Neuengamme, also near Hamburg. Neuengamme was the scene for medical experimentation on children[13] and it is estimated that a total of 82,000 prisoners died at the camp.[14] Unlike Albert, who was more than willing to talk about his experiences, Frank was unwilling to elaborate on what he saw either at Belsen or Neuengamme. Another Irish volunteer, David, saw the burying of corpses at Belsen and remembered that his team had to have injections before they entered the camp.[15]

Kenneth, the Dublin volunteer with the incredibly long military family tree, heard about the camp at Buchenwald second-hand from his friend and was still sickened:

> There was hardened soldiers there and they vomited on the ground with what they saw. Sick to their stomachs. Living corpses lying there, skin and bone. They threw up with what they saw. He said it was frightful, and the oven they burnt them in, men women and children, and they even had rooms there for to pick the gold teeth out of any of the Jews or any others that were executed. And they were all put there. Decent articles of clothing, jewellery, were put somewhere else. Everything was taken from them, they even cut their hair off, and *that* was used. He said it was frightful. To his dying day, he'd never ever forget what he saw in that place.

Few Irish veterans ever did forget.

Even those who did not see the cruelty of Nazi rule were damaged by their own, equally shattering, experiences. Kenneth found himself at the epicentre of anti-British riots in India just after the war ended. The twin sources of the agitation were the British attempt to prosecute Indian soldiers who fought for the Japanese – the Indian National Army (INA) – and Indian demands for self-government.[16] By 1945, the whole sub-continent seethed with tension and the situation was exacerbated by eyewitness accounts of British troops ill-treating their Asian allies.[17] Royal Indian Naval forces mutinied and six deaths occurred after shots were exchanged with British forces.[18] Street mobs rampaged through the major cities, killing anybody they found in an Allied uniform. Kenneth was in charge of an armed detachment of three trucks and was tasked with bringing supplies to a city-centre hotel in Calcutta which had become a refuge for foreigners in the city. During the journey he saw an American truck driver who was killed and set alight, and later witnessed the enraged mob descend upon a British machine-gun post on the street. A patrol stopped beside the soldiers and exchanged a few words with the men manning the post as the horde surged towards them. The machine-gunners urged their comrades to get out of harm's way: 'For God's sake, don't stop, get out, the hell out of here,' they said to them before they drove away, leaving them to face the wrath of the crowd. Kenneth didn't know what happened to them, but he suspected that they did not survive long. 'God, they must have been torn to shreds,' he reflected after the war.

One of the most painful aspects of going to war was being asked to kill. No matter how thorough the training and intense the preparation, taking the life of another human made a deep impression on many volunteers. Some Irish soldiers had their own ways of coping. Irving, who was an anti-aircraft gunner, found that when his gun detachment shot down an enemy aircraft, he found it

> exciting, it's not nice to say exciting, but to see a 'plane coming down, to see a German 'plane being shot down, we saw a few of them coming down alright. They weren't direct hits. It was nearly impossible to hit a 'plane, I know some did get the odd direct hit, but if the shell exploded near enough to the aircraft, it didn't need to have a direct hit to put it out of order and it spins down. You don't think if there is a man in it, or two men or ten men, you just say 'oh that's good…we're doing our job' sort of thing.

Others had less success dealing with the consequences. Upon witnessing Royal Navy destroyers attacking a U-boat with depth charges, Kenneth found himself sympathising with the German sailors: 'I felt sorry for the poor buggers that were down there in the submarines, Germans though they were, what a horrible death you get down there,' he said. Belfast native Sam McAughtry's memoirs recall a searing experience when his aircraft strafed and killed enemy soldiers on a Greek beach. 'Those soldiers didn't pose a military threat', he wrote. 'Somebody has suggested since that they posed a considerable threat to the Greeks on Rhodes. Maybe so, but I'd rather not have seen the men so clearly as they died. I'd never have made a foot soldier.'[19] Aircrew usually felt disengaged from the effects of their handiwork by the space between them and the target. One USAF veteran described it to British historian Laurence Rees as killing 'from a distance…it doesn't have that demoralizing effect upon you that it did if I went up and stuck a bayonet in somebody's stomach.'[20] They never saw the results of their actions. It was this disconnection that was missing in McAughtry's case and he found it an intensely distressing experience.

Kilkenny-born John underwent two deeply traumatic experiences during his time with the British army. First, he was aboard the Polish troopship HMS *Chobry* when it was sunk by German bombers off the coast of Norway in 1940, and had to throw himself overboard to escape. He was rescued by HMS *Stork* but the ship was under constant air attack and he was deafened by the ship's anti–aircraft guns. However, his war had only just begun. His unit next saw action in North Africa and after that, in January, 1944 he took part in the Anzio landings on the Italian coast. The attack was an attempt to break the deadlock around Monte Cassino, which was the lynch-pin of the German defences along the Gustav Line. The fighting focused on the monastery which overlooked the Liri valley and the Allied advance was held up around Cassino by fierce German resistance for five months. It was intended that the Anzio operation would outflank the defences and trigger a German retreat, freeing up Allied forces to advance on Rome and perhaps even encircle and destroy significant enemy forces. However, German strength was far

John in 2009.

more than the Allies anticipated
and the landing was soon bogged
down. The ferocity of the fighting
on the beach around Anzio led to
its being nick-named 'Hell's Half-
Acre'.[21] The Irish Guards were
badly mauled during the battle:
John's unit was under relentless
attack for two days and he was
shot in the stomach, groin and
legs. His comrades were forced
back and he was captured by the
Germans, who placed him under
cover in a destroyed tank and gave
him some medical aid. He was
then caught up in a British
counter-attack, and he was shot in
the hip when the RAF strafed the
position. His memory of the

John in 1939.

events was still clear, 66 years afterwards:

> And I was bleeding from the…my equipment. I was hit in the stomach as well, you see. Both my legs were shattered…There was plenty shooting going on, mortars and shellfire and everything else, but they all stopped, because a lot of it was our own stuff, our own artillery, so that was all right, we were on a sunken road, and the Germans rounded up these men and some of them were prisoners and took them with them, and they ran right into a company from my own Battalion, and the company wiped them out… They even killed some of our own fellas… There was a fight, hand fight, on the roadway, and they went away and just left us there, everything became quiet, I was bleeding like a pig, and I kept crawling off the stretcher and Moriarty kept putting me back again, and he gave me morphine, morphine tablets… They attacked with big scissors, cut the uniform, boots, everything off me, and I cried out for water, they couldn't give me water with stomach wounds. Oh God, it was an awful bloody place. It was a horseshoe perimeter, and at the back was a Navy, two Navies, Americans and the British, and on three sides were the Germans. They were hammering that beachhead day and night.

John was eventually found by a British army Medic, who turned out to have been a butcher from Tralee in his civilian life. He was rushed back to the casualty clearing station on the beach, before being evacuated. He eventually lost a kneecap and was invalided out of the forces, still only twenty-two years old. When asked if he suffered any mental damage, he mused, 'Post Traumatic Stress? Well, there was a certain amount of that, I suppose. I don't know, it was only reading about it afterwards…I think everybody suffers from that.'

Mental Illness

As John discovered, during combat both the mind and body are at risk.

The strain of waiting to go into battle, the shock of fighting and coming to terms with the aftermath can cause severe mental illness. 'Shell-shock' was first discovered to be a psychiatric condition during the First World War, and Irish writer Liam O'Flaherty, himself a veteran of the trenches, wrote a moving fictional account of a soldier sliding over the edge of madness in his novel *The Return of the Brute*. In that book, the main character's mania manifested itself in hallucinations and he imagined he could see hordes of hairy, ape-like creatures which eventually drove him to murder one of his comrades.[22] Those who had been disturbed by their experiences and who returned to Ireland after the Great War found themselves suffering multiple handicaps. Not only were some ostracised for having joined the British forces, but they were also labelled as weak in a society that was heavily militarised, and faced scepticism when they tried to claim benefits from the British government.[23]

Drawing on their experiences between 1914 and 1918, Allied military commanders expected that there would be a high number of psychiatric casualties during the Second World War. *Combat Exhaustion*, a report compiled by US army psychiatrists, pointed out that war produced a bewildering array of emotions in soldiers, as a result of which it was impossible for a person ever to be immune to the mental effects of fighting. The maximum that any soldier should be exposed to combat was generally held to be 180 days, and even then efficiency was seriously eroded after ninety days in the front line.[24] During the war, the combined psychiatric casualties of the US Navy and army totalled over 1.15 million.[25] However, there remained a stigma attached to the issue and a British Ministry of Health survey in 1946 discovered that only 5 per cent of veterans who were released because of mental illness received further treatment.[26]

It is impossible to say with any accuracy how many servicemen came back to Ireland after the Second World War suffering from mental illness as a result of their service, but it is possible to get a snap-shot of the period through the records of St. Bridget's Psychiatric Hospital in Ballinasloe, County Galway. In May 1946, there were four ex-British soldiers in the hospital whose treatment was being paid for by the London government.[27]

One was admitted in June 1944, suffering from 'Shell-Shock'. Another was suffering from 'melancholia', while a third, a 68 year-old man, was afflicted with 'Senile Psychosis (Supposed Cause: Worry)'.[28] Soldiers in combat were not the only ones at risk. Between January 1940 and October 1946, ten soldiers from the Irish army were treated at the hospital, for issues like neurasthenia, schizophrenia and manic depression.

Some veterans, like Jack, were treated with drugs which corrected their problem. Drugs such as insulin, sodium pentathol and barbiturates were widely used by doctors at the time to treat combat-related mental illness.[29] However, a lack of understanding of the condition meant that treatments varied considerably. Electro-convulsive therapy was still considered an effective treatment for depression, as was lobotomy.[30] Richard, whose story we encountered in the opening of this book, was one man who underwent brain surgery to correct his problem. One particularly cruel British military counsellor routinely locked nerve-damaged men in small rooms in darkness for three days, giving them only bread and water.[31] However, the rise of sophisticated psychiatric drugs in the 1950s meant that more archaic treatments were gradually phased out. There were places to turn in Ireland for men enduring combat stress: a small treatment and training centre for 'men suffering from psycho-neurosis' was established in Merrion Square, Dublin by the Soldiers, Sailors and Airmen's Help Society in conjunction with the British Red Cross. It was a small operation and catered for about a dozen men.[32] However, the lack of widespread counselling services meant that many ex-servicemen returning to Ireland did not seek help or receive treatment.

One such case was Patrick, who travelled to Enniskillen from Longford with his brother Michael in late 1939 to join the British Army. He enlisted in the Royal Electrical and Mechanical Engineers (REME) and was posted to France in 1940. There his unit was broken up by the German attack in May and, like hundreds of thousands of British troops, he ended up standing in line on a beach in France, waiting for evacuation. He remained on the open beaches for three days while under near-constant air attack. At one point he was temporarily buried alive when a Stuka dropped a bomb near him and he was engulfed in a wall

**Michael and Paddy, brothers who left the Midlands
to join the British army.**

of sand. When he finally got back to Britain, he immediately deserted and fled home to Ireland. His son described him as a nervous wreck who ran for cover every time an aircraft passed overhead. Disturbed survivors of the evacuations were so common that the British Army issued guidelines to service wives in 1940, instructing them not to 'worry if your man screams at night or throws himself down when a 'plane flies over the back garden'.[33] It is more than likely that Patrick was suffering from second-level battle fatigue, which usually affects troops upon their first exposure to severe stress. It makes a dramatic impact on the sufferer, but the major effects are only temporary, although it can leave a permanent mark.[34] In Patrick's case, it left him suffering from claustro-phobia for the rest of his life. Often, the trauma remained buried for many years and resurfaced unexpectedly: events such as the fiftieth anniversary of D-Day brought back some unpleasant memories. Frank Mc., a young Dubliner who joined the RAF, recalled that as the anniversary of D-Day approached and media coverage of the events were increasing, 'awful things come back…I have a lot of bad dreams occasionally'.[35]

While soldiers such as Patrick recovered, many others did not. Alcohol was a refuge for many, as it was for Larry. Others saw their marriages collapse or were unable to keep jobs. Inevitably, there were tragedies. Among the incidents recorded by historian Richard Doherty were two terrible events: in one incident, an ex-serviceman gassed himself, while another shot both his sons before turning the gun on himself.[36] One of the major problems facing Irish men and women who returned with psychological disturbance was the stigma which was attached to nervous disorders. During battle, those who fell prey to shell-shock were routinely isolated from the main troops, and were considered to be unreliable or even shirkers. In his memoirs, Jack inadvertently revealed how little sympathy combat troops had for nerve-damaged men: crammed into the hold on a German ship while being transported to a POW camp, Jack said that the situation wasn't 'helped by the whining of a couple of "battle happies", moaning about their predicament'.[37] John, who had come through the hell of Anzio, also remembered wartime discrimination. One of his comrades came across a small group of men in a military hospice in Italy who were refused food, because they had been diagnosed with psychiatric damage. They had been officially classified as 'Lacking Moral Fibre', and were looked down upon by their colleagues. Terrible as this may sound, it is an illustration that, in combat, there is little room for sympathy.

Guilt preyed on veteran's minds once they returned, usually guilt at having survived when so many had died. Death on the battlefield was completely random, and there was no logical explanation as to why one man survived while another died. Sometimes it was simply chance that dictated events. Kenneth, while on loan to the Royal Navy as a gunner, remembered that a German reconnaissance aircraft flew over his convoy, which was headed for North Africa. It was just good fortune that the airplane was out of range and so would not be able to direct the Luftwaffe to his position quickly enough. However, Kenneth knew that the next convoy would not be so lucky, and his instincts were correct. 'We found out that that convoy had been bombed by the Luftwaffe and been blown to pieces. Obviously the Luftwaffe was going to come after *our* convoy, which had been spotted by the reconnaissance plane; I suppose they thought that one convoy was as good as another.' Irving too reflected on the role luck played in his survival: 'when the bombs were dropping and you were firing the guns, you did say "very near"…it was all just luck, you know?…you never knew which day was going to be your last.'

Similarly, when burying the casualties of the battle for Leros, surrounded by death and destruction, Jack felt 'a sudden and desperate sense of guilt about being still alive'.[38] He had done nothing in particular to ensure his own survival and he could not understand why he remained alive when so many had been killed. Dermot, who hailed from Dublin and joined the British Merchant Navy, witnessed the aftermath of a devastating German air raid on the Italian port of Bari and afterwards couldn't face anything that reminded him of death: 'you usually feel guilt that it's not you…you can't let it get to you.'[39] He also felt as if he had done nothing special to survive, while so many of their comrades were dead. RAF man Martyn found himself after the war staring at his British-issue gas mask and imagining what happened to the Jews in extermination camps.[40] Irish writer Peter Cunningham depicted his father, a former captain in the British Army, staring into space as he got older, reflecting on the moment when he killed a German officer in Holland in 1944.[41] Guilt at his desertion in 1940, having survived Dunkirk, gnawed away at Patrick so much that he joined the RAF under an assumed name. The strain of combat on the volunteer's mind was tremendous, but trying to understand why they had survived when many around them had died was even more difficult.

Physical Health

One of the major benefits which Irish ex-servicemen drew from their time with the British forces was the fact that, if they were injured or wounded while on duty, London was willing to pay for their medical care, even while in Éire. In October 1944, the British government announced that Irish veterans would receive the same medical benefits as those who remained in Britain after the war. The British Legion was the conduit for much of the assistance handed out. Danny, an Irish army veteran, remembered one of his neighbours who returned from the British forces with a serious head wound, and that he was 'looked after well by the British Legion'. He needed frequent medical treatment, and the family spent much of their time travelling to hospital in Dublin or to Britain. Much of the Legion's efforts went into providing such care for Irish ex-servicemen. In its annual Poppy appeal in November 1945, the Legion journal noted that it had spent over £59,000 on ex-service welfare between October 1944 and September 1945.[42]

The main centre for the medical care of Irish ex-servicemen was Leopardstown Hospital, which had been established in 1917 to cater for wounded Irish soldiers, and which was administered by the British Ministry of Pensions. The first batch of soldiers cared for there in 1918 were nerve-damaged veterans of the First World War, and from 1926 onwards it also treated physical wounds as well; a function it carried out throughout the Second World War. Some men returned home with horrific injuries. Kenneth recounted seeing 'a fella once, poor devil, he had a plastic, half his face was shot away. Half his face was OK, the rest was covered with a plastic sheet like that, he was so horribly maimed. Terrible, terrible casualties. Particularly RAF fellas were terribly badly burned.' However, the hospital offered more than simply medicine. A strong emphasis was made on keeping patients active and there was a constant cycle of outings, competitions, sporting events and social evenings. Don, who worked in the Guinness brewery after returning from the Royal Engineers, recalled that they always provided free beer to the patients. Unfortunately, medical records are always highly sensitive sources and the archives of the hospital remain closed to researchers.

Conclusion

The experience of fighting and serving during the Second World War made a deep impression on Irish volunteers. Many found their outlook and attitude towards life altered forever. An unknown number of Irish ex-servicemen returned psychologically damaged by their exposure to war. The difficulty of re-assimilation into civilian life endured by every returning soldier was further added to by the lack of concern and a sense of apathy towards ex-servicemen from the Irish public. Although a by-product of war-time neutrality and not an illustration of animosity, it made it harder for Irish ex-servicemen to readjust to peacetime life. It was lonely and difficult for the volunteers to come home to a country that did not fully understand what they had experienced. For many, there was only a huge sense of anti-climax when they returned. Kenneth was disappointed that, after serving in the war, Irish veterans 'didn't come home the conquering heroes kind of thing'. Or, as Irving put it,

> when I came back *nothing* happened. I just came off the boat in Dun Laoghaire. I remember a porter, one of the porters on the mail boat, the mail boat used to come into Dun Laoghaire, and one of the porters said 'Soldier, can I carry your kitbag?' That was all that happened.

Chapter five

Money

*It is not contemplated that preference to any type of
employment will be offered to persons returning to this
country from civilian or other employment elsewhere*
Department of Industry and Commerce memo, October 1945

Southern Ireland is a depressed area for ex-Servicemen
Irish Times, 31 January 1947

The return to civilian life was not just mentally difficult for Irish ex-
servicemen, it was full of practical problems as well. In many cases, veterans
had grown used to items such as clothing, food, accommodation and
footwear being provided as a matter of course by the armed forces. When
a pair of boots wore out, another was provided from the stores; if you were
peckish between mealtimes in the barracks, you nipped down to the
subsidised canteen. However, in the post-war world, these things had to
be sought out, budgeted for, purchased and then preserved as best as
possible, as they were often in short supply. The transition from soldier to
job-seeker was made less of a jolt in Britain, as the government there
instituted a wide-ranging system of employment preferences, training
courses and low-interest loans to ex-servicemen looking to re-enter the
job market or set up their own businesses. However, for those Irish
veterans who chose to return to their own country, no such safety-net
existed. British re-employment schemes were not extended to Ireland;
Irish ex-servicemen returned to a country which was in the midst of a
deep economic slump and in which ex-members of the Irish Defence

Forces had a significant advantage when it came to finding jobs. Although the British and Irish governments cooperated to allow London to provide limited unemployment insurance to Irish veterans of the war, and firms such as Guinness strove to employ them, there is no doubt that ex-servicemen returning to Ireland after the war faced an uphill struggle.

The Irish Economy

By 1945, the Irish economy had been in difficulty for over a decade. The Economic War with Britain, which lasted from 1932 until 1938, and the economic impact of the world war from 1939 onwards produced high unemployment and severe emigration in independent Ireland. During the war, Irish industrial production shrank by 20 per cent.[1] From 1945 to 1948 there were successive strikes, fuel shortages, food crises and poor harvests which saw the reintroduction of bread rationing in 1947. A memorandum produced by the Department of Finance for the new Minister, Frank Aiken, illustrated the depth of the problem. It pointed out that Ireland lacked natural resources, suffered from a dearth of industrial development, had lost its place in the world agricultural export market because of the war, faced the prospect of an aging population and concluded by saying that the State was far too expensive to run. Department experts suggested that it would be 'much better to reduce the cost of living' than to increase public expenditure and unsurprisingly, Aiken took care to ensure that this memo did not leak to the press.[2] Furthermore, although there was a short-lived consumer boom in 1945, the economy as a whole was very slow to recover, and between 1938 and 1958 Irish industrial employment grew by only 10 per cent, hampering Ireland's economic performance in a rapidly industrialising world.[3] Prices had risen sharply as imports dropped away during the Emergency, and by 1945 the cost of living in independent Ireland had risen by two-thirds, but wages had only risen by one-third.[4] The de Valera government outlined an ambitious reconstruction plan in a White Paper after the war, proposing to spend a total of £71 million on roads, housing, hospitals, schools and hydro-electric power stations,[5] but few of these projects made it into reality. Probably the most bizarre was that drawn up by Frank Aiken, which suggested taking twenty years to pave all the roads in Ireland. Secondary roads and cul-de-sacs would be targeted first. 'It is on these roads that people get their feet wet,' he wrote, 'and that children suffer most hardship travelling to and from school.'[6] It is unclear if even Aiken himself took this seriously.

Returning veterans saw for themselves the extent of the problems facing the Irish economy, and what they would have to overcome to make a living in Ireland. Upon returning to Dublin from the Far East, Kenneth remarked that 'Ireland was pretty poverty-stricken. It was very poor.' John W., a post-war infantry recruit who fought in Korea, remembered having to make tea out of chopped carrots.[7] Danny, who joined the Irish forces, recalled that sweets were a rarity in his native Athlone at the time. Even members of the Irish political elite were feeling the effects. Garret FitzGerald, a future Fine Gael Taoiseach and son of one of the founding members of the Free State, recalled in his memoirs that petrol was hard to come by and that only 'doctors, diplomats, Ministers and key civil servants' could obtain fuel vouchers.[8] RAF veteran Joe, however, remembered that certain politicians did not allow this to interrupt their social life: his father used to meet on Sundays with Seán Lemass, the Minister for Supplies. Lemass would call to his house in Drumcondra 'with the squad cars in front and behind him and go down to Skerries' with Joe's father for a round of golf.

Historian Cormac Ó Gráda has memorably described the economic effects of the war on every day life in Ireland as resulting in an 'era of brown bread, damp turf, weak tea and unpleasant coffee substitutes such as Coff-o-era'.[9] But it was unemployment which was the eternal problem for the Irish government. In May 1945 61,604 people were out of work[10] and the figure would undoubtedly have been much higher had so many people not emigrated during the war. Of those who remained behind, many made their presence felt on the streets. Thomas, a part-time member of the Irish Defence Forces who was then employed in the Guinness brewery in the 1940s and 1950s, remembers the violence of enormous protest marches on the streets of Dublin soon after the war. He saw

> 50,000 lined O'Connell Street and O'Connell bridge, unem-
> ployed. Early fifties. 50,000. We were down, Maureen and myself,
> and they were F–ing everybody around and the police could do
> nothing with them. Lying on the ground. Buses, trams, nothing
> could go… Anyway, this fella had some kind of a placard, like that
> lamp there, something like that and he made a belt at a policeman
> that was coming down, the cap came off his head and the
> policeman whipped it off him and hit your man a belt with it
> and *his* head came up through it.

Concessions for Ex-Members of the
Irish Defence Forces

The poor economic state of Ireland at the end of the war had very
serious consequences for Irish veterans of the British forces. In January
1947, the *Irish Times* noted that

> Southern Ireland is a depressed area for ex-Servicemen. Their
> chances of obtaining employment are understandably small, with
> the competition of men released from the Defence Forces here,
> and it is no secret that great numbers of them have been
> compelled to return to England, after the expiration of the
> demobilisation leave, to seek employment there.[11]

Their difficulties were added to by the fact that the small Irish job
market was rapidly filling with demobilised members of the Irish
Defence Forces, all of whom had access to a comprehensive system of
employment concessions and gratuities that Irish men and women
returning from the British forces did not. The Irish military had
undergone a huge expansion since the outbreak of war; in 1939, its
front-line strength was estimated to be 7,600, with a further 4,300

reservists and another 7,200 in the part-time Volunteer force.[12] After the Low Countries and France had fallen to the Germans, the government awoke to the danger with a jolt. A strong recruiting drive was belatedly launched by the government in June 1940, and army numbers surged to 40,174 by June 1941.[13] After this peak, they declined to around the 30,000 mark; in March 1945, the total strength of the Defence Forces was 32,115.[14] Recruitment for the Irish forces was hampered by the fact that pay was lower than in the British and because there was a general feeling that the Irish Army would never see any real action.[15] Chief of Staff Dan McKenna deplored the low rate of enlistment and lobbied Oscar Traynor, the Minister for Defence, for 'some kind of compulsory military service', but to no avail.[16] Rather than try and attract recruits for the regular military service term, the Department of Defence decided that recruits should be offered the choice of joining as career soldiers or for the duration of the Emergency. Those opting for the latter became known as 'E-men' or 'durationists'. On 22 November 1944, recruitment of durationists was halted in the Irish army[17] and plans were drawn up for demobilisation. So great were the difficulties involved in this that a special resettlement section, named S.10, was established within the Department of Defence Secretariat. Post-war plans were developed to establish a small Defence Force of 12,500 front-line soldiers, with large numbers of part-time reserves. A large-standing army is an expensive instrument, so the government wanted it dismantled quickly and efficiently.

The White Paper on *Demobilisation and Resettlement of Members of the Defence Forces*, produced by the government in May 1945, proposed a number of concessions to former Irish army members. Soldiers who sat the civil service exams were awarded extra marks, which were in addition to those awarded to Irish speakers. Soldiers who exceeded the civil service age limit would have their service years subtracted from their age, up to a maximum of six years. Those men who had left employment to enlist were legally entitled to their jobs back upon demobilisation, and the Minister for Defence was given the legal power to impose heavy penalties if they were not.[18] A tax-free gratuity of three days' pay for every thirty days of Emergency service (up to a maximum of seventy-two Emergency periods) was awarded.[19] The total cost to the taxpayer was in the region of £4 million, of which £2.5 million would be spent on gratuities.

The Department of Industry and Commerce also arranged that ex-Irish soldiers registered at Irish employment exchanges would be given first preference in being allocated jobs. It was later agreed that even when soon-to-be-demobilised soldiers were *not* registered but were seeking employment, then 'the offers of employment should be notified to the Department of Defence so that serving non-permanent personnel (i.e. personnel due for demobilisation) could still be afforded an opportunity of applying for them.'[20] Officers were exempted from this scheme; it was pointed out that 'their former employment or Army employment has not been of an industrial nature' and that they should be treated differently than the ranks.[21] All preferences were to be left in place for five years to allow all Emergency soldiers to take advantage of them.[22] Companies such as Aer Lingus, the state Sugar Company, CIÉ (the State transport company) and the Post Office all agreed to give preference to Irish ex-soldiers.[23] Aer Lingus recruited clerks and administrators from the Emergency forces,[24] as well as some pilots from the RAF and Fleet Air Arm. CIÉ took almost all the released army drivers,[25] and Danny, a veteran of the Irish Defence Forces, was one of many ex-Irish soldiers given a job as a lineman on the railway after the war. In addition, the official Department of Defence history of the period noted that the 'Post Office absorbed nearly all available Signal Corps personnel'.[26] The army also gave personal interviews to offer advice to demobbed men who were having trouble finding work.[27]

The post-war rural electrification scheme also offered employment to ex-Irish army men, and in February 1952, Patrick McGrath, Fianna Fáil TD for Cork, asked the government to ensure that the scheme gave preference to Irish veterans rather than British ex-servicemen.[28] There was even a suggestion from the Department of Industry and Commerce that government posts such as employment clerks, prison wardens and district court clerks should be entirely reserved for Irish former army men.[29] In addition, in June 1946, the cabinet asked private contractors building houses in Dublin to employ demobbed Irish soldiers only, 'as far as practicable'.[30] These concessions were initially to be kept in place for five years, to allow all demobbed Irish soldiers to take advantage of them, but documents in the Department of Defence show that they were extended by almost eight years and only came to an end in December 1953.[31]

However, it must also be noted that these concessions were limited in a number of ways. The extra marks that were awarded to ex-soldiers applying for the Irish civil service were quite small. They were limited to 1/12 of a per cent for each month of service, up to a maximum of 6 per cent for full-time soldiers. If the applicant had been a member of the Reserve or any of the 'Auxiliary Defence Organisations', then he or she was limited to 1/40 of a percent for each month of service. None of these marks were to be awarded if the candidate was not fully qualified for the post.[32] The preference scheme also caused some intra-departmental tensions. For instance, the Departments of Defence and Local Government squabbled over the issue of priority housing for former soldiers. Peadar MacMahon, secretary of the Department of Defence, refused to hand over accommodation in army barracks to homeless civilians, arguing that Local Government had refused to allow ex-members of the Irish army to skip the queue for council housing in Dublin.[33] The conflict smouldered on until July 1948, when a compromise was reached: 46 houses were set aside by Dublin Corporation for demobilised soldiers.[34]

The raft of concessions for ex-members of the Irish army were much the same as those offered by other countries to their veterans. Governments had always offered extensive benefits to ex-servicemen. In Bismarckian Germany, any man who remained in the army beyond his term of compulsory service was entitled to State employment once he left.[35] The US government offered extensive concessions to its ex-servicemen[36] and had preference schemes for ex-soldiers dating back to the Civil War.[37] Canada's post-1945 incentive scheme compared favourably with Britain.[38] But the difference between Ireland and these other countries was that the concessions were aimed at one set of ex-servicemen only. What this meant was that the small Irish job market was tilted in favour of demobbed men from the Irish forces, and Irish men and women returning from the British forces found it increasingly difficult to find employment. They were left in no-man's land between the two governments: it was impossible for the British to extend their re-employment schemes to Ireland, and Dublin – not surprisingly – was committed to looking after the men and women who had joined the Irish defence and auxiliary forces.

We should also acknowledge that the de Valera government did not set out to reward Irish ex-servicemen simply out of the goodness of their hearts. There was also a political aspect to the concessions. De Valera and the Irish army authorities drew a direct line between the expansion of the Irish Defence Forces and the successful maintenance of neutrality. The White Paper spoke about 'men who so gallantly responded to the national call'[39] and de Valera's speech in May 1945 thanked a huge range of Irish Emergency services, from soldiers to volunteer medical staff. 'The ordeal of the past five years is over and all who joined the defence forces,' he said, 'have the satisfaction of knowing that they played their part in warding off the danger that menaced the nation for the whole of that period.'[40] By over-emphasising the role the Defence Forces had played in maintaining Irish neutrality, he was indirectly claiming credit himself, quietly reminding the Irish public that it was his government which had built up the armed forces. In addition, as thousands of soldiers left the army basking in the gratitude of the government and a post office book full of gratuity cash, perhaps de Valera calculated his generosity would be rewarded next time ex-soldiers went to the polls. If this was his intention, he was mistaken. With recession and shortages gripping the country in the immediate aftermath of the war, Fianna Fáil, for the first time in sixteen years, was ousted from power in the 1948.

Re-employment

The need to find a job immediately was offset for many ex-servicemen returning from the continent by the fact that the British forces handed out both a gratuity and demobilisation pay when releasing personnel. Belfast-born volunteer Sam McAughtry describes in his memoirs holding a roll of banknotes after he was demobbed from the RAF and feeling that the 'roll of notes was the first of the big differences in the way I joined the 1939–45 war and the way I came home from it'.[41] Being a veteran from the British forces could be quite lucrative. Servicemen who were defined as Class A (those who had been in the forces the longest) were handed eight-weeks' paid leave, ration allowance, family allowances (where applicable) and any foreign service entitlements they had accrued.[42] Demobilised men received £12 worth of clothing while women received clothes coupons and a variable cash amount.[43] Geoffrey recalled getting three-months' salary from the RAF when he was demobbed, meaning that he was able to take time to readjust when he came home.

However, this money would not last forever and jobs had to be found. Under the terms of the Reinstatement in Civil Employment Act, passed in March 1944, British employers were required to rehire conscripted servicemen after the war 'on terms and conditions not less favourable to him than he would have had in that occupation if he had not joined the Forces.'[44] While this could not be applied to Ireland, a minority of fortunate Irish volunteers left with the unofficial promise that their civilian job would be kept open for them until their return. Kenneth and Irving, both Dublin-born recruits into the Royal Artillery, came back to their old jobs; Kenneth in the Motor Union insurance company and Irving in the Royal Bank. Joe also walked back into his old job when he returned from the RAF. Intending to wind up his affairs and emigrate to South Africa, he contacted his former employers, who asked him 'When are you going to come back to us?' They gave him a lucrative new job as a field representative, with a car and an expense account. His one regret was not joining Aer Lingus which was recruiting ex-RAF and Fleet Air Arm pilots in 1946. Some historians have suggested that Irish companies may have encouraged their staff to join the British forces by keeping their jobs vacant, or even that veterans of the First World

War encouraged their younger colleagues to enlist, but this is difficult to prove.[45] However, one Irish company which was known to be veteran-friendly was Guinness.

Guinness

Guinness has a long connection to the British armed forces. The company gave its employees leave to join the forces during the Boer War[46] and did the same during the First World War. In 1915 there were around 400 Guinness workers at the front.[47] One half of the absent men's wages were paid to their families and were raised according to the fluctuating cost of living.[48] In 1919, the Guinness board officially sanctioned a policy of giving preference to ex-servicemen for brewery posts[49] and this was extended to cover the Irish Free State army when it was established in 1922. The company instituted a similar raft of schemes upon the outbreak of the Second World War. Unmarried employees who were granted leave to join the British forces were given one-third of the difference between their Guinness pay and their military salary, while married men were compensated for the whole difference, meaning that their families would not suffer any drop in income. A notice was sent to all heads of departments in May 1939 stating that 'while it is, of course, impossible to predict the future, the Board would do its best to re-instate employees at the end of their military service.'[50] On 5 September 1939, the Board reiterated its intention to try and re-employ all those who had left to join military forces. On the same day, it extended its payment scheme to employees who requested leave to join the Irish Defence Forces.[51] Reviewing the employment situation in mid-1945 after the end of the war in Europe, it was reported to the Guinness Board that out of a total workforce of 2,954, nineteen men had been given leave to join the Irish forces and eighty had left to serve in the British.[52] In May 1945, the Board sanctioned a bonus of 20 per cent of annual salary to be paid to all Guinness staff in the UK to celebrate the end of the war in Europe, and repeated it again in November after Japan had surrendered.[53]

All prospective employees applying for work in the brewery had to sit an exam, and the age limit for those wishing to apply was restricted to those between 18 and 22. In 1945, a separate exam category was created for ex-service personnel and the age limit for ex-military applicants was extended. Both categories sat the same exam, but an unspecified number of places were reserved for ex-servicemen, and the Board decided that it was unfair on ex-servicemen, whose education had been interrupted by the war, to compete directly against applicants who had just finished school. Don, who got a job in the brewery shortly after returning to Dublin from service in the Royal Engineers, remembered that he and his fellow veterans sat a separate exam and was assured by his supervisor that he would not be going head-to-head against recent school-leavers. He remembered the exam vividly as being both difficult and pointless. 'So we went back and did the three hours writing, reading, arithmetic, which was absolutely *useless*, completely useless. Anyway, you had an oral interview from the board and all the ex-service fellas, whatever there was, five of us, got in to the brewery and we were sent to different departments.'

Jack also got a job in the brewery, but was called back to his unit in England unexpectedly. Luckily for him the company agreed to defer his start date until he was fully demobbed. The separate exam policy continued until 1948, when the company decided to revert to a single category for applicants. This was done because the Board felt that ex-servicemen's exam results were dropping too low, on account of being 'too long away from school or university'. However, it was still willing to bend the age-limit rules for ex-servicemen, and the personnel department was instructed to allow veterans who were 'not much over the age limit' to sit the entrance exam.[54] By 1949, the limits of Guinness's generosity had been reached: that year's entrance exam results showed that although there were a number of ex-military applicants, none achieved the required standard and none were offered employment. The five available positions were awarded on the basis of merit and regardless of past military service.[55]

However, Guinness's leniency regarding ex-servicemen created some tensions within the company itself. While Don, the ex-Royal Engineers officer, felt that Guinness was a 'bloody marvellous company to work for', Thomas, who had worked in the brewery for twenty-five years, remembered being taken aback by the behaviour of ex-British veterans. He complained that they were 'clannish' and that non-British veterans were often overlooked for promotion. 'It was a sickening attitude,' he said. 'You'd swear they were from different countries. The attitude was, they looked at it as if they were from two different countries…as if they came over on the boat together from England.' Thomas was not an ex-serviceman, but had joined both the Local Security Force and Local Defence Force during the Emergency.

Religion

One of the most controversial aspects of the Irish ex-servicemens' attempts to find employment after the war was the impact of their religion. Research by historians has uncovered that some Irish firms after the war sought to filter job applicants along religious lines.[56] Ex-servicemen, too, remembered that their search for jobs was sometimes shaped by their religion. Albert was told by his friends shortly after his return in 1947 not to apply at places like Clery's department store or the Dublin Fire Brigade: '…the minute they ask you what school you went to and when they hear you went to a Protestant school, they clam up,' he said. He felt that it was religious discrimination, but pointed out that he also witnessed it in reverse: in his pre-war employment there was only one Catholic in the office, and was hired, it was rumoured, to refute the claim that the company employed only Protestants. Cathal, a Catholic, felt that Guinness, the distilleries 'and some of the Insurance Companies, basically the Protestant Unionist organisations…looked after both Protestants and "Castle Catholics"' returnees; historian Tom Garvin has defined Castle Catholics as 'those Catholics who had made their social and cultural peace with the British regime'.[57]

Job vacancies advertised in post-war Irish newspapers often asked for Protestant or Catholic applicants only. It has emerged in recent years that many employers did not actively discriminate against other religions, but that it never occurred to them to look outside their own religious circle. Protestants and Catholics in Ireland had existed within their own worlds for many years before 1945, and the habit was hard to break. In some cases, it was unconscious. As Geoffrey put it, 'I suppose if you're moving in a certain circle…it will always brush off, won't it?' Instead of outright bigotry, he suggested that people stayed within the same groups they were comfortable with, and hired people they knew. 'I wouldn't call it discrimination,' he said, but he acknowledged that '…there was that sort of barrier between one section and another.' It was a practical concern for some employers. Geoffrey applied for a travelling sales job, only to be told by the employer that he didn't want to hire a Protestant. It wasn't that the employer was sectarian; he was a Protestant too, but the sales territory was in the west of Ireland and he felt a Catholic would be better received by western clients. 'That was against me,' Geoffrey said, 'because I was a Protestant, he was a Protestant and it was a Protestant firm, but they didn't want a Protestant to represent them in Galway, the West.'

The lack of contact between the two religious communities some-times had comic consequences for ex-servicemen. When he finally did find a job working as a sales rep for a confectionary company after the war, Geoffrey told a wonderful story of an occasion he inadvertently walked into a Catholic business in Galway at midday. While he was chatting to his contact, the manager came out of his office and called the employees to say the Angelus. The staff all knelt and began their prayers and Geoffrey had no idea of how to react. So he and his colleague simply froze: '…and here's these two gobshites of Protestants standing there, you know? And, of course, all we could do was stand still and bow our head.' It never occurred to him to avoid going into Catholic businesses at midday, but it was a lesson which he did not forget.

Unemployment Insurance

But what of returning ex-servicemen who did not have the luxury of a job to come back to, or the good fortune to be hired by a firm like

Geoffrey in 1941.

Geoffrey in 2011.

Guinness? A minority of veterans who returned to Ireland were unable to find a job and had no recourse to either Irish or British unemployment insurance. Their situation was uniquely complicated. All people in employment in Ireland automatically paid into the Irish government's unemployment insurance fund. If they lost their job, they were entitled to claim back their contributions, until they either found another job or their contributions, or 'stamps' as they were known, ran out. However, once Irish workers left for Britain, either to join the Crown forces or to work in the British war industry, their contributions stopped; once employed in Britain, they instead paid into the British fund. Problems arose when they began to filter back to Ireland once the war ended. If they were unemployed upon their return, they had limited access to Irish unemployment insurance, as many had not contributed to the Irish fund for years, yet they could not claim British stamps either as London – understandably – refused to pay claimants outside of its jurisdiction.

This was not a new problem: in 1927, National League TD William Redmond had pointed out to the Cumann na nGaedheal government that Irish veterans of the First World War were unable to claim their British unemployment insurance, as the Irish Free State was no longer part of the UK. He also pointed out that it was deeply unfair that veterans who returned to Northern Ireland could claim their insurance stamps, but those in the south could not.[58] It was brought up again in the ex-servicemen's committee report in 1928. Sporadic attempts to reach a compromise faltered throughout the 1920s and 1930s, but remained unresolved until the 1940s. As the Second World War drew to an end, the scale of the potential problem began to dawn on the Irish government. De Valera and his ministers, particularly Seán Lemass, became increasingly alarmed that the country would soon be overrun by returning migrants who had little chance of getting jobs in Ireland and would have little or no access to Irish or British unemployment insurance.

The sheer scale of Irish wartime migration to Britain offered clues to the possibly severe situation Dublin was facing. Between 1940 and 1945, 198,538 travel permits were issued to Irish people to travel to Britain,[59] and a further 35,000 are estimated to have applied to leave for Northern Ireland.[60] This was on top of around 60,000 who left to join the British forces, which adds up to over a quarter of a million Irish men and women who left Ireland for Britain between 1939 and 1945. The Irish government facilitated this huge emigration, calculating that it was better to export the unemployed to Britain than to create jobs for them at home, or to run the risk of the unemployed drifting into the clutches of radical groups. Officials were occasionally very open about this; reflecting on a request from a British munitions company to recruit Irish workers, the assistant secretary at the Department of External Affairs, Frederick Boland, wrote that such a plan had 'positive advantage to us'.[61] Likewise, the Cabinet Committee on Emergency Problems decided in May 1941 not to stop Irish people crossing the border to join the British forces because it partially alleviated the unemployment problem.[62]

Irish migrants to Britain were classed as 'conditionally landed' by the British government, which meant that they had to return home every two years to avoid conscription and also – ominously for the Irish government – that they had to return home immediately if they became unemployed. The wartime demand for Irish workers was largely caused by British conscription, which drained the British labour force into the armed forces, leaving gaps that Irish workers were happy to fill. However, as the end of the war approached and the British government publicly promised to provide employment for the five million Britons now in uniform, the de Valera government became alarmed. The fear was that Irish workers would be forced out of their jobs by demobilised soldiers and the migrants would then have to return to Ireland, bringing economic chaos, and social and political upheaval with them. There was real fear within the Irish government that returning migrants would saturate the Irish job market, and that the government would have to assume responsibility for them. Supporting all these men and women, if they were forced to return home after the war, would put a strain on the Irish purse. As Frederick Boland put it, the only way to do it would be by 'asking the Irish taxpayer to put his hand in his pocket',[63] something which no government is ever eager to do. Even worse, from Fianna Fáil's perspective, was the prospect that the Opposition might be boosted by such a situation. It is well known that Boland at External Affairs worried about this and minuted during the war that Irish migrants would have 'imbibed a good deal of "leftism" in Britain'.[64] Historian Alan Allport has discovered that although the number of servicemen who were released to vote in the July 1945 British general election was too small to really influence the result, the vast majority of those who voted as newly-minted civilians cast their votes for the Labour party.[65] Perhaps de Valera feared the consequences of an upsurge in support for the Irish labour movement.

There was also the remote chance that they might gravitate towards radical politics. There were many groups – most notably the IRA and the right-wing group Ailtirí na hAiséirghe – which could potentially benefit from the presence of a large body of unemployed, angry and frustrated people in the country. Returning ex-servicemen routinely brought weapons back to Britain with them; a post-war police amnesty resulted in 17,000 weapons being handed into the authorities all over the UK.[66] Albert, who returned to Dublin from RAF service in Europe, almost made it to Dublin with a captured Luger in his rucksack. Afraid of being caught and charged, he threw it overboard, only to stroll off the mailboat without being searched. He also mentioned that he saw other soldiers flinging objects into the water before the ship docked. Kenneth carried a gurkha knife back from the far east with him, but handed it into the authorities. Both Albert and Kenneth were military trophy-collectors, not potential revolutionaries, but their cases illustrate how easy it would have been for veterans to bring home weapons with them. Fearful of the consequences of a mass-return of Irish migrants, de Valera struggled to come to an agreement with the London government and Irish ex-servicemen played a key role in his plan.

Interestingly, it was not only Dublin that was prey to fears of a post-war deluge of potential welfare-seekers and trouble-makers. Harry Midgley, the Stormont Minister for Labour, worried that ex-service-men from independent Ireland would look for work in Northern Ireland, thus competing with reliable Protestants returning from the war. Some of these might 'gravitate to the disloyal element in our population and increase our political difficulties'.[67] Northern leaders reasoned that those from Éire enlisted 'owing to economic pressure and without any sense of loyalty to the Empire',[68] thus it was assumed that if they settled in the province, they would naturally identify with the nationalist minority. He suggested banning southern veterans from moving to Northern Ireland after the war. In March 1947, Ronald

Ross, the unionist MP for Derry, asked the House of Commons if its members were 'not ashamed that…ex-Servicemen should be sacked from their jobs in order to keep the citizens of a neutral State, who never served this country, in their employment?'[69] Even the most powerful nation on the planet was preparing to feel the pinch. American economists calculated that there would be twenty million veterans from the recent war, plus four million from other wars, and their families to care for, adding up to an estimated annual bill which would run into the billions.[70]

De Valera began to take tentative steps to face the situation in 1942, when he wrote to the Minister of Finance, Seán T. O'Kelly, pointing out that they might have to contend with 250,000 returnees after the war.[71] The story was then picked up by the press, and Fianna Fáil's party paper, the *Irish Press*, printed an interview with de Valera in October 1942, in which he said that one of the biggest problems facing Ireland was that of absorbing demobilised soldiers and 'perhaps the more difficult task of providing for the thousands who had emigrated because of the closing down of industries'.[72] The *Irish Times* editorialised in November 1942 that 'work must be provided for the returned "exiles", or the nation will be confronted with an unemployment problem which will surpass anything of the kind it has ever known.'[73]

Seán Lemass, the wartime Minister for Supplies, and from 1941, Industry and Commerce as well, was also worried and he began dropping hints to British officials in Dublin in 1943 about the estimated quarter of a million Irish migrants in Britain.[74] The British Legion in Ireland also began to press the government on the issue, writing to Lemass in September 1945 and pointing out that some thought be given to those in the Crown forces because 'these men will under existing legislation not be entitled to Unemployment Assistance Benefit to tide them over a most difficult period.'[75] The Legion was eager for a solution, as it was under considerable financial strain; in 1945 alone, it spent over £71,000 on welfare for Irish ex-servicemen.[76] Lemass wrote to Maurice Moynihan, secretary at the Taoiseach's office, reaffirming that all returning ex-servicemen who had unused contributions to the Irish unemployment insurance fund would be able to claim benefit, but he was adamant that it was 'not contemplated that preference to any type of employment will be offered to persons returning to this country from civilian or other employment elsewhere'.[77]

Lemass, however, did take steps to make sure that returning migrants could claim their stamps. Pre-war legislation stated that Irish workers who were absent from the country for more than five years lost all claim to any contributions they had made; Lemass amended this in June 1943 so that any worker returning to Ireland within twelve months of the end of the war could claim back all their unemployment insurance if they became unemployed. Significantly, he made sure to define 'employment' as encompassing both civilian and military.[78] Irish veterans of the British forces reported after the war that this had been the case, and that they had no problem claiming back any contributions they had made in Ireland before they left for Britain.[79]

The debate over returning migrants was made more heated by the publication of the British government's White Paper on Full Employment in 1944, and divisions were revealed within the hitherto seemingly-monolithic Fianna Fáil party. The British White Paper proposed stimulating economic growth by large-scale public spending during times of recession. Seán Lemass was intrigued by the idea, but ran into predictable opposition. J.J. McElligott, secretary of the Department of Finance, who argued that the agricultural industry was sufficient to absorb Ireland's unemployed, and that the Beveridge plans were better suited to an industrialised economy such as Britain. In this, he joined forces with Seán MacEntee, Minister for Local Government and Public Health, who had also served as Finance Minister between 1932 and 1939, who vehemently opposed the plan and said that State intervention in citizen's lives pointed the war to totalitarianism.[80]

The Catholic hierarchy, who were appalled at the prospect of 'leftist' or vaguely socialist ideas taking root in Ireland, also took umbrage at the idea. Adding further fuel to the debate was the questions from Fine Gael on what steps the government were taking to safeguard against a mass return of migrants. In November 1945, Eamon O'Neill, TD for Cork

West, asked de Valera in the Dáil if he was aware that '250,000 German prisoners of war are to be allocated for the rebuilding of bombed areas in Britain' and because of this Irish workers would 'be repatriated in bulk as soon as their jobs can be filled by British ex-servicemen or German prisoners of war'.[81] De Valera dismissed the suggestion, sardonically replying that 'not everything that appears in English papers is correct...'[82] but, despite his nonchalance, behind the scenes, the Irish government was trying to strong-arm London.

What de Valera really wanted was to persuade the British government to repay unemployment insurance contributions to workers who returned to Ireland from the UK after the war. Starting in 1939, the Irish government made repeated attempts to open talks with London about the unemployment insurance problem for *all* Irish migrants, only to be rebuffed every time. These requests were initially informal and low-key, but as the end of the war approached, they became more and more insistent. The first was in April 1939 but nothing came of it. However, in October 1942, when the British Home Secretary Herbert Morrison announced that London reserved the right to dismiss civilian workers in favour of demobbed men, the news landed like a bombshell on the corridors of power in Leinster House. A sense of urgency gripped the Dublin government and the requests to enter into negotiations became ever more frantic, but the British were in no rush to give in to Irish demands. They had no intention of talking about post-war arrangements while the conflict was still in the balance: according to British cabinet minutes, 'During the war the question had little practical or immediate importance.'[83]

In February 1943, Ernest Bevin, the UK Minister for Labour and National Service, refused to open discussions on the issue, promising to look at it again in the future.[84] In April 1945, the secretary of the Department of External Affairs, Joseph Walshe, wrote that the 'matter is now regarded as one of great urgency'.[85] Events began to pick up pace in May 1945, when Bevin revealed to the House of Commons that the first contingent of British troops would be released from service on 18 June.[86] Within two months, 200,000 had been discharged to civilian life.[87] Although officials within the Ministry of Pensions felt that 'it would not be decent to keep the Irish worker's contributions',[88] the Treasury steadfastly refused to even consider paying unemployment benefits outside the UK, and there were some inside Whitehall who considered all Irish wartime migrants as nothing more than job-seeking mercenaries.[89] During December 1945, the Treasury strongly resisted the proposals, sharply pointing out that they found 'the case of the Irish civilian particularly unimpressive'. They felt that Irish worker–migrants 'came here to make money and made it' and that Britain's responsibility towards them was over.[90]

The confusion was added to by frequent interventions by the Department of External Affairs and the Irish High Commissioner in London, John Dulanty. At one point, Dulanty suggested that the British either implement a full set of benefits for Irish migrants returning home, or pay a lump sum for the total of all Irish emigrant contributions to the British Unemployment fund from the Treasury to the Department of Finance.[91] Interestingly, there was a precedent for this. In October 1938 when the 'Treaty Ports' had been handed over to Dublin, some members of the British garrisons stayed behind to act as advisors to the Irish Defence Forces. These men were paid by the Irish government under the terms of an agreement in June 1938 which stated that Dublin would pay these troops at the correct British rate and would give them 50 per cent of their special British allowances, such as servants and fuel allowances. Pension contributions were taken from these British soldiers, which were refunded to the British Treasury every three months by the Department of Defence via External Affairs.[92]

However, like all attempts made during the war, this one failed. In desperation, de Valera decided on a change of tactics. Britain was clearly not going to be persuaded to do a deal on all Irish migrants. Accordingly, in September 1945, in a meeting with the British Minister for National Insurance, James Griffiths, Dulanty suggested that if London did not want to come to an agreement for *all* Irish migrants, then de Valera was willing to accept one for *wartime* migrants only, i.e. those who had left for Britain since the war began. Dulanty followed this up in June 1946 with a personal visit to the Ministry of National Insurance, in which he reiterated his desire to compromise on the issue of war migrants only. He also illustrated that Dublin was still wary of a flood of returning emigrants, and left the British officials with

> the strong impression that as respects industrial workers the Eire Government's main concern at the moment was to ensure that as many as possible should be retained in employment in Great Britain for the next two years or so rather than they should be returned to Ireland to face almost inevitable unemployment.[93]

Griffiths was in favour of such a solution, as was Christopher Addison, the Dominions Secretary, but they faced stiff resistance from Hugh Dalton, the first post-war British Chancellor. He had little time for Irish migrants, arguing that Britain had already provided them with employment, as well as attractive wages, and thus did not owe them anything.[94] Griffiths and Addison took their case to the cabinet, arguing that the British government had a moral duty to look after Irish migrants who had assisted with the British war effort. Their case was helped by outside pressures, particularly a petition sent directly to Prime Minister Atlee, pointing out that many would have limited access to Irish unemployment insurance. The petition wildly over-estimated the total number of volunteers at 300,000 and was signed by such notables as Hubert Gough, Seán O'Casey and George Bernard Shaw, among others.[95] After days of discussions, compromise was reached. It was agreed that while London would not pay unemployment insurance to Irish *workers* while in Ireland, they would agree to pay Irish ex-servicemen who returned home.[96] On 10 May 1946, Griffiths formally informed Dulanty, who relayed the news to Dublin. De Valera and his colleagues, who had hoped for a much wider-ranging agreement, reluctantly agreed; Lemass noted that he hoped this would be a stepping-stone to reciprocal unemployment insurance arrangements between the two countries. The official government bulletin released to the press illustrated the cabinet's hope for a wider arrangement: it noted that 'Certain arrangements were tentatively agreed to...' and that, 'It is proposed that further discussions will take place later in the year in respect of persons who have returned here after working in Great Britain during the War.'[97]

At a conference held in London on 17 and 18 July 1946, the two sides hammered out the outlines of the deal. The issue was a complex one, but both sides were eager to reach agreement, relations were cordial and a scheme was quickly agreed. If Irish ex-servicemen returned home and became unemployed, they were entitled to claim back British unemployment insurance stamps for a total of 180 days. To be eligible, applicants had to be already demobilised; they had to have been resident in the twenty-six counties of independent Ireland before enlistment; they had to have served in the British forces between 3 September 1939 and 14 August 1945; and they had to have had made at least thirty contributions to the British national insurance fund in the two years before they made their claim. The maximum rate of pay was twenty-four shillings a week, with additional payments for dependents and children. Those who qualified would be paid out of the Irish fund, at the British rate, and the money would then be reclaimed by Dublin from the British Treasury. Remarkably, there was to be little British oversight and a great deal of trust was placed in Irish officials to run it correctly. Ernest Bevin expressed his confidence in Dublin's ability to run the scheme 'faithfully and efficiently'.[98] As a whole, the scheme was only to last two years. On 15 October, de Valera officially but reluctantly accepted the arrangement.[99]

Legislation had to be rushed through the House of Commons in order to make the scheme work; the Unemployment Insurance (Éire Volunteers) Bill was placed before the Commons in October 1946 and passed through both houses relatively speedily. Speaking about the Bill in October 1946, James Griffith pointed out that it was 'in the interests of men and women who came forward spontaneously to join our Forces during the war. We want to make them feel that the United Kingdom is not unmindful of the services they rendered.'[100] Osbert Peake, the Conservative MP for Leeds North, asked if there 'was a possibility, almost amounting to a likelihood, that there would be some discrimination against these men in Eire';[101] he was answered that the British government concerned itself with the scheme itself and nothing else.[102] In the same debate, there were also a considerable amount of political swipes taken at Éire. For instance, Ronald Ross, Unionist MP for Derry, ridiculed the 'extraordinary inadequacy' of southern Irish social services.[103]

In Dublin, the Irish half of the legislation, the Unemployment Insurance Act of 1946, also ran through parliament without many hold-ups. It was different from the British legislation in one respect: Lemass estimated that there were twelve veterans of the Emergency forces who needed Irish unemployment benefit, but who were resident in Northern Ireland. He suggested, in view of the small number involved, that they should be paid directly out of Irish funds. Lemass was repeatedly questioned in both the Dáil and the Seánad if the agreement covered both ex-servicemen and workers, prompting him to sarcastically enquire if his colleagues were listening to him.[104] He was also tackled by Labour's William Norton and Fine Gael's Richard Mulcahy about non-military migrants. Lemass replied that he hoped the veteran's agreement would lay the foundation for a larger reciprocal scheme, and that the Irish had to keep a very close eye on the scheme as a whole:

> It is important to us that we should enforce the Bill in that spirit, as if there should appear, to the British authorities, to be an inclination on our part to pay out their money to claimants here, without proper examination of their eligibility, they would be less reluctant to enter into a reciprocal arrangement of wider application and of a permanent character.[105]

He was right to be cautious, because British documents show that officials in London were prepared to cancel the whole scheme if Irish adminis-tration was not up to scratch.[106] Political sniping aside, the Bill met little resistance in the Oireachtas. It was signed into law by the President, former Minister for Finance Seán T. O'Kelly, on 19 December 1946.[107]

As soon as it was up and running, it almost immediately ran into a problem. Because of the stipulation that at least thirty contributions had to have been made to the UK unemployment insurance fund in the two years prior to a claim, Irish service personnel who were in Class A (and therefore had been discharged first at the end of the war in Europe) were automatically disqualified. Because they were released so quickly from the forces, they did not have the time to make the thirty contributions required to apply for the benefit. William Boyle, the Earl of Cork and Orrery, who was himself a veteran of the war, brought this up in the House of Lords in June 1947. As he phrased it, 'the men who joined up first and served longest fell between two stools.'[108] This was eventually solved and the affected men – estimated to be only fifty veterans – were given special dispensation to apply.[109]

The economic situation in Ireland at the time meant that there was a great demand for the scheme and by March 1947, 1,678 claims were being processed. Despite there being a number of invalid applications (some optimistic Irish veterans of the Boer War applied and were rejected), the scheme was a success and by March 1948 4,461 Irish veterans had applied for and received unemployment insurance. By the time the scheme was wound up in early 1950, 6,509 men and women had claimed the benefit and over £187,817 had been paid out.[110] No new claims were accepted after 24 February 1949.[111] For the men and women involved, it was of great assistance, easing their passage back into civilian life. For the Irish government, it was a template to be followed for other Anglo-Irish agreements; documents in the Irish archives, proposing cooperation with London on social welfare reforms in 1948, specifically refer to the ex-servicemen's unemployment agreement.[112] For London, it was a chance to build bridges with Ireland after diplomatic relations had been strained by Irish neutrality. In a memo in March 1946, Addison stressed that ex-servicemen were 'a much-needed stabilising and friendly element' in Ireland and that it was in Britain's interest not to alienate them by refusing them welfare. He added that

> during their stay over here [they] will have unlearnt many of the prejudices which they were taught and will to that extent, on their return to Eire, contribute to the improvement of relations between the two countries which we have at heart. It seems false

economy to run the risk of destroying this good will by sending these men home with a feeling that they have been treated in a manner more worthy of a swindling hotel-keeper than of the Government of a great and honourable country.[113]

It also improved the professional links across the Irish Sea: in April 1949, J.F. Danielli at the British Ministry of Pensions wrote approvingly of the efficiency of the Irish civil service and felt that the 'authorities in Eire were most cooperative'.[114]

Far from being a diplomatic triumph for de Valera, the unemployment agreement with Britain was probably the best he could salvage at the time. As the war went on, his negotiating position was slowly but steadily eroded: at first, he wanted an all-encompassing agreement for *all* Irish migrants, then suggested wartime migrants alone, and finally settled on Irish ex-servicemen only. The British government held all the cards. They had the money which de Valera wanted paid to Irish migrants; they had plenty of jobs available to attract ever more Irish people to the UK; and they had the threat, however remote it was, of sending thousands of emigrants back to Ireland, which Dublin was anxious to avoid. In addition, Britain's prestige was high, its leaders were savouring total victory on all fronts and Ireland's international standing had taken a hammering during the war. De Valera was probably lucky to have extracted such a good deal from the British, as he was certainly negotiating from a position of weakness.

The British government also attempted to prepare Irish ex-servicemen for life at home before they were released from the forces. In December 1945, the Department of External Affairs received word that all Irish POWs were eligible to be sent on vocational training courses, to upskill them before joining the job market. Downing Street wanted to know what courses to send Irish veterans on, and asked what trades might be useful in post-war Ireland. At the time, there were discussions going on within the Irish government about prospective rebuilding programmes, and an anonymous official in the Department of Industry and Commerce brusquely replied to London that it was impossible to predict when the Irish economy would return to normal, and the government already had its hands full dealing with the demobilisation of the Irish forces. The only crumb of advice which was offered was that the building trade was expected to expand again.[115]

Conclusion

Despite the apocalyptic fears of the de Valera government, the mailboats from Holyhead to Dun Laoghaire were *not* crammed with Irish returnees in 1945. Britain was rebuilding in 1945 and needed workers from all over Europe. The Irish answered in their droves. In July 1946, the British Ministry of Labour began a drive to recruit Irish workers for British coal mines and by August was processing 2,200 men a week.[116] By December 1945, the Irish government had finally realised that they would not be facing the flood of returnees they had feared. Joseph Walshe at External Affairs forecast that the reverse would occur and that people would continue to stream *out* of Ireland. British plans for rebuilding and the reorientation of their economy would need even more Irish workers and, in Walshe's opinion, would result 'in a definite shortage of at least certain classes of labour in this country'.[117] Walshe also noted that Lemass and his officials at Industry and Commerce were edgy because the flood of returning emigrants they had predicted had not materialised. 'The problem is not primarily one for this Department,' he noted smugly.[118] By September 1946, Lemass had also accepted that the emigrants would not be flooding home. 'Irish civilian workers in Britain,' he wrote, 'are not expected to return home in any large numbers for eighteen months or so.'[119] In fact, most did not come back at all. Between 1945 and 1960, an estimated 500,000 Irish men and women left in search of work, the majority of them destined for America or Britain, where employment was plentiful, wages were good and a ready-made support network of expatriate Irish existed to draw them in. And it was no wonder that they did; the economic historian Cormac Ó Gráda has estimated that in 1946, Irish men's wages lagged behind their equivalent in Britain by 32 per cent and women's by 31 per cent.[120]

The great majority of Irish veterans of the Second World War opted to make their homes in Britain after 1945, to take advantage of the generous concessions being offered by the British government. However, many of those who decided to return to Ireland found themselves facing economic difficulties. A lucky few came back to jobs which had been held open; others had the good fortune to be hired by companies such as Guinness. For the rest, the Anglo-Irish unemployment insurance agreement provided relief for over 6,000 men and women who, through no fault of their own, found themselves in limbo between the Irish and British unemployment insurance systems. Whatever their economic circumstances, many found solace in remembering their fallen comrades and their ex-service organisations. But in Ireland, this had never been an easy or straightforward issue.

Chapter six

Remembrance

It is…a well known but nonetheless deplorable fact that
the administration of the British Legion in Ireland is
entirely in the hands of a small Protestant and Freemason
minority

John A Belton, September 1945

You knew bloody well that people didn't like you

Testimony of Geoffrey, RAF volunteer

In November 1945, the Fianna Fáil government controversially allowed the Gardaí to prohibit the annual march held by Irish ex-servicemen from Smithfield Market in Dublin city centre to the war memorial park at Islandbridge. Defending the ban in the Dáil, the Minister for Justice, Gerald Boland, argued that the ban was a necessary measure taken by the government to prevent public disorder. Among the most vehement critics of the ban was James Dillon, a former member of Fine Gael who had been forced to resign from the party for his outspoken criticism of Irish neutrality. Dillon argued that the ban was an insult to the Irish men and women who had fought and died for the Allied cause. The heat of the debate across the Dáil chamber – at one point, Dillon accused Fianna Fáil of being 'ignorant fools' – was an illustration that, despite Ireland's long connection with the British forces, the commemoration of the dead was a deeply divisive and contentious issue in Ireland.

Cumann na nGaedheal and Commemoration

The first governments of the Irish Free State, from 1922 to 1932 under the leadership of W.T. Cosgrave and the Cumann na nGaedheal party, were deeply uncomfortable with the issue of commemoration in general. Cosgrave led a country which had been in turmoil since 1914. In nine turbulent years, Ireland experienced the First World War, a revolution from 1919 to 1921 and a bitterly contested civil war between 1922 and 1923. The question of whom to remember and how best to commemorate them was thus a highly-charged and emotive issue. Cumann na nGaedheal sought to celebrate figures who cemented their legitimacy, such as Michael Collins, Arthur Griffith and Kevin O'Higgins. Anti-Free State groups, republicans, Sinn Féin and later Fianna Fáil preferred to commemorate anti-Treaty figures or nationalist figures. Both sides of the Treaty divide defined themselves against each other, constructing their own pantheons of heroes and decrying the other side as traitors.[1] There was an almost constant three-way battle for memory: monuments to the Irish dead of the Great War faced competition for public spaces from both the Free State government and the anti-Treaty republicans. With pro- and anti-Treaty battles being fought out in statues, biographies and newspaper articles, there was little room left for those who wished to pay tribute to Irish veterans of the British forces.

Because Ireland was so deeply involved in the First World War – with over 200,000 men taking part and around 27,000 of those being killed – post-1918 Armistice Day commemorations, traditionally held annually on 11 November, saw thousands of people gathering in Dublin and around the country. Photos from Dublin in the 1920s show Armistice parades of up to 20,000 people, all packed into College Green outside Trinity College. The ceremonies were generally organised by the largest ex-service organisation in Britain and Ireland, the British Legion. The Legion had been formed after the First World War when the British government, wary of the revolutionary potential of disgruntled ex-servicemen, persuaded the three largest ex-service organisations – the Blackburn Association, the National Federation and the Comrades of the Great War – to merge under the leadership of Earl Douglas Haig. The resulting organisation was founded in Britain and Ireland in 1921 and its charter was to provide welfare and relief for ex-servicemen and women who had fallen on hard times. Its most attractive trait, from the government's point of view, was that it was avowedly non-political. The method of raising funds mostly rested on the selling of paper replicas of the poppy flowers which grew on the battlefields of Flanders. In Ireland, the Legion took a little longer to establish itself as the country plunged into political upheaval and violence after the war. However, by the mid-1920s, it was firmly established.

In 1924, with memories of the world war still fresh in Ireland, the British Legion announced that it had sold almost 500,000 poppies in the Dublin area alone.[2] However, Armistice Day was also the scene for violence and disorder, as the IRA and other republican groups regularly attacked parades, or snatched poppies from veterans' and onlookers' lapels. This led some enterprising people to stitch razor blades inside the petals to deter or injure potential poppy-snatchers. In 1925, the veteran's march was stopped by firebombs.[3] In 1926, after two years of disorder in Dublin and seeking to avoid further chaos, the government ordered the ceremonies be moved to the Phoenix Park, away from the city centre.[4] While the capital generally saw widespread violence on Armistice Day, it usually passed off peacefully around the rest of the country. For instance, in November 1928, when there was a series of bomb attacks on British symbols in the capital, commemorative parades and ceremonies were held in Sligo, Carrick-on-Shannon, Wexford, Kilkenny and Tralee without incident. In Cork the only disturbance involved a house in which poppies were stored being broken into and set on fire. The following year ceremonies were staged in Cork city, Fermoy, Mallow, Longford town, Athlone, Tralee, New Ross, Waterford, Tramore, Kilkenny, Bandon, Bray, Naas, Thurles, Drogheda, Monaghan, Boyle, Sligo, Galway city, Ballinasloe, Mayo, Donegal and Limerick without there being a single reported confrontation.[5] Dublin remained the epicentre of disturbances: in 1930, the ex-servicemen were attacked on their way back from the memorial park and their flag was thrown into the Liffey,[6] while in November 1932 shots were fired during an anti-Imperialism march and buses within the city were boarded by vigilantes, searching for poppies to confiscate.[7] Geoffrey recalled something similar about poppy appeals in the 1930s: in spite of the trouble, collectors still 'took out poppy boxes, but they kept it under their coat, didn't want to be seen with it because there was a element that might pass disparaging remarks at them, and even try to whip the box from you'.

The IRA itself admitted that veterans were not being singled out simply because of their service, but that some republicans wanted to reduce the appearance of British emblems in Ireland. Throughout the 1920s and 1930s, the IRA waged an intermittent campaign against British symbols, targeting Boy Scout camps, British beer companies, royal monuments and cinemas showing British films. A booklet of IRA attacks compiled by the Department of Justice illustrated that the movement spent as much time dispersing Baden-Powell Scout meetings and forcing businesses to remove British images as it did destroying British Legion halls and clubs.[8] Republican leaders such as Frank Ryan claimed that the republican movement was not trying to deny ex-soldiers their *right* to remember their fallen comrades, and organised alternative ceremonies, stripped of their British trappings, for Irish ex-servicemen.[9] In November 1925, Seán Lemass made almost exactly the same point: Armistice ceremonies, according to him, were 'attempts to seduce the Irish nation and win support for the British connection...Though Irishmen might have their differences...they stood when the Union Jack was waved in their faces as uncompromisingly against British rule as they ever did.' However, he did point out that he 'meant no disrespect to the Irish survivors of the Great War who wished to honour their dead comrades',[10] words which Gerald Boland would echo in November 1945, when defending the Remembrance Day march ban.

Cosgrave and his government were uneasy about publicly engaging with Armistice Day celebrations, and despite being invited to attend, usually declined. During the ten years that Cosgrave was in office, minor government representatives attended Armistice ceremonies on five occasions: in 1924 and between the years 1928 to 1931. When he himself was invited to the Armistice Day ceremonies in Dublin in 1924, Cosgrave replied that 'the time was not ripe for the Government to publicly associate itself with functions of this nature' and that neither himself, nor the Governor-General, Timothy Healy, could attend.[11] Civil servants who requested leave in order to attend the ceremonies were normally refused[12] and it was with the greatest of reluctance that the Free State government agreed to finance British military graves in independent Ireland.[13] Ironically, Cosgrave's counterpart in Northern Ireland, James Craig, was initially dubious about publicly associating his government with either 12 July or Armistice Day, worried about completely alienating the nationalist community,[14] but as the years went on Stormont became deeply involved in remembrance ceremonies. After the Second World War, Remembrance Sunday became a graphic illustration of the union with Britain.

It was politically impossible for any nationalist government in newly-independent Ireland to overly associate itself with a ceremony which was replete with British flags, British symbols and which routinely concluded with the singing of the British national anthem. Throughout the 1920s, there were a series of confrontations between the government and representatives of ex-servicemen. In 1927, Minister for Justice Kevin O'Higgins strongly opposed the building of a memorial for those who died during the First World War within sight of government buildings. Instead, the government set aside a large plot of land at Islandbridge, a peaceful spot beside the river, which was also conveniently a considerable distance away from the city centre. O'Higgins feared that the close proximity of the memorial to the seat of power would suggest that independence was won as a result of Ireland's contribution to the First World War; instead, he argued, it was the Home Rule party and the revolution which brought freedom. Cumann na nGaedheal's opponents consistently painted the party as a British puppet: in 1925, Seán Lemass thundered that 'Ireland today is ruled by a British garrison, organized by the Masonic lodges, speaking through the Free State parliament, and playing the cards of England all the time.'[15]

In 1929, the Department of External Affairs instructed the then Governor-General, James McNeill, to boycott a function at Trinity College, as the Provost of the university had refused to play 'Amhrán na bhFiann', instead playing 'God Save the King'.[16] In addition, Cosgrave ordered a number of restrictions be placed on the annual commemoration ceremonies on 11 November. A complete ban on the use of military words of command to marshal parades of any kind was introduced under the Treasonable Offences Act in 1925, a measure that was aimed at anti-Treatyite demonstrations, but which encompassed ex-servicemen as well. The public display of Union flags was also prohibited by Cosgrave's government and the British flag was routinely removed from films by the Irish censor from the early 1920s onwards.[17] Poppy sales were also usually restricted by the authorities to three or four days in November.

There were several confrontations between the Gardaí and ex-servicemen in parades throughout the 1920s. One, in Clare, was serious enough to be reported to the Garda Commissioner by the Chief Superintendent in Ennis. The police had stopped a large parade of ex-servicemen and requested that they stop using military words of command. He was confronted by a vicar who 'approached and excitedly said "To Hell with the Free State"'. The report concluded that the parade 'was a definite Imperialistic display, and not a commemoration to the war dead...the continuance of exhibitions of this kind which are hateful in the eyes of nine-tenths of the people will undoubtedly court trouble.'[18] The Gardaí regularly reported that they were worried, not about the parades and ceremonies themselves, but about the reaction to them. In 1928, the Garda Commissioner wrote to the Department of Justice, pointing out that 'these 11th November displays led to drilling and other activities of a military nature on the part of the Irregulars.'[19]

Fianna Fáil and Commemoration

The coming to power of the Fianna Fáil government led by Eamon de

Valera in 1932 did not see a major change in Irish government policy towards Armistice Day or ex-servicemen's commemorations. In fact, the new administration seemed anxious not to antagonise ex-servicemen, much like the Cumann na nGaedheal government. When Garda Commissioner Eamon Broy called on de Valera to ban all parades on Armistice Day in 1933, he was informed that the Fianna Fáil leader was 'slow to arrive at a decision which might give offence to the large body of ex-servicemen in this country'.[20] By way of contrast, the new government in August 1933 suppressed a parade commemorating Arthur Griffith, Michael Collins and Kevin O'Higgins, fearful that clashes between the IRA and the Blueshirts would lead to disorder and possibly even a coup by the Blueshirts. In 1938, de Valera even indicated that he would attend the official opening of the Islandbridge war memorial park, but did so under certain conditions. He stipulated that there be no British flags and that the British anthem not be played, because he would not tolerate anything which might 'tend to create ill feeling or resentment or to embarrass the Government in the slightest degree'.[21] He did not make this condition without reason: Union badges were sold in the memorial park and 'God Save the King' was sung at the ceremony every year, which the Legion leadership said they were powerless to prevent.[22] In November 1946, when the official band did not play the British anthem, the crowd sang it anyway at the close of the ceremonies.[23] Fianna Fáil largely continued the same restrictions on parades and celebrations; in September 1932 the Department of Justice recommended that all flags should be banned from the parades and that sales of poppies should be restricted to 10 and 11 November. Both of these restrictions originated under the Cumann na nGaedheal governments and both would be features of Fianna Fáil government policy again after 1945.

In common with the UK, all public parades were prohibited once war was declared in September 1939. Ex-service ceremonies were still allowed to go ahead in the memorial park at Islandbridge, but the by-now traditional parade from Smithfield Market to Islandbridge was banned for safety reasons. Small parades were routinely allowed during the war: in November 1939, for example, a British Legion parade was allowed to march from St. Stephen's Green to St. Patrick's Cathedral,[24] as were others around the Pro-Cathedral.[25] However, Irish neutrality meant that there was a clamp-down on overtly pro-British symbols. In 1940, the ban on British flags was extended to include anything with the Union symbol on it; as many British Legion banners and regimental standards incorporated the Union flag, this meant they too were prohibited. In 1941, all Armistice Day leaflets and posters were prevented from mentioning the current war.[26] From 1943 onwards the V-sign, made popular by Churchill as a sign of British defiance, was also banned.[27] Newspapers were forbidden to print details of the ceremonies the day afterwards.[28] Despite complaints, the ceremonies still concluded with the playing or singing of the British anthem.[29] British flags could be carried if kept rolled, and could be displayed once in the war memorial park.

Easter 1941

The preservation of the appearance of neutrality and fears for public safety were the major reasons why Armistice parades were halted during the war, but this did not stop de Valera taking advantage of their absence. With ex-servicemen out of sight for the duration of the war – even their annual ceremony was hidden away at the peaceful but remote memorial park at Islandbridge – the Fianna Fáil government took the opportunity to use the vacant public space to present their own version of Irish history. The best example of this was the elaborate 25th anniversary celebrations of the Easter Rising in April 1941, which was carefully choreographed and controlled by de Valera to the benefit of Fianna Fáil.

Despite the furore in European capitals on 1 September 1939, the Taoiseach still found the time to send a memo to all government departments, asking them for their thoughts on what form the 25th anniversary celebrations should take. On February 1940, he wrote directly to the Department of Defence, asking for their opinion. It was a busy time at Defence, which was engaged in reorganising the forces and expanding the army. It took three months, but when Daniel McKenna, the Chief of Staff, finally answered it lacked nothing in thoroughness. Writing back on

6 May 1940, McKenna recommended that a whole week be given over to the commemoration. He also suggested:

1) Religious Services be held all over the country
2) Memorial Services at Arbour Hill
3) A Military Review in the Phoenix Park
4) Presentation of Campaign Medals to veterans of the war of independence
5) Pageant of History be staged by the army, culminating in a re-enactment of the Rising
6) A special programme of nationalist education be developed for school children
7) A Gaelic festival, under the banner of 'Not Merely Free but Gaelic as well'
8) Victory parade to consist of army troops and old IRA
9) A State Ceilidhe
10) Athletic functions with the cooperation of the GAA
11) A National Museum exhibit
12) An army development exhibition to 'stress the development of the army since 1916'
13) An Industrial Pageant 'to stress the industrial development of Ireland since 1916'
14) A Commemorative Stamp
15) A Souvenir Handbook
16) Press and Propaganda – As Defence put it: 'Attempts should be made to get newspapers to publish special Commemoration issues or supplements, or to give a distinct national bias…during the week. The outstanding Border issue could be stressed also.'
17) Plays & Films, including the 'Plough & The Stars' and plays by Pearse
18) The GPO to be floodlit and a Flame of Remembrance to be kept lit on the roof
19) Special transport to be provided for all attendees.

Finally, it was felt that a 'definite motif should run through the entire Commemoration. This would be based upon the fact that the national resurgence and all subsequent developments were only made possible by the sacrifice of Easter Week. This motif should underlay all ceremonies and be impressed upon the public throughout.'[30] Enlistments into the Irish Defence Forces were dropping off as the risk of invasion passed: McKenna probably hoped to reinvigorate recruitment by stimulating a wave of patriotism.

De Valera rejected the majority of these ideas out of hand. Replying on 9 August, he wrote that 'in present circumstances the holding of a commemoration on elaborate lines would not be appropriate' and he ordered the whole issue to be dropped until October, when a 'much less ambitious' plan could be drawn up.[31] He then wrote to McKenna on 25 October 1940, pointing out that 'the commemoration should be on a very much more restricted scale than that originally contemplated and should only take place if circumstances generally be favourable.' He also wanted the ceremony to be purely military and to be confined to one day only.[32]

Taking this reprimand on board, Michael Beary, the assistant secretary at Defence, wrote to the Taoiseach's office in December, putting forward a much more limited plan. The new suggestions were more in line with de Valera's inclinations. Defence now confined its proposals to three: religious services around the country, presentation of medal to revolutionary veterans and a Victory Parade. As before, it was again recommended that this parade consist of a mixture of regular army troops and IRA veterans. There would be more discussions before April 1941, but essentially this was the format that the ceremony would eventually take. Significantly, Beary took care to point out that the Minister for Defence, Oscar Traynor, had signed off on these proposals.[33] This suggests that Traynor had not authorised McKenna's original and extravagant recommendations. Three weeks later, de Valera signalled his acceptance of these new slimmed-down plans. He also said that he did 'not desire to have any views on points of detail communicated officially to the Department of Defence at this stage. He wishes the Minister of

Defence to be requested to take an early opportunity of discussing matters of detail with him personally.'[34]

A cabinet meeting on 27 January 1941 finalised the format of the commemoration, which was along the lines suggested by Defence. It was decided that there would be a memorial mass at Arbour Hill, and that medals would be awarded to both survivors of 1916 and those who took part in the war of independence. More significantly, the parade was not to be called a 'Victory Parade', but instead the '1916 25th anniversary commemoration parade'. This would consist of a mixture of regular army troops, Old IRA men and veterans of 1916.

De Valera's reasons for wanting to scale back the celebrations are not recorded, but we can speculate with some accuracy. The first and most obvious is cost – Defence's week-long republican jamboree would have consumed a great deal of money. Quite apart from the cost, however, was the possible diplomatic impact of any ceremonies. Irish neutrality caused a great deal of tension between Dublin and London throughout the war and the overly nationalistic and belligerent tone of Defence's suggestions could conceivably have added to it. At its core, any Easter Rising commemoration is a celebration of a battle against British forces. This by itself had the potential to be sensitive, but in the midst of a war in which Britain was struggling for survival and which Ireland had refused to join, it could have further complicated already heavily strained Anglo-Irish relations. Trumpeting a 'Victory Parade' would only have caused further antagonism. When de Valera spoke of Defence's plans not being appropriate 'in the present circumstances', this is more than likely what he meant.

The parade was one of the biggest that had been seen in the capital for many years. Air Corps aircraft performed a flypast, before armoured cars, Bren carriers and truck-towed artillery trundled down O'Connell Street. They were followed by two brigades of troops, mixed with Old IRA men, Local Defence Force personnel, Local Security Force men, Air Raid Precautions members, the Marine Inscription, Gardaí, ambulances and members of the Red Cross – approximately 20,000 personnel in all.[35] Before the parade, de Valera inspected a guard of honour and then was presented with his medal for participating in the Rising, before he went on to award medals to other revolutionary veterans. He was then joined on the platform by high-ranking army officers and other government ministers and watched for two-and-a-half hours as the parade marched by.[36]

It was his speech, however, which revealed the most about his motives. Broadcast from the GPO to the nation, it was, for the most part, conventional, beginning with a ringing tribute to the men of 1916 and then moving onto an examination of the dangers facing Ireland while the Second World War raged around them. He made a determined effort to link the Rising with neutrality, declaring that if Ireland was invaded, the modern Defence Forces would fight as well as the men of Easter Week. Two phrases, however, stand out. Firstly, he declared that the 'freedom we now enjoy is the direct fruit of the courage and sacrifices of the leaders of Easter Week'. It is significant to note that he did not say the *executed* men of Easter Week. Although de Valera was not the only insurgent to escape execution – Countess Markievicz and Fine Gael leader W.T. Cosgrave, among others, did as well – de Valera was the only major battalion leader to avoid the firing squad. By reminding his listeners that he was the sole surviving commandant, he was posing as Patrick Pearse's successor. This image would have been bolstered by the fact that he was, at that moment, wearing his newly-presented 1916 campaign medal. This was further reinforced by the editorial in the *Irish Press* the next day, which pointed out that de Valera was 'himself one of the military leaders of the small insurgent army'.[37] The Taoiseach was also at pains to place himself at the centre of veterans of the independence struggle and the modern Defence Forces, thus portraying him as the point of contact between Ireland's history and Ireland's present. The juxtaposition of veterans of 1916–1923 and the Emergency Army conveyed a clear message: the independence struggle made neutrality possible. By taking the salute from both at the same time, de Valera was placing himself deliberately at the intersection of past and present. It is worth remembering that this idea had originated in the Department of Defence, and was one of the few of their original suggestions to survive.

Adding to this theme, in his speech to the nation he said that the present Irish were 'the first generation in centuries to have a freedom which is worth defending.' This was a bold statement to make. What he was claiming was that the strange hybrid Dominion-republic that he had created since 1932 was more valuable than anything that had gone before. By doing so, he was not only dismissing any contribution the British state made to Ireland, but also denigrating the achievements of the Free State under the Cumann na nGaedheal government. What de Valera was clearly trying to do was to create what historian Douglas Peifer described as a 'memory beacon': a historical event that is carefully chosen by government or leaders to resonate with the public.[38] The year 1916 was destined to be the foundation stone of de Valera's new Ireland, and he was keen to persuade his listeners that Irish history flowed in a serene and linear fashion from Easter Week 1916 to Easter Week 1941. This narrative of Irish history would allow de Valera to project several different images of himself at once. There was de Valera the soldier, wearing his 1916 medal; de Valera the republican theorist, guarding Pearse's legacy; de Valera the state-builder, creating a vision of Ireland worth fighting for; and de Valera the leader, charting a course through the Second World War. Perhaps we should not be surprised at de Valera's insistence on his place in the republican blood-line: Diarmaid Ferriter has already discovered that the Fianna Fáil leader consistently recycled the speeches of past republican leaders, such as Wolfe Tone, Thomas Davis and Pearse, for his own benefit.[39]

The major victims in all of this were Irish ex-servicemen. If de Valera's theory was correct, then Irish volunteers in the First World War had played no part in the independence movement; and if neutrality was the inevitable consequence of Easter 1916, then the Irish men and women who were fighting in British uniform in the Second World War were excluded from Irish history also. After all, President Douglas Hyde's radio broadcast to the nation spoke of the Rising breaking 'the chains that bound us'. Although both Hyde and de Valera were careful not to actually mention Britain in their triumphal speeches, there was no doubt what both men were referring to. The 1941 celebrations were designed to be a showcase of Irish independence from British colonial rule: there was no way to incorporate Irish ex-servicemen into this nationalist paradigm. And because all other major parades were banned during the war, there was public space available to de Valera to stage his enormous celebration. The striking visual images of aircraft flying overhead and thousands of troops marching down O'Connell Street added force to de Valera's argument.

The government's ambivalent attitude towards commemoration created some surreal and incongruous situations during the war. For example, the 1942 Armistice Day ceremonies in Dublin were attended by representatives from Belgium, France, Britain, America, Czechoslovakia, Yugoslavia, Holland and Poland.[40] The majority of nations attending the ceremony had virtually ceased to exist. All except America and Great Britain had been conquered by Nazi Germany. Even stranger, Czechoslovakia, Yugoslavia and Poland had not taken part in the Great War as independent nations and their countries had only been formed in the post-war settlement at Versailles. Likewise, Ireland had participated as a part of the United Kingdom and independence only came after the war. What was strangest of all was that it was a commemoration of Irish war dead of a war in which Ireland participated, taking place in the Irish capital and which was boycotted by the Irish government. The cross-currents of loyalty and obedience created by the war meant that similarly odd situations were generated all across Europe. In France in 1941, the head of the collaborationist Vichy state, Marshal Petain – a veteran himself and heroic defender of Verdun – solemnly commemorated the French who died during the First World War[41] while his bitter enemy Charles de Gaulle, whom Petain sentenced to death *in absentia*, did the same thing in London. Even stranger, in 1943, the brutal German governor of occupied Poland, Hans Frank, gave the green light to ceremonies commemorating the Polish soldiers who died fighting against the German invasion in 1939.[42] These bizarre situations were also replicated on an individual level. Brian Inglis's memoirs recorded a complex situation in Dublin generated by neutrality. He had left the *Irish Times* to join the RAF and, when back on leave, had visited the editor, R.M. Smyllie. He ended the evening sitting in a bar in the city centre, having a drink with both Smyllie and the German Press attaché – a national of the country Inglis was at war with.[43]

VE Day

As the end of the Second World War approached, de Valera feared that there would be some disturbances in Ireland once the war in Europe was concluded. Anticipating trouble, the Department of Justice instructed Gardaí on 24 April 1945 to place extra protection on the German and Japanese Legations as well as on the residence of Eduard Hempel, the German Minister to Ireland.[44] On 5 May, Secretary of Justice Stephen Roche suggested that the Gardaí should, as far as possible, head off disturbances before they erupted. He asked that individual Gardaí 'intervene in both directions': people found flying Allied flags were to be asked to tone down their revelry, while those offended by the flags were to be asked to not react violently. Flags in large processions were to be seized and large crowds were to be dispersed. Roche suggested that Gardaí should use 'tact and discretion' when dealing with VE Day celebrations which seemed likely to cause trouble.[45]

The government's suspicions were correct and VE Day on 8 May 1945 saw a series of riots and disturbances in Dublin city centre. Celebrating the Allied victory, a group of Trinity College students College flew the British, Soviet, French and Irish flags over the college; according to the *Irish Press* the Union flag was at the top and 'a rather dirty Irish Tricolour' was at the bottom of the flagpole. After some protestors tried to break in, the students partially burned the Irish flag and flung it off the roof, before they eventually removed all the banners.[46] In retaliation, a Union flag was torched soon after in the Phoenix Park by a group of University College Dublin students. These flag-burnings kick-started a cycle of violence in which twelve people were injured.[47] The next day Trinity College came under sustained attack from a large crowd of stone throwers, and houses or shop windows displaying Union flags were smashed. When the Gardaí guarding the university buildings were targeted, they charged the crowd to disperse it.[48] Also on 9 May, a mob shattered the windows of the British Representative's office and those of the US Consulate-General. Across the country Gardaí removed British and Allied flags from houses and public places when they felt riots were brewing. In Westport on 9 May a rally was held in the town to protest against the display of Allied banners and a crudely drawn swastika flag was hauled down by the Gardaí from the town clock tower. A day later in Cork a crowd of 200 people gathered in the city centre to witness the public burning of a British flag. The leaders of the protest delivered a speech specifically mentioning the burning of the Trinity College tricolour.[49]

The following days were filled with official apologies and letters of protest. Joseph Walshe, secretary of the Department of External Affairs, apologised to both the British and American governments; on 10 May, the Provost of Trinity apologised to de Valera and the head of the Student Representative Council wrote to the *Irish Press*, affirming that the flag-burning had been carried out by a small minority of students.[50] It became clear that the violence was generated in large measure by fringe groups: along with the IRA, one of the main culprits was the right-wing political group Ailtirí na hAiséirghe ('Architects of the Resurrection') which was profoundly anti-British and defaced street signs and attacked British monuments throughout the war. College rivalries also played a part. Students from the mutually antagonistic Trinity College and University College Dublin taunted each other and scuffled in the streets. Further unrest occurred in Sligo on VJ Day, where there were more punch-ups; another tricolour found its way onto a bonfire and a public meeting outside the town hall decried the 'burning of the National Flag by Sligo Imperialists'.[51] By way of contrast with another neutral, the Portuguese capital Lisbon was relatively quiet on VE Day and the Irish representative there, Colm O'Donovan, noted that the population waved Allied flags eagerly.[52] An even more embarrassing contrast was the festivities in Belfast on VE Day, where large jubilant crowds gathered to celebrate the end of the war, amid the ringing of church bells and fireworks.[53]

Remembrance Sunday, 1945

These events were surely on the government's mind as November 1945 approached. It was clear that the Remembrance Day parade, the first since the end of the war and also the first in six years, was going to be sizable, much bigger than any previous event. (Armistice Day became known as Remembrance Sunday after 1945, and the ceremonies were held on the Sunday nearest to 11 November.) There were hundreds of Allied ex-servicemen on leave in Dublin at the time, and representatives from several European countries were set to attend. As VE and VJ Day had shown, tensions were high in Ireland at the time, and Ailtirí na hAiséirghe or the IRA might not have been able to resist the prospect of attacking such a large parade, which would have doubtlessly been heavily laden with British flags and Allied symbols. In October 1945, the Minister for Justice, Gerald Boland, took a decision which was controversial then and has remained so ever since: on the advice of the Gardaí, the ceremony in Islandbridge was allowed to go ahead, but the parade from Smithfield Market to the park was banned.

The decision raised a storm of protest in the Dáil, particularly from James Dillon, formerly of Fine Gael. Dillon accused the government of victimising ex-servicemen and said that he was proud to say that Irish men and women had fought against Nazism. In reply, Boland pointed out that his decision was based on secret information from the Garda Commissioner and he was worried that violence would result from the parade going ahead. He also said that he was mindful of the VE Day violence when he made his decision. Dillon later asked if a 'body of law-abiding, decent citizens are to be made responsible for the act of a brat, one isolated, ignorant brat who, from the top of Trinity College, burns the National Flag?'[54] Tempers flared and at one point, Boland snapped at Dillon to 'keep cool'. Dillon retorted, amidst interruptions, that 'It is hard to keep cool…when one beholds ignorant…fools rejoicing in the trampling down of minorities.'[55] Boland replied heatedly that he was not 'trying to prevent these people honouring their dead'.[56] When Dillon asserted that the protection of the Constitution had been withdrawn from the veterans, Boland replied that he was 'not capable of following the line that Deputy Dillon adopted, and there is no necessity to do so'. Boland eventually admitted that he was not privy to the secret information the Gardaí had acquired, much to Dillon's frustration. He also sarcastically asked Dillon if the army should have been mobilised to protect the march. Dillon repeatedly question whether if it was a Fianna Fáil parade which had been scheduled, instead of a British Legion one, if it would still have been banned. The debate eventually came to an end with Dillon shouting across the chamber that 'It is mob rule if the police will not protect the individual.' Ironically, the ban itself caused disturbances, as Trinity students took to the streets to protest against it. The British Legion itself did not make a public protest, and the Legion conference in February 1946 stressed that the organisation had 'always obeyed the instructions of the authorities'.[57]

The threat of violence was taken very seriously and armed Gardaí patrolled the park during the ceremony. The event was so well attended that the city bus service struggled to cope with the numbers and approximately six thousand people filled the memorial park. Nearly 1500 ex-servicemen took part in a march past the monument in the park.[58] Large numbers of Allied servicemen in uniform were seen at the ceremony. Also present were representatives from the UK, US, Belgium, Canada, Spain, Italy, Czechoslovakia, Holland, Poland, as well as members of the British Legion in Northern Ireland.[59]

Was the government over-reacting to the threat of violence in 1945? Ex-servicemen reported that there was little animosity towards commemoration activities after the war. Kenneth, who was the standard-bearer for the Royal Artillery Association, remembered that there were 'a few protests, but never any trouble'. Geoffrey also recalled few problems in the immediate post-war period, but as he astutely pointed out, the average parade consisted of a few hundred ex-military personnel; 'it wouldn't be very sensible to attack them.' In fact, there seems to have been some public support for the parades. Cathal remembered people waving British flags and remembers one woman in particular who used to wave a red British cavalry jacket out of her

**The Guinness Ex-Servicemen Association
at Islandbridge, 1950s.**

window when the parade passed, although other onlookers booed or threw stones. Kenneth recalled that at one point the IRA 'put a bomb against the cross in Memorial Park to try and blow it up. They didn't succeed, but it was all marred with the smoke...I thought it was a terrible thing to do when you're just commemorating your dead comrades.' It also helped that Irish companies contributed towards ex-service ceremonies. Don, who returned from the Royal Engineers to a job with Guinness, often marched down the quays to Islandbridge as part of the Guinness ex-Service Association on Remembrance Sunday, where they would lay their own wreaths at the memorial park. They had their own flags and banners, which escaped government sanction as they did not contain the Union flag. The brewery also used to pay for an annual dinner for all ex-servicemen in the company.

As the issue became less and less important for the government, restrictions on Remembrance Sunday were relaxed and, in 1945, it was decided that all banners would be allowed, except for those which contained the Union flag. From 1947 onwards, the Department of Justice stopped referring to the cabinet for guidance on Remembrance parades and issued guidelines on its own authority.[60] However, the restrictions were not totally removed. In August 1948, a group of ex-servicemen from Britain sought permission to hold a small commemoration ceremony at Islandbridge while they were on a tour of Ireland. The service was extremely small and only 160 ex-service men and women planned to attend. The long-serving secretary of the Department of Justice, Stephen Roche, reminded the new Inter-Party government (Fianna Fáil had been ousted from power in the February 1948 election) that 'there were displays of sentiment which caused breaches of the peace' during commemorative ceremonies in the past. Permission was eventually granted for the private service, but the Tanaiste, Sean MacBride, insisted the party travel to the memorial park in private transport. He also insisted that 'there be no display of any kind – the latter is, of course, an invariable condition in these cases', and there be no banners or decorations.[61] This provoked a furious response from E. Oliver Humphries, the Chairman of the British Legion in Ireland, who pointed out that 'such restrictions are against National Interest' and that the ex-servicemen left with 'a poor conception of the government of our country'.[62]

The British Legion

The Irish government's uneasy interactions with ex-servicemen's commemoration were mirrored by its strained relationship with the

British Legion in Ireland. The Legion was the largest ex-service organisation in Britain or Ireland and was set up in the aftermath of the First World War. It was mainly concerned with looking after the welfare of ex-servicemen across the two countries and its main source of revenue was the selling of poppies. Throughout the 1920s and 1930s, it existed in a strange state of stasis in Ireland: the government was generally suspicious of an organisation which was so openly tilted towards Britain, while the Legion tried to conduct its business unobtrusively and avoid government attention. Generally, Dublin was content to allow the Legion to fundraise and to organise commemoration activities, as long as it stayed out of Irish politics and avoided overly pro–British sentiments or displays.

Irish neutrality in the war made the government even more suspicious of the Legion. Although the organisation officially called on ex-servicemen to join the Irish Defence Forces during the Emergency,[63] it also provided references to men and women who wished to volunteer for the British forces. G2, the Irish military intelligence organisation, suspected that the Legion was helping deserters from the Irish army to join the crown forces, and during the war undercover investigators caught some Legion officials assisting deserters. The men involved were fined and officially warned to stop the practice, but avoided further sanction.[64] In general, as long as the Legion did not flout neutrality, it was allowed to function in peace.

Although de Valera accepted the existence of the British Legion and allowed it to function without major restrictions, there was still some suspicion towards the organisation from within his government. In particular, there were those who believed that it was a conduit for British influence in Ireland and was an anti-national body. In 1939 it was suggested that the Irish President, Douglas Hyde, would attend the war memorial opening ceremony, and reports appeared in various newspapers saying that Hyde would accept the gardens on behalf of the Dublin government. This drew a very sharp response from Michael McDunphy, the President's secretary.[65] At the time the incident occurred, he wrote,

I was inclined to attribute the statement to the stupidity of an old man, but it was so precise in its terms that in the light of other events I am now inclined to think that it was inspired by that very active group in the community who are anxious to associate the President with British and Imperial matters.[66]

In October 1940, McDunphy again vented his feelings on paper, explaining that there existed in Ireland 'a number of people, mostly ex-Unionists, some of them titled, many of them wealthy, who because of past connections with British institutions, or lack of national outlook, consider themselves the custodians of British imperialism in Ireland'. He went on to say that some 'of them…hold the view that Ireland is still a subordinate dominion of the British Empire, that people of this country are British subjects; that their ideal of British domination must be kept in the forefront at all times and that it is their duty to act as apostles of this out-of-date cause.'[67]

Nor was it only alleged unreconstructed unionists who were on the receiving end of McDunphy's acerbic pen. In late September 1939 he fulminated against the Irish Red Cross (IRC), accusing the committee of the organisation trying to degrade Ireland's neutrality because its head, Sir John Lumsden, sought to send aid to British troops. McDunphy placed the IRC and St. John's Ambulance Brigade in the same bracket, and described the ambulance brigade as being 'purely British in outlook'.[68] In 1942, the President's doctor, Dr. Boxwell, brought a poppy with him on a visit to the Áras, which led McDunphy to write sharply that this was 'lacking in good taste': he felt that Armistice ceremonies were 'a denial of the neutrality of this country'.[69] In the same vein, Frank Aiken justified the ban on newspaper advertisement for the poppy appeal by saying that it was prohibited 'in order to prevent the growth and development of such competitive organisations…to the detriment of national unity'.[70] However, this did not surprise some veterans. Cathal, who met Frank Aiken in the 1960s, got the impression that 'he was really *very* anti-British…a man whose attitude towards Britain was an anti attitude, you know, it was an anti-attitude.'

The debate continued and intensified as the war ended. In August 1945, a letter arrived at the Department of External Affairs in Dublin from John Lucy, a Cork native who was a Lieutenant-Colonel in the British Army, which forced the de Valera government to reassess the British Legion in Ireland. Lucy alleged that the Legion was discriminating against Irish Catholic veterans. Of particular concern to him was the fact that the British anthem was played at Legion ceremonies, despite protests from some members, and that the leadership of the organisation was almost wholly Protestant. Even worse, he revealed that some of the leading Legion figures were not just Protestants, but also Freemasons, members of 'a secret society not acceptable to the majority of Irish exservice [sic] officers and men who are Catholic'. He suggested three main changes. Firstly, the charter of the Legion had to be replaced; secondly, representation was to be extended to all religions; and thirdly, the name needed to be changed to drop the 'British' tag. He cited the example of Canada, where the Legion had been re-badged as 'Canadian War Veterans'. He concluded that the charter provides for political loyalty to the Crown and as such it prevented many southern Irish from joining. As a result,

> Legion affairs in the Republic are run by the representatives of a small minority, who accept the Title unreservedly, who confuse loyalties, and who certainly are not representative of the vast majority of Irishmen who fought for Britain, and who are in the Irish and Catholic tradition.[71]

An anonymous official in External Affairs drafted a reply to Colonel Lucy, which was highly critical of both the nature and the function of the British Legion in Ireland. He argued that the Colonel's suggestions could not be acted upon and that the Irish government

> should not be too unhappy at the very defective manner in which the Legion is organised in this country. While not suggesting for a moment that Irish members of the Legion cannot be excellent

Irishmen, the very raison d'etre of their membership rather suggests a qualification to their national sense and must, if only to a minute extent, act as a brake. To assume that those in charge of the British Legion will ever abandon an effort to maintain alive some sense of loyalty to either Britain or the British Crown would be naïve and even a reformed Legion in this country would therefore always be somewhat of an exception to the ordinary course of national life.[72]

The memo also accused Legion members of being nothing more than unreconstructed unionists, and the smaller and less efficient it was, then all the better for Dublin, as its corrupting influence would not be spread. The report went on to mention that any reform of the Legion had to come from within the organisation itself, or from Britain. Any attempt to do so from Dublin would be naïve and even if it was reformed, it would still remain outside the mainstream of Irish life. It concluded by stating that 'In so far as the Legion is a British influence here, the less active and effective it is, perhaps the better.' Nor did the matter rest in Dublin: it was passed along to the Irish High Commission in London to comment on. It drew an appraisal from John A. Belton, the Counsellor of the High Commission, who asserted that 'It is…a well known but nonetheless deplorable fact that the administration of the British Legion in Ireland is entirely in the hands of a small Protestant and Freemason minority.'[73] In the aftermath of the war, there were people within the de Valera government who were opposed to the British Legion and were deeply distrustful of its motives. This idea that service in the British forces eroded the recruit's sense of Irish identity is present in some veteran's testimony. One ex-serviceman said he felt as if he was regarded as 'slightly less than Irish, having been in British service' upon his return from the front.[74]

The tension between the government and the Legion came to a head in February 1946 when the chairman of the Legion in Éire, A.P. Connolly, gave a speech at the British Legion conference in Belfast, which was attended by the Northern Ireland prime minister, Basil

Brooke. In the course of his talk, Connolly pointed out that many Irish ex-servicemen were facing hard economic times and that the 'Legion was a Godsend…there was no part of His Majesty's Dominions that had such a need for that organisation as Éire.' He praised the preference schemes operated by Stormont for Northern Irish veterans, but condemned the lack of any concessions for ex-servicemen in the south, and faintly criticised Dublin when he said that he 'supposed they could not find fault with any Government in looking after its own soldiers'. By way of reply, Brooke listed the ways in which the Stormont government was looking after its veterans, and said that he thought his government 'probably had done more than even the British Government for ex-Servicemen'.[75]

Connolly's speech would probably not have aroused any attention except for the fact that his main occupation was as a civil servant with the Revenue Commissioners. In June 1946 Frank Aiken, who had been installed as Minister for Finance in the post-war Fianna Fáil cabinet, wrote to Connolly, instructing him to resign from his civil service post. In the Dáil on 25 June, Aiken was challenged by Fine Gael's T.F. O'Higgins about this, and Aiken replied that Connolly had 'crossed the political line'.[76] Asked why it had taken him so long to act, Aiken ducked the question, speaking about the need to get 'final direction' on the matter.[77] As was common when Aiken sparred with his Fine Gael opponents, the debate quickly became heated and insults flew across the chamber. Daniel Morrissey, Fine Gael TD for Tipperary, accused Aiken of being a 'jack-boot Minister', while Aiken parried with snide remarks about 'Deputy O'Higgins' Blueshirts'.[78] The *British Legion Journal's* Irish supplement in August 1946 ran a banner headline 'Mr. Connolly forced by Éire authorities to resign chairmanship of Southern Area' and stated that this had 'created a first-class sensation in the British Legion in Dublin'. The Legion, as we have seen, generally took care to avoid controversy, but sailed close to criticising the government in this issue. 'It is felt that if holding office in the Legion is incompatible with being a public servant', the article ran, 'it is time the position was clarified.'[79] (The article also strangely made reference to the fact that Connolly was 'one of the tallest men in Ireland'.) In truth, Connolly's speech was not particularly incendiary or even consistently critical of Dublin, but the fact that his remarks were made in front of Basil Brooke probably sealed his fate.

It was not only the Legion that the Dublin government was worried about. In November 1944, Henry Frazer of the RAF (Comrades) Association ('RAFA') requested permission to set up operations in Ireland. He pointed out that he had already received enquiries from Irish RAF personnel about an organisation and he was eager to get to work. De Valera replied in February 1945 that it 'would more appropriately be left over for determination by the men themselves, in consultation with the Irish Government, when hostilities have ceased'. A follow up to the initial enquiry was sent later in the year, which then was shunted from External Affairs to Defence and on to the Taoiseach's office, before being lost in the Byzantine labyrinth of the civil service and seemingly never replied to. Concluding the internal correspondence on the subject was a handwritten note from an anonymous official in May 1946 stating 'Dúirt Rúnaí na Roinne G/E liom inniu go mb'fhearr an scéal seo a thagairt marbh – Go socródh an aimsir é!' ('The Secretary of the E/A Department told me yesterday that he would rather if this story was killed – time will settle it!')[80]

Similarly, in August 1944, one Austen Braudenfield-English requested permission to meet de Valera to discuss the setting up of the 'Men of Éire' association for ex-servicemen in Ireland. Trying to appease the Taoiseach, he wrote that he was not 'Cromwellian trash' and that he 'may claim to be "Auld Irish Stock"' as he had Irish roots. Joseph Walshe was singularly unimpressed, writing that Braudenfield-English had 'Dáil ambitions'. Predictably, de Valera refused the request in February 1945.[81] A month later, Walshe complained to Maffey that the organisation's committee was composed 'of Lords and marquises whose sole purpose was to get some social kudos for themselves in Britain' and that he did not believe they 'had the slightest interest in the men themselves'.[82] Maffey urged him to allow all the associations to continue working and assured him that none of them were anti-Irish in any way. Despite the reassurances, the government was wary of new and possibly radical ex-servicemen's organisations taking root in Ireland. The Legion generally went about its business relatively under the radar; as Maffey wrote to Eric Machtig in February 1945, 'The Eire Government does not and will not oppose the work of voluntary and unofficial organisations, provided these do their work unostentatiously and objectively.'[83] There was no guarantee that new associations would be so accommodating.

The British Legion was also alive to the potential problems which a noisy new veteran's association might cause. A.P. Connolly, the chairman of the Legion in independent Ireland, pointed out that the Men of Eire should 'be extremely careful about starting any new organisation which in the exceptional circumstances of the situation might, in the long run, do more harm than good'. He had no intention of allowing the new organisation to provoke the ire of the government. The Legion was deeply engaged in planning for the post-war situation and he thought it was

> not desirable at this stage that anything should be done to cut athwart their efforts. With the best intentions in the world, the promoters of the 'Men of Eire' Association might create difficulties it would not be easy to overcome. Hence, they should be exceedingly careful to avoid taking any action which might be subversive or harmful in its effects. Accordingly, he [Connolly] suggested to those who had promoted the 'Men of Eire' that they should seek the advice and counsel of the leaders of the British Legion before they proceeded further. Otherwise, they might raise very dangerous issues which, in the interests of those most deeply concerned, were best avoided.[84]

Connolly spoke these words at the annual meeting of the Dublin metropolitan branch in January 1945, and the minutes record that 'Mr Connolly's views met with the complete approval of the meeting.'

There was also tension between the organisations for ex-British servicemen and the Organisation of National Ex-servicemen (ONE), which represented those who had served in the IRA or the National Army. In 1953, the World Veterans Federation invited President Sean T. O'Kelly to send a message to their annual conference. In response, Michael Rynne, the legal advisor to the Department of External Affairs, minuted that ONE had not been permitted to join the Federation. At the 1952 conference, the RAF association had objected to the presence of ONE, because 'the Irish War of Independence was not an international war as envisaged by the rules of the Federation.' It was clear that ONE was needled by this and had 'lost interest' in the Federation. Both de Valera and O'Kelly refused the Federation's invitation on Rynne's advice.[85] As with so much regarding commemoration in Ireland, this tension has largely been defused over the years and relations between the various veteran's organisations are now very close. Geoffrey is a member of ONE, despite never having served with the Irish forces, and Joe often attends Air Corps functions at Baldonnel.

Little wonder, then, that many returning Irish veterans felt ignored and isolated in post-war Ireland, as their commemoration services were restricted and there were divisions between the various ex-service organisations. However, despite the fact that de Valera carefully kept British ex-service organisations at arm's length from the government and the State after 1945 that did not mean that he ignored them completely. For instance, he agreed to meet a delegation from the British Legion in February 1947. However, no notes were kept of the meeting and it is unknown what was said. Indeed, the only evidence that it ever happened was a handwritten note by an anonymous civil servant, who noted that the delegation arrived at Leinster House at 11am, and that a letter of thanks from the Legion was 'Léite don Taoiseach'.[86] Typically, we are given no insight into de Valera's own attitude.

There were other private bodies in post-war Ireland that were pondering how to cater for the thousands of expected returning migrants. The Irish Commonwealth Association submitted a plan to the Department of External Affairs that called for the setting up of a 'Shamrock Benevolent Fund' – to be registered as a charity, funded by the British government, but run by a board of trustees within Ireland.

Reaffirming that such an arrangement would save Dublin from 'certain embarrassments', the Association suggested that the board of the fund would consist of representatives of the two governments, of the three British military services, a number of people who were experienced in civilian charity work, as well as an accountant. There was no recorded reply from Dublin to the Association, but de Valera, if he even considered the scheme, was probably turned off by the demand that the fund have the power to determine its own organisation and be fully in control of its relations with government departments.[87] The British were also dismissive of the idea. When asked to comment on the proposal, the perceptive Maffey said that although the Irish Commonwealth Association imagined it was a popular organisation in Eire, 'it would not be far wrong to say that the reverse is the case.'[88]

Throughout the 1950s and 1960s, the uneasy truce between the Irish government and veterans associations continued. Ex-service clubs and annual commemorations continued all over the country, although often behind closed doors; church services were offered in the town of Ballinasloe every Remembrance Sunday and the town's ex-servicemen's club house lasted until 1969, when the membership was reduced to three. The *British Legion Journal* records that branches in towns such as Athlone, Clonmel, Tullamore and Galway continued to hold fundraising events, such as golf tournaments, concerts and cake sales. Many of these branches had a very small membership, often fewer than fifty people. However, relations were shattered by the explosion of violence in Northern Ireland during 1968–69. The poppy became increasingly viewed in Ireland as a unionist symbol and the events of Bloody Sunday, in which British troops shot dead thirteen unarmed civilians in Derry in 1972, saw a rise in anti-British sentiment in the Republic. This impacted directly on ex-servicemen, whose halls and clubs were often the focus for anti-British protests. For instance, the Legion club in Dun Laoghaire was picketed by Sinn Féin just after Bloody Sunday. Joe recounted that the new situation meant that 'for instance on Poppy Day, you couldn't sell poppies, and you had to keep your head down and all this sort of thing.' Likewise, for Geoffrey, it meant that he could no longer openly sell poppies on the street; instead it had to be done clandestinely.

> You had your collecting box and a plastic bag, and you had your poppies in the bag, and you only take out your poppy box and put it in your hand. You wouldn't have a display thing or box, you know, with all the poppies in it.... You'd be very foolish to go out to certain places and shake a poppy box, have your poppies; you'd be only asking for trouble, you knew bloody well that people didn't like you.

Even more ominously, two men posing as ex-servicemen stole the membership list of Geoffrey's Legion branch around the same time. Some of the names on the list were men who had been high-ranking officers in the British forces and with the situation so unstable at the time Geoffrey was genuinely worried about 'getting a firebomb or something thrown at you'. Cathal felt the same way, pointing out that the Northern situation made people who had relatives in the British forces feel 'as if you had joined the enemy'.

It was not that the Irish public blamed Irish ex-servicemen for the situation in Northern Ireland, but their position became increasingly complicated as the violence spiralled out of control and tensions mounted between Dublin, Belfast and London. When it was suggested that the Irish Defence Forces would participate in the Remembrance ceremonies in 1983, a small group of ex-officers protested and called on the government to reverse the decision.[89] Politics and remembrance had become intertwined. One of the protesting officers was Captain James Kelly, who had been involved in the infamous Arms Trial of 1970, but who had been found not guilty of smuggling arms to the IRA. It also cut across the professional bonds which had been forged between the militaries in Ireland and Britain. In 1969, the RAF Association proposed donating half the proceeds of the premier of the film 'The Battle of Britain' to the Irish Air Corps Benevolent Fund, saying that it was in recognition of the close ties between the RAF and the Irish search and

**Kenneth and Irving, the last remaining members of the
Royal Artillery Association.**

rescue service. The Department of Defence speedily turned this down, doubtlessly with one wary eye on Northern Ireland and the Chief of Staff wrote that he did not want the Air Corps associated with a film which had 'political overtones'.[90] Despite an appeal by the RAF, the Taoiseach, Jack Lynch, declined to get involved.[91]

Atrocities, such as the IRA bomb attack on the Enniskillen war memorial in 1987 which killed eleven civilians, embittered people on both sides. Ex-servicemen endured a difficult time while the Troubles continued, and it was only towards the end of the 1990s that situations began to improve. In 1998, the Good Friday Agreement laid the basis for a peaceful settlement to the Northern conflict; the same year the Messines Peace Tower was opened by the Irish President Mary MacAleese and Queen Elizabeth II. Within Ireland, attitudes also changed. The Irish national day of commemoration was moved to July, to coincide with the anniversary of the battle of the Somme. It was an inclusive ceremony, which was dedicated to remembering *all* Irish soldiers who died in war, regardless of which army they fought in, including UN service. In addition, the government regularly sent representatives to the annual Remembrance ceremonies at Islandbridge in November.

Conclusion

The bitterness and controversy over commemoration in Irish history is both deplorable and understandable. Ireland's past is too fractured and violent for there to be a national consensus on who or what to remember, or even how to remember them. It has often been a political and partisan issue: the Easter Rising celebration in 1941 is a good example of an Irish government using the memory of the dead for its own purposes. Relations between veterans' organisations and the Irish government have been frosty and sometimes confrontational. The inevitable victims were the ex-servicemen themselves, who faced restrictions on their services and their activities. The rapprochement in recent years is welcome, but with the passage of so much time before old wounds healed, it has come too late for many Irish veterans of the Second World War. Of the estimated 600 members of the Royal Artillery Association in Leinster just after the war, only two – Kenneth and Irving – are still alive.

Chapter seven

Uniforms

*It is probable that the presence of British soldiers in
uniform in this country would lead to breaches of the peace*
Stephen Roche, secretary of the Department of Justice,
16 November 1939

*We all fought in the same war…it would have been nice
to come back in your uniform*
Irving, Dublin-born Royal Artillery gunner

The large number of Irish citizens in the British forces during the
Second World War presented a unique optical problem for the Irish
government: independent Ireland was officially neutral, but British
uniforms were a common sight in towns, villages and cities across the
country. Men and women in British uniform moving freely throughout
Ireland made Irish neutrality appear very biased indeed to outsiders.
Every month, the boats chugging across the Irish Sea contained
hundreds of Irish volunteers, either being demobilised from the forces
or coming home on leave. Demobilised personnel usually had access to
civilian clothes, having been given a demob suit upon their release,
although many managed to hold onto their military greatcoats, rucksacks
or boots. Those on leave, however, often came back in uniform, despite
the best efforts of the British and Irish authorities to stop them. The
determination of the Dublin government to restrict the practice of
wearing British uniforms in Ireland both during and after the war
presented a problem for Irish volunteers and ex-servicemen. Many, like
Cathal, had left their civilian clothes behind when they had enlisted –

what use were casual shoes, jackets and pullovers while on duty with the RAF in the jungles of Burma? Others, like Albert, wanted their parents and friends to see them in their uniforms. Irish volunteers became practiced at avoiding Irish uniform regulations, regulations which had precedents dating back to the foundation of the state in 1922.

The Free State and Uniforms

Even after independence was granted in 1922, the new Irish Free State remained closely militarily tied to the United Kingdom: thousands of Irish men and women joined the British forces every year; the Free State army was closely modelled on the British; the Royal Navy was responsible for the seas around Ireland, which maintained three bases in independent Ireland at Lough Swilly, Berehaven and Cobh. British ships and troops regularly passed through Irish ports and contemporary newspapers carried many reports of columns of British troops marching through town centres to their bases. Aware that W.T. Cosgrave's government was sensitive to the issue of British uniforms – Cosgrave himself was a veteran of 1916 and his Cumann na nGaedheal government contained many ex-rebels – the British government did its best to restrict the wearing of uniforms in public. When a British army boxing team visited the Free State in 1926 for a series of bouts with a combined Army-Garda team, they came ashore without their uniforms[1] and the British War Office issued a circular in 1927 to all commands, ordering all soldiers on leave in southern Ireland to wear civilian clothing. In reality, this order had little effect. There were occasional backlashes against uniforms: in 1924 the IRA ambushed a party of British troops in Cobh, killing one and Cosgrave had to answer angry questions from London about the ability of the Free State to police itself.

In 1928, Cosgrave decided to make a stand against the appearance of British uniforms, but was forced into an embarrassing climb-down. The initial spark was a letter from the Dominions Office, which arrived at the Department of Defence in March 1928, requesting that on-duty British soldiers in Cobh be allowed to wear their uniform into the town. The letter went from Defence to External Affairs and on to Justice while a decision was being made. On 24 April Stephen Roche, secretary of the Justice Department, wrote back, refusing permission, citing 'the possible inflammatory effect of the British uniform on extremists'. He also went on to say that 'large parties of emigrants from remote parts of the country pass through Cobh and to these people the sight of a British uniform is unusual. In all circumstances the Minister feels that it is desirable to avoid the slightest excuse for any disturbance.'[2] It subsequently turned out that British troops in Cobh had always worn their uniforms when they went into town while on duty, and there had never been any incidents. Joseph Walshe, the secretary of External Affairs, suggested that the whole thing be quietly dropped and no more be said about it. The Cumann na nGaedheal government followed his advice and did not comment again on the wearing of British uniforms in the state.

Fianna Fáil and Uniforms

The de Valera government, which took over the reins of power in 1932, was also slow to react to the issue. For a party which trumpeted its republican credentials, this was surprising. However, it was not as if de Valera was blind to the uniform issue at the time. Throughout the 1930s, he took steps to stop the quasi-fascist Blueshirts from parading in their uniforms, and also prohibited the public appearance of the British Union of Fascists appearing at Armistice ceremonies in their black shirts.[3] British uniforms, seemingly, were not a threat and therefore not a priority for him. This probably explains why, despite coming under pressure from republican and ex-IRA groups,[4] it was not until 1936, after four years in office, that de Valera made any move to restrict the appearance of British uniforms. In September 1936 the Irish High Commissioner in London, John Dulanty, was instructed to complain to the Dominions Office and to urge them to take early action 'to prevent the wearing of uniforms by British soldiers on furlough in Saorstát Éireann'.[5] This was despite the fact that Secretary of the Department of Justice Stephen Roche admitted that his department had no legal power to arrest uniformed soldiers[6] and the visit of a German boxing team in 1937 led him to confess that 'the wearing of foreign uniforms in the Saorstát is perfectly legal and could not be prevented'.[7] Because the Gardaí were unable to officially confront uniformed servicemen, Roche suggested that

> if members of the British forces in uniform are observed in Dublin, they will be asked for their names, addresses and particulars of their unit and advised in a friendly way to get into civilian clothes in their own interests. If circumstances render it necessary, persons appearing in British uniform may have to be temporarily detained by the police for their own protection: but you will appreciate that the police are not entitled to arrest such persons or even to insist on their giving their name.[8]

In his memos, Roche candidly admitted that the Gardaí had no legal power to stop soldiers wearing their uniforms. Instead, he insisted that the appearance of British uniforms was a menace to Irish public order and that 'violence will be directed against such members parading the streets of Dublin',[9] but official documents fail to support this claim. When directed to compile lists of sightings of uniformed British soldiers, numerous Garda stations all over the country reported that British uniforms were readily accepted by the Irish public and that there was little chance of disorder.[10] A typical one from the capital on 13 October 1936 pointed out that a large number of soldiers from the Irish Guards regiment had been seen in the city, 'but they have not occasioned any attention from the public'.[11] Another from Cork stated that a young Irish Royal Navy sailor had been spotted in uniform, but that there was little chance he would be attacked. 'Practically every family of the small farmer and labour class in the area have members in the British Navy', the report ran, 'and little notice is taken of these members when appearing in uniform in the area concerned.'[12] One exception was an Irish volunteer from Kilkenny whose appearance *was* likely to cause trouble, but only because he was, according to the Garda, 'inclined to say too much in praise of England and to ridicule this country and it is evident that his reason for wearing the uniform is to defy people here and let them see he doesn't care about them.'[13] In other words, the vast majority of the Irish public in the 1920s and 1930s had no problems with the sight of British uniforms and those wearing them were only likely to spark disorder when they caused it themselves.

All these Garda reports were subsequently forwarded to Sir Henry Batterbee, the permanent under-secretary at the Dominions Office, who replied rather tersely on 3 March 1937. He pointed out that Royal Navy uniforms were unmilitary in appearance and that the Admiralty was reluctant to ban their members wearing them in Ireland. The granting of leave from Royal Navy ships was at the discretion of the captain, and the First Lord was not inclined to interfere with the traditional freedom of decision given to British captains. Batterbee concluded that if such a ban was issued, it would soon become public and 'would suggest to most people that there had been a sudden deterioration between the relations of this country and the Free State'.[14]

It is perfectly clear that Fianna Fáil action against uniforms was motivated by political and diplomatic calculations. There was literally no law against the wearing of British uniforms in Ireland. However, by ordering the Gardaí to take even unofficial measures, it allowed the government to claim that it was trying to tackle the problem. It was not responding to public pressure; in fact all the evidence points to the opposite direction, that the Irish public had no issue with British uniforms. There *were* some letters of protest from IRA veteran's organisations, but these were very few and far between. The instructions to the police in 1936 were probably designed for Fianna Fáil followers and activists, to be seen to be doing something. Diplomacy also played a role. In December 1934, the government swiftly refused permission to a German officer who wished to wear his uniform while hunting in Ireland. 'The President does not wish this permission to be granted', wrote Walshe. 'It would create an awkward precedent.'[15] In the same year Colonel Wilhelm Fritz Brase, a German who was the director of the Irish Army School of Music, was refused permission by the government to take over as the Irish branch of the Nazi Party.[16] De Valera was, however, swift to take up the advantages offered by foreign uniforms.

For instance, in November 1934 he speedily facilitated the request of a young French army lieutenant (and son of the famous French General Marquis de Brantes), to be married in his uniform in Ireland. De Valera even instructed that the wedding party was to be sped through customs, a gesture which brought thanks from the General himself.[17]

The War and Uniforms

When war broke out in September 1939, the government moved to restrict and finally outlaw the wearing of foreign uniforms in Ireland. Neutrality called for stricter measures and the government could hardly claim to be neutral when soldiers of one of the belligerents passed freely through the country in uniform. On 15 September 1939 Frank Aiken, the Minister for the Co-ordination of Defensive Measures, bluntly instructed Frederick Boland, assistant secretary at the Department of External Affairs, to halt British soldiers wearing their uniforms in the country either by diplomatic means or by having them arrested. 'I hear that there are a number of British servicemen appearing in the city in British uniform,' he wrote. '…it is most important that it should be stopped.'[18] The sight of British uniforms was being questioned by some revolutionary veteran's associations as well: on 26 September, the Old IRA Men's Association in Cork wrote to de Valera, complaining about the issue, and received an answer from Frederick Boland, who wrote that 'the wearing of uniforms in this country by members of the belligerent forces has not the approval of the Irish Authorities' and that 'measures have already been taken with a view to bringing about a discontinuance of the practice.'[19]

The problem was, as the Department of Justice freely admitted, that 'there is no law prohibiting the wearing of foreign uniforms in this country.'[20] Despite being in office since 1932, and taking unofficial measures against uniforms, the situation was the same as that confronted by the Cosgrave government; the wearing of British uniforms was not illegal and could not be stopped by ordinary legislation. De Valera got around this problem by using the powers that he had been granted by the Emergency Powers Act, passed on 3 September 1939, which allowed him to bypass the Dáil in certain cases. Legislation would be too long and complicated to draft, therefore on 16 November Stephen Roche formally proposed banning *all* foreign uniforms in Ireland by emergency order, in order to maintain neutrality and preserve public order. 'From the point of view of neutrality,' he wrote, 'it is obviously undesirable that…persons should be allowed to wear in this country the uniform of the armed forces of any other State and particularly of a belligerent State.' He went on to further justify this by claiming that 'that the presence of British soldiers in uniform in this country would lead to breaches of the peace. Such incidents would be almost certain to occur if, for instance, British soldiers in uniform indulged in provocative language in public-houses.'[21] He also said that there was little the British authorities could do to stop the practice, as soldiers about to head into battle were unlikely to care about a minor wartime regulation. Despite this, in November the British government agreed to help stop troops travelling to Ireland in uniforms, and Maffey asked to be given 'the name and regiment of each delinquent in future' so he could forward it to London.[22]

The ban on uniforms was eventually introduced as an Emergency Powers Order (no. 17). Exceptions were made for diplomats, and for those who had to attend religious or ceremonial functions in independent Ireland. Those convicted were to be fined £25 for a first offence, £50 for a second, or were to serve three months in prison. Those who knowingly transported soldiers in foreign uniform into Ireland were also liable to be prosecuted. There was some doubt in Dublin whether women's organisations, such as the Auxiliary Territorial Service (ATS) and the Women's Auxiliary Air Force, were actually military in nature, and it was decided not to apply the ban to them. Another area of difficulty was the Great Northern Railway Line, parts of which ran through Éire. The Railway was informed that the ban applied to the portions of the railway line that lay in the twenty-six counties, but that no action would be taken if the train was moving from one part of Northern Ireland to the other.[23] The prohibition on uniforms caused the de Valera government many problems during the war. A request from the British Embassy in Washington to allow the British Air Attaché, who was travelling to Ireland as part of a party of diplomats, to wear his uniform sparked near-panic in Dublin. Telegrams were dispatched to the Irish Legation in Berne, to see how the neutral Swiss dealt with the matter: the answer was that military Attachés were always allowed to wear their uniform, but that they had to be accompanied by a Swiss officer when they travelled. Liam Archer, the Assistant Chief of Staff of the Irish Defence Forces even got involved, pointing out the 'risk of incident' made it inadvisable to allow Attachés to wear uniforms. In the end, normal administrative paralysis set in: no decision was made, and all requests to wear uniforms were to be assessed on a case-by-case basis.[24]

To further complicate matters, US troops began to arrive in Northern Ireland from 1942 onwards, and often came south to Dublin on leave. Technically they were also subject to the ban, but an enterprising civil servant in External Affairs realised that they had no idea what American uniforms looked like. It was not until January 1943 that the Irish Legation in Washington was able to forward the required information: farcically, the best thing they could find were two patriotic American posters, produced by the Commercial Credit Company of Baltimore, which depicted US uniforms, ranks, insignia and medals for the US army, Navy, Marine Corps and Coast Guard.[25]

Enforcement of the ban was patchy at best. Many Gardaí were satisfied if Allied personnel, Irish or otherwise, made an effort to cover up their uniforms with an overcoat. Albert came home on leave with his uniform concealed underneath a long coat and was allowed to disembark. Cathal made sure he had a long raincoat which he wore to cover his RAF blues. Other police were not so lenient. One particularly zealous Garda was notorious for hiding at Dun Laoghaire harbour and surprising servicemen as they tried to get off the mail boat. In March 1940 he complained to his superiors that he was being obstructed in his duties searching for uniforms by the customs officials working at the pier. They often let the passengers off the boat quickly, in order to sabotage his search, even though he could see men and women in uniform and was unable to catch them. Even when he stood at the end of the exit and searched the passengers one by one, he found that other exits were being opened to allow the passengers off. Eventually, he wrote to the Commissioners Office, complaining at the obstruction and pointing out that he could

> only suggest that this present antipathy on the part of these men may be perhaps attributable to the nature of the Emergency Powers Order (No.17) 1939, in so much as to be distasteful (patriotically) to the general atmosphere that permeates this Port from ship to shore, especially as some of this present Customs staff are ex-British service men and some of whom may have relatives at present serving with the British Army.[26]

He was probably also irritated by the fact that sometimes there was a special gangway on the pier marked 'H.M. Forces this way'.[27] He later had a heated confrontation with two British soldiers, again in Dun Laoghaire, in which one of them told him that the uniform ban would not last long because 'England would be shortly taking over this country!' It turned out that both men were survivors from Dunkirk and had been drinking.[28]

The issue may have been a diplomatic one for the Fianna Fáil government, but it was a practical problem for many Irish volunteers. Cathal, for instance, left all his civilian clothes behind in Ireland when he joined the RAF.

> And this was fine for fellas who lived in Britain and Northern Ireland, but when you sent your clothes home to the Republic, to Éire as it was then, it meant that if you were going to go on leave, you didn't have any civilian clothes. I only came on one leave, home on one leave, which was before my embarkation, that was embarkation leave, so I was faced with a problem. I only had my uniform. When I made this point…our adjutant he said 'all right, go into the stores and see if anybody has a raincoat'. So I got a raincoat which I wore over my uniform.

The British government tried to stop the practice by providing Irish personnel with temporary civilian suits for their journey home at Holyhead and other ports, and Irish volunteers dealt with the situation in several different ways. Some obeyed the injunction: Albert remembered leaving his uniform behind at a barracks in London, but hated the practice because the civilian clothes rarely fitted properly. Kenneth kept his uniform at an Irish club in central London, but arrived back in the UK after a trip home to discover that the building had been destroyed by a bomb. Geoffrey kept a civilian suit with his relatives in Watford. Others simply ignored the ban entirely. Don returned to Ireland twice on leave during the war, both times strolling off the boat in full Royal Engineers uniform, and never had any trouble: 'I walked off the mailboat, down to my house here, and I never had any trouble at all. I wasn't, I shouldn't have done it, but there you are, you do these things.' Hilda, who enlisted as a military nurse, described how easy it was to evade the rules:

> We got on board [the boat to Britain] and everybody was like me, in ordinary clothes. We were out about ten minutes, or more, probably ten minutes, and suddenly...there's paper bags everywhere. The overcoats were all put in paper bags and left on the deck, and everybody is in uniform... And I put *my* coat in a bag and left it. It was so funny, a boat full of uniforms and only ten minutes before you'd think they were ordinary civilians. They were dressed in them because everybody wouldn't have a suit to wear, come home just for that. I suppose they took their army stuff and wore it, just like me.

Post-war Ireland and Uniforms

The situation regarding uniforms changed completely once the war had ended. Dublin in 1945 was flooded with Allied servicemen on leave, in and out of uniform. So many American soldiers visited the Irish capital that US Army magazine *Yank* ran a special feature on the city in October

**Don in Royal Engineers
Uniform.**

Don in 2011.

1945.[29] Allied servicemen came looking for cheap food and alcohol, as well as to visit relatives: the phenomenon of uniformed Allied soldiers in cars or more usually on bicycles, stopping to ask directions in small towns all over Ireland, appeared in several local papers after the war.[30] These men and women brought with them much-needed tourist income to Ireland, and the Irish Red Cross organised a Tourist Association to provide transport and accommodation for visiting servicemen. De Valera was reportedly delighted with the success of the scheme. The secretary of the Department of External Affairs, Joseph Walshe, took the precaution of checking with the Irish Legation in Switzerland, to see if visiting US troops there had brought any loose morals to the host country.[31] With so many Allied servicemen coming to Ireland and providing a timely boost to the local economy, the government decided that it would be too embarrassing to enforce the ban on uniforms and decided that it would be temporarily lifted. The Government Information Service's public statement emphasised the government's pragmatic approach:

The Irish Government have been informed by the American Government that a number of American soldiers desired to visit relatives in Ireland before returning finally to the United State[s] but that they would experience great difficulty in providing themselves with civilian clothes. The Irish Government have accordingly decided to suspend in respect of such American soldiers the regulations concerning the wearing of foreign uniforms in Irish territory.[32]

However, they insisted that this did not apply to Irish veterans who were returning home. The British authorities provided civilian clothes to returning veterans, so the government did not wish to change the rules for them. In the Dáil, Justice Minister Gerald Boland flatly refused to extend the exemption to returning Irish servicemen, brusquely pointing out that the 'special considerations…did not exist in the case of Irish citizens serving in the British forces.'[33] Many Irish veterans felt victimised by this. Irving was particularly annoyed by the situation. Justifiably proud of his service, he wanted to show his uniform to family and friends and was irritated to see Australians, New Zealanders or Canadians walking about Dublin in uniform. '…we thought it was a bit ridiculous', he said. 'We all fought in the same war, it was the same cause… Why should they be allowed back? It was only a small thing in a way, but it would have been nice to come back in your uniform.' Cathal too was frustrated by the measure: '…it was common enough to see Yanks in uniforms here in Dublin. And, indeed, Canadians from the North of Ireland came down in their uniforms,' he said. Men who had served abroad for years and only wanted to return home to their families and friends in their uniforms were 'bloody furious'.

The reasons why the government chose to single out Irish ex-servicemen are not clear, but we can speculate. The maintenance of the public face of neutrality was probably the dominant factor. The free movement of Irish troops in British uniforms into Dublin and other cities around the country might conceivably have provoked 'welcome home' ceremonies or unofficial parades as khaki-clad Irish men and women streamed off mailboats. By forcing veterans to return home in civilian clothes, thus making them indistinguishable from Irish worker-migrants, perhaps the de Valera government was trying to conceal just how many Irish citizens chose to disregard neutrality and join the British forces. Another explanation was that the Irish ex-serviceman in uniform offered a vision of Irish citizens with multiple loyalties: to Ireland, to Britain, to the Allies.[34] Perhaps de Valera felt that his vision of Ireland as Gaelic, Catholic and morally superior to the warring nations was threatened by this. Whatever the explanation, the ban was formally reintroduced in the Defence Forces (Temporary Provisions) Act, which came into force on 1 April 1946. The act prohibited the wearing of all foreign uniforms in Ireland. The only exception was 'the consent in writing of a Minister' and it also made it illegal for anyone to knowingly transport persons in foreign uniform into the state. The penalty for being convicted was £25 or six months in prison.[35]

The debate continued long after the war was over. Among the files of the Taoiseach's office is one containing just two letters: one from a man in Donegal, asking why members of the British forces are allowed to travel over the border in uniform, 'whereas members of the forces of the Republic cannot go into the Six Counties in uniform',[36] and another from a Corporal in the British Army, asking to be allowed home to Cork in uniform as he has no civilian clothes.[37] No reply was recorded in the archives, but attached to both letters was a copy of the 1946 prohibition on uniforms. It had become the standard reference point for post-war uniform problems, but, as the letters show, the issue had not gone away.

Conclusion

People reading the *Longford Leader* local newspaper on 5 January 1946 would have come across an advertisement reading 'Always the best. British Army boots, reconditioned and restudded, 6 to 9, 12/6 and 14/.'[38] Whether for practical purposes or for pride, and whether they were permitted to or not, Irish volunteers came home from the Second World War in uniform. Some, like Don, came back in full uniform;

others, such as Albert, covered them up with overcoats; still others, as the advert above suggests, only took home what could be used in their post-war lives. De Valera's policy towards ex-servicemen and their uniforms in 1945 was a complex mixture of measures inherited from the Cumann na nGaedheal government and concerns about the façade of neutrality, but whatever the reasons, the government's decisions victimised Irish veterans and made them feel unwelcome when they came home from the war.

Chapter eight

Deserters

The Deputy wants us to bring out bands and banners to
meet these fellows and give them a welcome home
Minister for Defence Oscar Traynor, October 1945

we were fed up working in the bog…we were supposed
to be soldiering
Testimony of Danny, Irish Army soldier

While all Irish ex-servicemen faced a host of problems when they
returned to Ireland after the war, there was one group of returnees who
were more anxious than the rest: deserters from the Irish Defence
Forces. Throughout the war, a steady stream of Irish soldiers left their
posts, the majority of which either joined the British forces, or travelled
to Britain to seek employment in the war industries. In all, six thousand
men are estimated to have deserted during the war. Irish volunteers
abroad consistently met fellow countrymen who had swapped Irish for
British uniforms. Albert heard of a platoon in the British artillery which
was composed of 'Irishmen who resigned or deserted from the Irish
forces and joined the Royal Artillery'. As they had already undergone
basic training, they were kept together as a unit and when the day's work
was over, 'they'd sit in their tents and sing their rebel songs at night'.
Cathal also ran into a deserter while in the RAF: a man from Dublin
who fled 'out of sheer boredom'. Richard Doherty has recorded the tale
of an Irish man who enlisted in Belfast along with thirty deserters.[1]
Many deserters were eager to return to Ireland after the war, but were
fearful of the consequences, as they faced prosecution and impris-

onment. The Irish government struggled to come to grips with the problem in 1945, torn between punishing deserters for their offence, and the economic/diplomatic consequences of pursuing them. Eventually a solution was found which dealt with the deserter issue quickly and cheaply, but which generated a great deal of controversy, both then and now.

Deserters, 1922–1945

Under the terms of the Anglo-Irish Treaty in December 1921, the British military presence in independent Ireland was almost completely removed, with the Royal Navy retaining just three bases. However, with the scale of Irish involvement in the British forces, the link was far from severed and one of the live issues between the Irish and British military authorities was that of deserters in each others territory. It was a matter of some concern for the British: in 1924, the Colonial Secretary, the Duke of Devonshire, estimated that almost 5,000 men had vanished in Ireland between 1916 and 1924[2] and the British military authorities were understandably anxious to trace them. Investigations revealed that many of these men were dead, having either been killed in accidents or by the IRA, but there remained a significant number of British service personnel who were presumed to be deserters.

While the evacuation was underway in 1922, the British military forwarded details of suspected deserters to Michael Collins, the chairman of the Irish Provisional Government, which had been established by the Treaty. Collins initially had little time to deal with deserters, and the issue received little Irish attention, and it was not until 1923 that a semi-permanent procedure was put in place. The War Office forwarded the details of individual deserters to Dublin, where the government would instruct the Gardai to arrest the men. They were then detained and handed over to the British at the nearest available port or the Northern Irish border. At the same time, the Home Office refused to consider the idea of apprehending Irish Army deserters in Britain.[3] The foremost opponent of the arresting of Irish military deserters in the UK was Leslie Brass, the legal advisor at the Home Office, who wrote in 1925 that

> The Home Office is indifferent as to whether deserters from the I.F.S. Army in this country are recovered by the I.F.S. or not…the Home Office however feels it necessary to point out that deserters from Dominion military forces are not recovered in this country and that the British Army is quite different from the I.F.S. Army since the former is Imperial in character and the latter only local.[4]

On the Irish side, the Free State Minister for Defence, Richard Mulcahy, was deeply uncomfortable with the idea of arresting and handing over deserters to the British. Many of those detained were Irish; even worse, some had IRA service to their name and it galled the new military authorities in Dublin to have to deport them to courts martial and possible imprisonment in the UK. On one occasion in May 1923, Mulcahy refused to take any action when a British Army deserter was discovered in the Irish forces, and clashed with Kevin O'Higgins over the matter.[5] But despite Mulcahy's objections, the rest of the Free State government cooperated with British requests over deserters. The men were either arrested and deported or were asked to sign a Form of Confession, in which they admitted their offence and were not liable to prosecution, but forfeited all pension and gratuity rights. Files in the Irish military archives show that throughout 1923, several deserters were either arrested or presented with confession forms.

In November 1923, Mulcahy travelled to London and came to an informal agreement with the Duke of Devonshire over the deserter issue. According to a letter which Mulcahy wrote to the Executive Council of the Free State, from 1 November 1923 the Irish Free State government undertook to

> make every effort to apprehend and arrest deserters from the British Army who seek refuge in Ireland. They will not, however, be called on so to apprehend and return deserters from the British

Army who deserted at any date prior to the 1 November 1923 and gave service in the Irish Forces, whether pre-Truce or in the present National Forces.[6]

Under this new agreement, there was much closer collaboration between the two governments. Between November 1923 and November 1925, a total of thirteen deserter cases were investigated by the Gardai; four of these men were traced and signed forms of confession; one was in the Free State army and so exempt from prosecution; four had emigrated; two could not be traced; one was known to have fled, and one was arrested and handed over to the British authorities.

This new-found spirit of cooperation came to a shuddering halt in September 1926. The Irish police had arrested a British Army rifleman and was preparing to hand him over at the border, when the soldier's father issued a writ of *habeas corpus* and the Attorney-General – future Fine Gael Taoiseach John A. Costello – advised the government that Dublin had no defence against it.[7] By Costello's reckoning, British deserters in Ireland had not broken any Irish laws and were therefore not liable to arrest. The practice of tracking down deserters was swiftly stopped. Acrimonious intra-departmental debates ensued in Britain, as the War Office complained that Ireland had technically become a safe haven for military deserters, while the Home Office stubbornly refused to make any concessions to Ireland. Leslie Brass continued to insist that it was not the duty of the British police to arrest Dominion deserters and his refusal to budge hampered efforts to reach a compromise. Interventions by the Treasury, the Colonial Office, the Dominions Office, the Law Officers and the Treasury Solicitor made no headway against what was a tortuously complicated legal issue. The matter remained unresolved when the Second World War broke out in 1939. But whereas the problem in the lead-up to 1939 was a flow of British deserters to Ireland, the war saw the trend reverse itself. The major issue now was Irish deserters fleeing to the UK, either to work or to join the British forces.

Deserter's Motivations

Irish soldiers were both pushed and pulled out of the Irish forces and they travelled to the UK during the Second World War for several reasons. Pay in the British forces, and in the munitions factories, was higher than anything on offer in Ireland. The basic salary for a new recruit in the Irish Army was eighteen shillings, while it was twenty-two shillings in the British forces.[8] According to the list of deserters held in the Irish military archives, most of the men who absconded during the war had been unskilled workers before they had enlisted in the Irish forces, and most of them had been classified as 'labourer'. This suggests that they had been attracted to the Irish army principally because it offered a steady wage, but that they had then deserted to take advantage of the higher rates available in the UK. Peadar MacMahon, a former Chief of Staff and wartime secretary of the Department of Defence, felt that the desertion problem was intimately linked to the wider issue of recruitment for the British forces in Ireland and throughout the war kept a careful watch on the figures for both. At the core of the issue, he felt, was that most defections from the army and 'enlistment generally in the British Forces by Irish citizens is almost wholly governed by economic considerations'.[9] However, his pleas for higher pay in the Defence Forces generally fell on deaf ears.

The course of the war also influenced deserter's decisions. During the initial phase of the expansion of the Irish forces, from June 1940 to early 1941, the threat of invasion was thought to be high and desertions from the army remained at a relatively low level. The most prevalent offence during this period was short-term absence without leave, which accounted for 60 per cent of all military offences.[10] The Irish Chief of Staff, Daniel McKenna, suggested that the large number of new recruits, many of whom were training in barracks far away from their homes, accounted for the spike in absences. In this period, the army authorities were delighted with the response and the Department of External Affairs received many queries about enlisting from abroad.[11] However, in the case of men from Northern Ireland wishing to enlist in the Irish

Volunteer reserve, government officials were more cautious. Responding to one request in 1939, Peadar MacMahon suggested that because Volunteers were allowed to keep their uniform and equipment, it would be 'inadvisable' to allow these out of Dublin's 'jurisdiction and control'.[12] However, once the focus of the war shifted away from Britain and Ireland from 1941 onwards, particularly after the German invasion of the USSR in June 1941, the trickle of deserters became an out-and-out flood. In the period April 1941 to March 1942, 2,731 men disappeared from the Irish forces,[13] 450 of them in August 1941 alone.[14] In July 1943, 196 Irish soldiers were declared deserters[15] and G2, Irish military intelligence, estimated that 200 civilian recruits a week were also leaving the country.[16] It was no wonder that the Irish commanders worried about the levels of manpower left in Ireland. As the war went on, and the tide of the war began to run against the Axis, more and more men decided that the threat to Ireland had passed. In 1943, said one deserter, 'there was no risk of invasion of Ireland…our time in the army seemed a waste of time'.[17] The military authorities were under no illusions about the effect that the news of the war was having on the Irish forces: 'The course of the war in Europe has convinced most people that there is little danger to this country of immediate invasion,' wrote McKenna in 1943, 'and the patriotic urge to join the Army which was so noticeable during the summer of 1940 has almost completely disappeared.'[18]

However, the dominant reason for desertion was simple: boredom. The German victory in western Europe triggered an invasion panic in Ireland, and recruits flooded into the forces. Even after the danger had seemingly passed, there was still plenty of excitement caused by the amount of aircraft which crashed in neutral Ireland as the war raged around the island. Danny, a wartime recruit who joined the Emergency army and eventually served for thirty-eight years, recalled his infantry unit being sent out into the Donegal hills to track a German bomber which had crash-landed, and discovered the Luftwaffe crew having tea in a local's cottage. However, once the initial momentum of 1940–41 had faded away, life in the Irish forces settled into a fairly dull routine. Even worse, the army was more and more deployed on non-military duties. With the threat of invasion receding, the government succumbed to the temptation of using the large pool of trained but under-used manpower in the army for duties such as helping with the harvest, disposing of animal carcasses after foot-and-mouth outbreaks, cutting timber or providing transport. Even worse, soldiers were sent to work in bogs as supplies of imported fuel dried up and the government launched a major campaign to harvest turf as an alternative. In the twelve months between April 1942 and March 1943, the army was responsible for cutting and transporting 23,880 tons of turf and 662 tons of timber.[19] For men who had joined for patriotic reasons, were seeking adventure or had just enlisted because it was a regular wage, labouring in the bogs of Ireland quickly lost its appeal. As Danny put it '...we were fed up working in the bog, cutting turf...we were supposed to be *soldiering*, we weren't soldiering... We spent months, two months in the bog, maybe more, and we were camped in the bog, we had all the canvas in the bog.'[20] Irving, who joined the Royal Artillery, recalled that his pal was very dissatisfied with life in the Irish army:'...he told me afterwards, "If I'd known I was going to be just sent down to the bog lands", I think they cut turf and everything.' Irish men and women who volunteered from civvy street also sensed that the major events would bypass Ireland and that if they stayed at home they would miss them: Kenneth, when asked why he chose the Royal Artillery over the Irish army, said that he 'knew there'd be a bit of action going on if we joined the British army, while there was no chance of it here'.

Defence and Deserters

The Irish military's attempts to stamp out desertions were hampered by the fact that the Irish army was in a unique position as regards the British forces. Both the British forces and the British war industries were still hungry for manpower as the war went on, and both offered very high wages. The British forces were a particularly attractive option for men who were sick of life in the Irish army. The huge number of Irish volunteers already serving in British uniform provided a ready-made support network for would-be recruits, and acted as a powerful magnet to men who were fed up of toiling in the bog. In addition, the recruiting centres for the British forces were close, well within the reach of deserters. Irish army units stationed near the border with Northern Ireland consistently suffered the highest rates of desertion.[21] The Éire–Northern Ireland border was porous and difficult to police; when several of Danny's Irish army comrades deserted late in the war, they simply left the bog they were working on and walked across the border. Danny later heard that many of them had been killed at the Anzio beachhead. The problem became so bad that there were rumours that Irish army patrols were detailed to collect the piles of discarded Irish army uniforms, which had been cast aside as deserters fled across the border into Northern Ireland.[22] It was also a constant headache for British intelligence, who admitted in their post-war review of Irish neutrality that the 'actual crossing of the Border…could not be prevented or even controlled.'[23]

The Department of Defence tried various ways to tackle the deserter problem during the Emergency. Undercover investigators were sent into the offices of the British Legion to see if they were actively assisting the deserters in their escape. The Military Police increased cooperation with the Gardaí and intercepted hundreds of men every year. Dublin further asked the British military authorities in Belfast not to accept deserters, and the British responded by sending a notice to all potential recruits, stating that they would not be accepted if they were already members of the Irish army. 'If you are in the Free State Army (or on the Reserve),' ran the British leaflet, 'it is useless proceeding further in the matter, since in that case if you come to Belfast you will be rejected and no expenses will be refunded.'[24] However, as we have seen, many Irish enlisted under false names, so this warning was useless.

McMahon and McKenna also tried to raise army wages and both brought the issue to the attention of the cabinet. McMahon urged that Irish military pay be raised to British levels, but ran into a stubborn refusal from the Department of Finance. The secretary of Finance, J.J. McElligott, consistently ordered Defence to rein in its spending, regardless of the international situation. During the Sudetenland crisis in September 1938, McElligott told McMahon that there was no need to expand the Irish army because Britain would inevitably defend Ireland[25] and in April 1940, at the same time as the Germans attacked Scandinavia, McElligott piled pressure on the Adjutant General, Colonel James Flynn, pointing out that the forces were 1,500 men over budgetary estimates. Flynn responded by ordering that the numbers be cut to 1,500 *under* the budget.[26] McElligott had been handed the authority to cut staff in all government departments by the Taoiseach on 5 September[27] and he was not about to give in to McMahon's request for higher wages in the army. In any case, with so many other factors also combining to pull recruits out of the army, a pay raise was not guaranteed to stamp out the problem.

The Department of Defence was not blind to the fact that the lack of excitement was a major motivation for desertion, and Dan McKenna's reports to the government during the Emergency mention it several times. His report for 1942–43 noted that 'those who have a natural taste for military life are more inclined to join the British forces, where a more exciting career is expected.'[28] A year later, he admitted that it was becoming more and more difficult to keep up the morale and 'interest of the troops who are for so long in an Army which is at peace, but is surrounded by armies at war.'[29] In an attempt to raise spirits, the army tried to organise regular 'Step Together' recruiting fairs and in August – September 1942 held major exercises in the south of the country between Dublin and Cork. Both divisions of the army took part, as well as armoured car squadrons, the Air Corps and the Local Defence Force. Soldiers remained out of barracks and living on the ground for most of the month and HQ judged the whole enterprise a great success, despite the accidental death of four soldiers in the Blackwater river.[30] However, a lack of equipment and funds soon bit again. Shortages of petrol meant that the forces sank back into immobility and the excitement generated by the exercises quickly faded away, to be replaced by apathy. Nor was the government under any illusions: in June 1944, the Defence Minister Oscar Traynor steadfastly refused to deploy soldiers to help with the harvest. Individual soldiers were already being given, upon application, two months' leave at planting and harvest time.[31] He did not say it openly, but we can assume Traynor knew that sending army units into harvest fields may have prompted even more troops to desert.

Matters were made worse by the fact that there was a lack of coordination between the various branches of the government. Despite the close collaboration between the army and the Gardaí, some still slipped through the net. In November 1941, MacMahon complained to Joseph Walshe that an Irish army fugitive had been apprehended on a mail boat bound for Britain, but that he had been carrying a valid travel permit issued by External Affairs. Walshe replied tartly that it was the job of the police to check emigrant's backgrounds and that 'no additional enquiry can be made in this Department regarding the bona fides of the applicant.' In January 1942, MacMahon suggested adding an extra question to the travel permit application form, asking if the applicant was a member of the Defence Forces, but it was not until April 1943 that even a draft was drawn up.[32]

Dublin did not just have to contend with Irish soldiers absconding to the UK. As had been the case before 1939, there were also cases of Allied service personnel fleeing to Ireland and on this issue it seems that there was a reasonable amount of cooperation between the two governments. In the case of an RAF deserter apprehended in Cork in March 1941, it was almost seamless. The young American, a volunteer in 1939, was arrested as a result of mysterious 'information received', the source of which was not revealed, and he was put on the train to Dublin, where he was met by more Gardaí and put on the Belfast train, after being given five shillings for personal expenses. The total money expended, £2.0.7d, was billed to the Department of External Affairs, who passed it along to the Irish High Commission in London, where John A. Belton, the legal advisor to the High Commissioner, swiftly received reimbursement from the British permit office.[33] Unfortunately, most of the files dealing with British deserters in Ireland during the Emergency remained sealed, as they contain names and details of men and women who are potentially still alive.

However, Dublin did not routinely track down British deserters in Ireland, for one important reason: many of those deserters were Irish. During the war, Irish officials did not protest too vigorously to British authorities about the appearance of British military uniforms because many of the offenders may have been deserters who fled home, a point noted by an anonymous official in External Affairs in 1940. Raising the issue might, he noted, 'conceivably provoke discussion of the question of the return to Britain of deserters from the British Army'.[34] By February 1946, it was thought that over 15,000 British troops were AWOL in Britain,[35] and half of this total had given addresses in Ireland when they enlisted, suggesting that many had simply returned home without waiting to be demobbed.[36] Like Richard Mulcahy in the 1920s, de Valera did not want to arrest Irish military deserters and deport them to Britain. In one case, however, the Irish government deliberately distanced themselves from an Irish deserter from the British forces. In May 1944 the Department of External Affairs was contacted by an Irish soldier who had absconded because his commanding officer had made anti-Irish comments. He wrote several letters to Dublin asking for help. For External Affairs, however, it was far too controversial to meddle in the internal operations of the British Army: officials suggested that the correspondence 'neither merits nor requires a reply'.[37]

Returning Deserters, 1945

As the war drew to a close and British demobilisation began to pick up speed, both of de Valera's offices – Taoiseach and Minister for External Affairs – began to receive enquiries from relatives of deserters, asking the government's policy towards them. In the absence of any clear orders to the contrary, the Gardaí and Military Police began to arrest deserters as they returned home from the UK. In June[38] and July 1945[39] newspapers carried stories of Irish deserters being detained by the police. But arresting and prosecuting all returning deserters was not a viable solution; it would have been far too expensive to pursue the hundreds of men who were expected to return home, to say nothing of the time and resources that the Gardaí would have had to have poured into it. Far more importantly, it would have had disastrous diplomatic consequences. Ireland's international reputation had taken a battering during the war. The refusal to grant the Allies use of Irish bases, official complaints about US troops in Northern Ireland, the refusal to expel Axis diplomats, violence on the streets on VE Day and de Valera's visit to the German Legation had combined to make Ireland very unpopular indeed by 1945. Prosecuting all deserters upon their return to Ireland, having either fought in the British forces or helped the war effort, would have only brought even more bad publicity.

As it was, British newspapers were already running stories about it: in June 1945, the *Daily Express* published one under the headline 'Éire puts war heroes in jail', detailing how eight men were detained by the police as they came ashore at Dun Laoghaire.[40] The British government was also interested in the fate of Irish army deserters, and there were several intra-service notes sent on the subject, speculating about what would happen to them. Unsurprisingly, the War Office was most interested.[41] But at the same time, the Irish government could not allow these men to escape unpunished. Although Dublin had placed few obstacles in the way of Irish civilians who wished to leave for Britain, Irish soldiers were another matter entirely. Allowing them to desert and to join the British forces without consequence would have called neutrality into question, and could even have undermined the existence of the Irish Defence Forces: why have an Irish army at all, if the soldiers were free to simply walk out of the barracks gate and join the British?

Emergency Powers Order 362

De Valera had to carefully balance punishment with publicity when deciding how best to deal with the deserter problem. The government had faced questions in the Dáil in May 1945, and Oscar Traynor, the Minister for Defence, answered that deserters were 'worthy of very little consideration'. He also added that they would be excluded from government jobs 'for a long time to come'.[42] The first concrete proposals came from the Department of Justice in June 1945. In a memo circulated to all departments, Secretary of Justice Stephen Roche laid out a series of proposals. In his preamble, Roche stated that the majority of deserters 'have been serving in the British Forces or are in civilian employment in Great Britain or Northern Ireland'. To arrest them all was too costly and, in any case, the army was not interested in recovering them, as they had proved themselves unreliable by deserting. Therefore, according to Roche, the simplest solution was to simply dismiss them all from the forces *en masse*. All those expelled would forfeit some types of pensions and gratuities, would not receive a discharge certificate (vital for securing post-war employment) and, most controversially of all, would be disqualified from any sort of government-funded employment for a period of seven years. Roche proposed that 180 days be the threshold for deserters; if they were not caught before that, then they were automatically dismissed. All of these suggestions were adopted and became part of Emergency Powers Order (EPO) no. 362, which de Valera signed on 8 August 1945 and with a stroke of his pen, expelled 4,634 soldiers from the army. In March 1946, a further 149 deserters who had passed the 180-day limit were dismissed.

The measure provoked a backlash from Fine Gael in the Dáil and in October 1945, T.F. O'Higgins put forward a motion calling on the government to reverse the Order. O'Higgins argued that the Order was very unfair and effectively discriminated against men who had left to join the British forces: as they were out of the country, they had no chance to hand themselves in and would therefore be automatically subject to the Order. He characterised de Valera's actions as 'stimulated by malice, seething with hatred, oozing with venom' and declared that the men were being penalised 'not for the crime of deserting this nation in a time of danger, but for the crime of going to assist other nations in what they believed was a fight for survival of Christianity in Europe.'[43] It was, he said, 'a brutal, unchristian and inhuman Order'[44] which reduced Irish army deserters to 'pariah dogs…outcasts, untouchables'.[45]

As his argument developed, it became clear that he was also expressing the frustration of the Fine Gael party at being powerless to make any impression on the Irish political scene since the beginning of the Emergency. At the outbreak of the war, de Valera had put forward an amendment to the constitution to allow the government to assume emergency powers. He justified this by saying that although Ireland was not involved in the war, it was still an emergency situation as war was raging all around it. The Emergency Powers Bill was passed and the government was granted an extraordinary array of special powers. It could raise temporary forces, order the compulsory cultivation of land, impose curfews, limit public assemblies, ration supplies, enforce censorship and, as we have already seen in EPO no. 17, ban the wearing of foreign military uniforms in Ireland. Emergency powers meant that Fianna Fáil could effectively ignore the Dáil, while oppressive censorship stifled dissent. Thus de Valera and Fianna Fáil took a tight grip of the political system in Ireland during the war and Fine Gael, although the main opposition party in the Dáil, was in electoral decline and was powerless to prevent it. Their contribution to wartime government policy was to be members of the powerless National Defence Conference, a cross-party Dáil committee that debated a lot but achieved very little. O'Higgins himself was a member of the Conference and must have realised that it was a pointless exercise. Fighting against EPO 362, O'Higgins likened Fianna Fáil to a 'junta' and declared that the deserters measure was both unconstitutional and illegal. His frustration was clear when he shouted at Traynor 'Legislation can be discussed, altered, amended, reduced or extended but an emergency Order cannot…That is the position into which the Dáil was forced.'[46]

Speaking for the government, Oscar Traynor did not mince his words. He had little incentive to be gracious in victory or to offer the Opposition any favours; Fianna Fáil had an overall majority in the Dáil and their grip was buttressed by Emergency legislation. He also had little love for Fine Gael, having fought against the Treaty in the civil war. By 1945, the leader of the Fine Gael party was Richard Mulcahy, who had been in charge of the Free State army during the civil war and many Fianna Fáil deputies would have regarded him with particular loathing. Echoing Roche's memo of June, Traynor pointed out that it would place a huge burden on the army to have to prosecute the many hundreds of returning deserters. He also declared that the government's sole aim in depriving the deserters of their pensions and allowances was to fully reward the men who resisted the temptation to desert. Traynor himself said that he saw the mass expulsion as an act of charity by the government. If all the deserters went before military courts martial, there was a possibility that they would be sentenced to penal servitude. In other countries, he added, deserters were simply shot.[47] However, despite his attempts to sound reasonable, some anger did seep into his remarks. O'Higgins's repeated charges of Fianna Fáil vindictiveness clearly irritated him, and at one point Traynor asked his opponent if he had taken into account

> that these men, voluntarily, without any compulsion, took an oath of allegiance to this nation which they did not respect, and which the Deputy now suggests that there was no necessity for them to respect. The Deputy wants us to bring out bands and banners to meet these fellows and give them a welcome home for all the gallant deeds they did in China, Japan or the other places he referred to.[48]

Fianna Fáil repeatedly raised the issue of conscription of Irish in Britain as a way of defusing Fine Gael's argument, and pointedly asked O'Higgins if his party was as concerned with Irish citizens abroad as it was with deserters. When O'Higgins pointed out that deserters who had gone on to liberate German concentration camps deserved a second chance, he was attacked by Michael Moran, Fianna Fáil TD for Mayo south. Moran sneered that O'Higgins was making a 'song and dance about Belsen camps and so forth and about the glorious place the Irishmen who were in the British Army won for themselves'.[49] Moran further argued that the Order was not harsh enough and that 'the State should go further and make it clear to all citizens of the State that crimes of this character during a period of national emergency will be severely punished.'[50] In comparison to Moran, Traynor's stance seemed moderate, but perhaps that was the plan all along.

Fianna Fáil also argued that deserters had joined an army which could potentially have invaded Ireland. At the height of Anglo–Irish tensions in 1940, when German victory seemed on the cards, this may have been a plausible argument, but it was a patently absurd one by 1945. The most obvious explanation why Fianna Fáil continually brought it up was to rationalise the continuation of Emergency legislation. By 1945, there was not the slightest danger of German invasion; if the danger to Ireland had passed, then the state of emergency could be ended; if it ended, then de Valera would have to relinquish his considerable emergency powers and returned Irish democracy to normal. By repeatedly pointing to the possibility of an Allied invasion, Fianna Fáil was attempting to justify the maintenance of Emergency powers, which in turn reinforced their grip on Irish politics. De Valera was not about to waste a good crisis. In the end, O'Higgins's and Mulcahy's arguments were in vain and the proposal to annul the Order was defeated.

Deserters and Diplomacy

The law of unintended consequences is a strange phenomenon and de Valera was lucky enough to benefit from it when dealing with deserters in 1945. EPO 362 was designed as a quick, cheap and relatively quiet way of disposing of the deserter problem, but it actually played into the hands of those in Downing Street who argued in favour of paying British unemployment insurance to Irish migrants. Ireland's international standing was weak in 1945 and London was determined to take advantage of it. Christopher Addison, the post-war Dominions Secretary, urged the cabinet in September 1945 not to waste the strong position 'in relation to world opinion' that Britain held over Ireland. 'Eire's position has never been weaker,' he wrote. 'We should be very careful not to lose this great advantage.'[51] Sir John Maffey also wrote to the cabinet along much the same lines, saying that neutrality 'reduced Ireland's credit with the Allied Nations'.[52] It would have been extremely hard to entice the British to the negotiating table when pursuing and prosecuting army deserters at the same time.

Instead, EPO 362 gave Addison the chance to argue that the British government needed to take quick action to take care of Irish ex-servicemen. In March 1946, the British cabinet considered a joint memorandum on Irish volunteers from Addison and James Griffith, the Minister for National Insurance. In it, they strongly criticised Dublin for its attitude and pointed out that

> The Eire Government are not concerned to look after the interests of these men who from their point of view have been guilty of leaving Eire to join the service of a 'Foreign Power'. In fact the only contribution to the problem has taken the form of disqualifying for seven years from any employment in or under the Government or any local authority of some 4,000 ex-service-men who 'deserted' from the Eire Forces to join the United Kingdom Forces-a measure described in the Dáil by the Deputy Leader of the Opposition as equivalent to a sentence of seven years['] starvation.[53]

The dismissal and disqualification of deserters was presented as evidence of Dublin's indifference to veterans from the British forces. De Valera would not look after them, Addison and Griffith argued; the harsh nature of EPO 362 was ample illustration of that. It was up to the British government to take care of their interests. De Valera had been trying since 1939 to entice the British to the negotiating table, and had been consistently rebuffed. The swift dismissal of Irish army deserters lent urgency to the arguments of those who wanted to open talks with Ireland, and handed de Valera an unexpected bonus.

The Seven-Year Ban

Of all the provisions of EPO 362, the one that has generated the most controversy is the seven-year disqualification from government-funded employment. It is easy to think that it was a straightforward attempt to discriminate against deserters by a spiteful and vindictive Fianna Fáil government, but a closer look suggests an alternative explanation. The government put together a significant package of concessions for ex-members of the Irish Defence Forces after the war, and many government jobs were reserved for them. To avail of these, ex-army men had to possess a military discharge certificate, stating that they had a clean service record. Those dismissed under EPO 362 were not entitled to a discharge certificate, and were therefore barred from government jobs in any case. They were placed in the same situation as Irish volunteers, who had left civilian life to enlist in the British forces. They too, having not served in the Irish forces, were at a disadvantage when it came to getting state jobs in Ireland. The employment concessions for ex-Irish army men were left in place until December 1953, eight-and-a-half years after the end of the war – and one-and-a-half years longer than the seven-year disqualification. This meant that even when the seven years were up, a deserter still had little chance of landing a state job because of the lack of the discharge certificate. In a way, then, the seven-year disqualification was redundant. It may have been designed as a way for the de Valera government to look as if it was taking stern measures to punish deserters, while in reality it had a limited impact on them.

Furthermore, had the Fianna Fáil government really put its mind to it, there were several other ways in which it could have victimised returning deserters. Under the Order, they were still allowed to claim unemployment benefit in Ireland, if they had sufficient contributions to the fund. The Order specifically stated that 'such dismissal shall not constitute a discharge for the purposes of the Unemployment Insurance Act, 1945'. Defence Minister Oscar Traynor later explicitly and sarcastically confirmed this in the Dáil.[54] They were also given all pay and allowances due to them up to the day they deserted – and we can safely assume that the Department of Finance would have welcomed the chance to recoup that money. They were not exempted from the ex-servicemen's Unemployment Insurance Agreement with Great Britain in 1946, nor did they forfeit their citizenship when they left. By contrast, US citizens and deserters who enlisted in the Canadian forces before December 1941 were stripped of their citizenship and there was a $10,000 fine or imprisonment for anyone caught recruiting for outside armies.[55] There can be no doubt that there were some in the government who were hostile towards deserters, but de Valera did not allow the punishment to get out of hand. In fact, all the parties in the Dáil, Fine Gael included, agreed that it was necessary to punish deserters in some fashion, and the Labour leader William Norton said in May 1945 that deserters should not get pensions at all.[56]

It is also possible that the seven-year ban was designed to be a stern deterrent to any future deserters. The Irish army was being reduced to its peace-time level of approximately seven thousand men as the war ended: a force of this size could not sustain the high rates of desertions suffered during the Emergency. Historian Liam Canny has illustrated that between April 1945 and March 1946, 252 soldiers out of a total strength of 6,662 left their posts, a desertion rate of 3.78 per cent.[57] The British forces, despite being in the process of demobilising their war-time forces, were still recruiting and attracting a high number of Irish enlistments. Department of Defence estimates showed that in April 1945 around thirty men a week were leaving Ireland to sign up.[58] Cathal remembered 'at least twenty' others from independent Ireland joining with him in 1945. He knew the RAF would still be recruiting even during the last days of the war because Britain still had world-wide military commitments: 'they needed replacements so they were glad to get anybody.' The British government itself estimated that a total manpower of over two million would be needed for the forces after the war.[59] EPO 362 was revoked by the SR&O (Statutory Rules & Orders) No. 95 in 1946, but was then built into the Defence Forces (Temporary Provisions) Act of 1946. The fact that it was included in regular military legislation after the war suggests that it was not intended for Irish Emergency deserters alone, but as a disincentive for any potential future deserters. De Valera's solution to the deserter issue was undoubtedly harsh, but it was also pragmatic and limited.

Conclusion

Responding to an enquiry from a British Army major as to the potential treatment of deserters in post-war Ireland, the Department of Defence wrote that since EPO 362 dismissed deserters from the army, 'The question of arresting such ex-soldiers on their return to Éire after a period of absence from the State does not, therefore, arise.'[60] This would have come as a relief to many who absconded during the war. Many had left in a hurry, disillusioned with life in the Irish Defence Forces which had become more and more arduous and boring as the war went on. When they wanted to return in 1945, the government had to find a way to appropriately punish deserters without inviting diplomatic complications. By choosing to use emergency powers legislation, rather than military law, de Valera chose the path of least resistance, ensuring that the problem was dealt with swiftly, cheaply and with the minimum amount of adverse international publicity. The seven-year ban was undoubtedly harsh, and may also have been redundant, given that Irish ex-servicemen from the British forces would have limited access to government jobs in any case. Pragmatism, not malice, guided de Valera's hand in dealing with the deserter issue, as it had with so many other issues in post-war Ireland.

Conclusion

On 29 March 1927, the Minister for Justice in the Irish Free State government, Kevin O'Higgins, rose in the Dáil to speak on the motion before the House. The Senate had recommended that a Joint Committee be created to consider whether or not to hand over the grounds of Merrion Square to the Irish National War Memorial Trust, in order to build a memorial to the Irish men who had died during the First World War. O'Higgins opposed the proposal on the government's behalf. The grounds for their resistance was that any monument built in Merrion Square would be directly opposite Leinster House and, as O'Higgins put it, 'that any intelligent visitor, not particularly versed in the history of the country, would be entitled to conclude that the origins of this State were connected with that park and the memorial in that park, were connected with the lives that were lost in the Great War in France, Belgium, Gallipoli and so on.'[1] This clashed with how the men who ran the Free State viewed themselves and the origins of the country they had taken over in 1922. Rather than the First World War, they saw the Free State's roots lying in the Home Rule party, through to the Easter 1916, which was then embraced by the Irish population in the 1918 election, which in turn lead onto the Treaty in 1921. Although O'Higgins' speech was long and somewhat incoherent, on this point he was clear.

> It is on that Treaty won in that way that this State and its Constitution are based and I submit to Deputies it is not wise to suggest that this State has any other origin than those...It would be lacking in a sense of truth, in a sense of historical perspective, a sense of symmetry, to suggest that the State has not those origins,

but that it is based in some way on the sacrifice of those who followed the advice of the Parliamentary representatives of the day and recruited in great numbers to the British Army to fight in the European War.[2]

In other words, the existence of the Irish Free State owed nothing to hundreds of thousands of Irishmen who had volunteered to fight in the First World War. O'Higgins was quick to point out that he had nothing against the men themselves, and that he hoped that 'their sacrifice will always have respect and reverence in Ireland'.[3] O'Higgins himself had two brothers in the British forces, one of whom was killed on the Western Front. It was ironic that O'Higgins was effectively dismissing their service when he opposed the building of the Merrion Square memorial.

In the immediate aftermath of the Second World War, Eamon de Valera trod a very similar path to O'Higgins, who ironically would have been a bitter opponent of the Fianna Fáil leader. De Valera had already made his opinion plain during the Easter Rising celebrations in April 1941, in which he – like O'Higgins before him – claimed responsibility for Irish independence for himself, in the process sidelining both his political opponents and Irish ex-servicemen of both world wars. This process was continued at the end of the Second World War. On 13 May 1945, Winston Churchill spoke to the British nation, recapping the course of the war and Britain's part in the ultimate victory. However, the issue of neutrality clearly still frustrated him and he launched a scathing attack on Ireland, de Valera's refusal to allow the Allies to use Irish bases, and the presence of Axis diplomats in Ireland during the war. He suggested that the British government was tempted to invade Ireland when denied use of Irish ports, but he also praised the 'temper and instinct of thousands of Southern Irishmen who hastened to the battle-front to prove their ancient valour' and singled out 'Lieutenant-Commander Esmonde, VC, or Lance-Corporal Connolly, VC, and Captain Fegen, VC, and other Irish heroes that I could easily recite'. Although the reference to Ireland was short – only 283 words in a speech which was 3,547 words long – it caused uproar and anger in Ireland. De Valera's reply three days later was deliberately measured and understated, and he was determined to seize the moral high ground from Churchill. Dublin was still reeling from the storm of protest that de Valera's visit to the German Legation had provoked, and Churchill's speech gave the Taoiseach the opportunity he needed to recover. He defended Irish neutrality, explicitly linking it to partition, and invoked the 'spoliations, famines, massacres in endless succession' of British rule in Ireland to justify his policy. Like O'Higgins, he sidelined the contribution of Irish ex-servicemen during the war. In fact, despite Churchill's direct mention of Irish volunteers in the British forces, de Valera ignored them entirely. In his own speech to the Irish nation at the end of the war, he showered thanks on the Irish Defence Forces, the auxiliary formations, the coast watchers, the Air Raid wardens and the Knights of Malta; Irish ex-servicemen were entirely absent. The Fianna Fáil party organ, the *Irish Press*, was full of praise for the speech, and sold commemorative copies of it from their offices. De Valera's speech set in stone the dominant narrative of Irish neutrality: Ireland had escaped the war through its own efforts, Fianna Fáil's leadership and the strength of the Defence Forces.

The actions of both O'Higgins and de Valera are examples of how Irish ex-servicemen have consistently been victims of how the Irish government presented Irish history. In the 1920s, the deaths of Irishmen in the First World War contradicted O'Higgins's story of the purity of the nationalist bloodline, from the Home Rule party down to the Free State government. In 1945, Irish veterans of the Second World War had the potential to expose the extent to which Irish neutrality – which Fianna Fáil was claiming full credit for – relied on the goodwill of the Allies. Between 1939 and 1945, a rigid censorship, assiduously manipulated by Fianna Fáil for their own benefit, removed the moral framework of the war and reinforced de Valera's biased version of neutrality. This meant that by 1945, many Irish people saw the war through the distorted looking-glass of their own experiences. For instance, in November 1946, the *Connacht Tribune* ran a two-part series pointing out that 'the first concentration camps known to history' had been established by Oliver Cromwell on Inisboffin and the Aran Islands. 'The experiment of liquidating a whole nation by means of mass murder and deportation is not unknown to the student of Irish history,' said the author, after pointing out that 'Belsen, Dachau and Auscwitz [*sic*]…were the worst features of World War No.2.'[4] Similarly, one woman, writing to the *Irish Press* in October 1945, pointed out that Ireland had a duty to help the victims of the war in Europe; the Irish public understood their suffering, she said, because of 'our own sorrowful heritage of "to hell or to Connaught"'.[5] Attitudes such as these had an immediate impact on Irish veterans of the war. Kenneth felt that he and his comrades had been 'airbrushed out of history' and Albert said it was as if he had been 'frozen out' of Irish society. Kevin, who left Dublin to join the Royal Fleet Air Arm, detected what he described as an 'indefinable feeling, of not really being welcome' when he came home in September 1946.[6]

This focus on neutrality meant that there was no space left in public discourse for Irish ex-servicemen. Unlike in Britain, they were not an integral part of Irish society, but peripheral to it. Their economic and physical well-being was not the focus of government policy, as it was in the UK. Nor did they have unrestricted access to public spaces for their Remembrance ceremonies. The November commemorations were often contested and disrupted by republicans or right-wing groups, who saw ex-servicemen and their symbols – particularly the Poppy – as agents of British imperialism. Certain classes of ex-servicemen were singled out for special treatment by the Irish government. Those who were caught returning in uniform and deserters from the Irish army were sanctioned, even if the penalties for being caught were not too severe or, in the case of the seven-year ban, arguably redundant.

Irish ex-servicemen reacted to being sidelined in a number of ways. Thousands returned to the UK after the war, dissatisfied with their life in Ireland. Those who remained behind developed their own coping mechanisms. Frank simply returned to work after the war and gave his time in the Irish Guards little thought. Despite there being a British Legion branch close by in Longford, Frank never joined. When interviewed in 2008, he revealed that he had never worn his medals and that he had not kept any photographs of himself in uniform. Cathal, on

Danny, the Irish soldier who was fed up working in the bog, cutting turf... 'we were supposed to be soldiering'.

the other hand, became determined to succeed despite the obstacles placed in his way. He drew strength from his time in the RAF and went on to become a successful journalist and broadcaster, both in Ireland and in the UK. He never hid the fact that he had been a volunteer and sometimes used his demob pass in order to obtain extra cigarettes from a shopkeeper who was friendly towards veterans.

For the most part, however, Irish ex-servicemen turned to their organisations and clubs for comfort in the chilly atmosphere of post-war Ireland. Although the British Legion was the dominant association, there were a host of others: the Men of Eire, the Aircrew Association, the Burma Star, the Royal Air Force (Comrades) Association, the Royal Artillery Association, just to mention a few. All of these existed within a tight-knit veteran community. In effect, veterans created what could realistically be called a sub-culture within Irish society: they built up a whole network of associations, clubs and celebrations for ex-servicemen only. They carried on their own commemorative ceremonies, replete with flags, banners, decorations and songs which had special significance to themselves. Their service in the British forces set them apart from the Irish public at the end of the war and their participation in ex-service associations further emphasised their separateness. These connections permeated the workplace, and LDF veteran Thomas's testimony shows that ex-servicemen sought each other out in the Guinness brewery. The sociologist Michael Clarke has argued that sub-cultures are 'clearly defined by the evidence as to who is in and who is out...and most importantly that there is a feeling that being in is significant.'[7] Irish ex-servicemen used this feeling of belonging to something bigger to carve their own niche in Irish society.

It is no wonder that ex-servicemen sought to recreate the feeling of comradeship and togetherness generated by the forces. Time and again veterans spoke warmly of the friends they had made and the bonds they had created while in uniform. Irving fondly remembered his comrades: 'You never, no matter how friendly you are with people in civilian life, you never get the same comradeship that you get in the Army or Navy or Air Force. I presume it was because you were all in it together, and you didn't know if you'd be alive the next day', he commented. Kenneth had great memories of the African soldiers who were under his command, men whom he trained, fought and drank alongside with. His extensive photo collections of his time in Africa show an enduring fascination and fondness for his comrades.

Kenneth Salutes his Comrades.

Benedict Anderson, in his classic study *Imagined Communities: Reflections on the Origins and Spread of Nationalism*, described all nations as 'imagined' because 'the members of even the smallest nation will never know most of their fellow-members, meet them, or even hear of them, yet in the minds of each lives the image of their communion.'[8] It could be argued that Irish volunteers, by enlisting in the British forces, wearing the uniform and partaking in the Allied war effort (even if it was only in a small capacity), became part of a larger imagined *Allied* community. They built up connections with all sorts of people from all over the world – Albert with the Canadians, Kenneth with Africans – and the only thing most of them had in common was that they were all fighting on the same side. This imagined community included British civilians as well: those who were on the 'Home Front' endured their own type of war, and even the term 'Home Front' implies parity with the fighting men. Romie Lambkin felt this sense of solidarity; while standing in a roomful of soldiers and sailors waiting for a radio broadcast by Churchill, she thought '…it is a good feeling…being part of a whole uniformed audience standing to attention in wartime.'[9] They came home with an extra dimension added to their sense of identity: Irish men and women who had experienced the Second World War. This only served to increase the distance between ex-servicemen and Irish society. The majority of Irish civilians were not members of this 'imagined community'; they experienced the 'Emergency' in Ireland, shortages of tea, petrol, unemployment and emigration instead.

Irish ex-servicemen also unwittingly threatened to undermine the foundations of the basic myth of independent Ireland. Irish nationalism rested on the assertion that the Irish and British were two separate peoples, and that the British colonisation had interrupted the development of Irish culture. In much the same way as Kevin O'Higgins had suggested the First World War was irrelevant to Ireland, in September 1939 de Valera declared that Ireland wished to remain outside the war to 'rebuild her own civilisation'[10] and during the war spoke about Ireland spending 'seven and a half centuries…in chains'.[11] Dublin pursued policies such as the revival of the Irish language and the protection of

Irish industries, all of which highlighted Ireland's distinctiveness from Britain. As we have seen, de Valera was also willing to provoke the anger of Allied leaders to emphasise Ireland's separateness and independence, as his visit to the German Legation in May 1945 demonstrated. However, the fact that so many Irish citizens chose to join the British forces dented this image.

Even worse, from Fianna Fáil's point of view, many volunteers saw no contradiction in fighting for Ireland and supporting neutrality while wearing a British uniform. Irish veterans proved that Irish people could have multiple loyalties – to the Allies, to London, to their regiments, to their associations, to their comrades – and still be loyal Irish citizens. Over and over again, interviews with veterans illustrated the multi-layered nature of Irish identity. Kenneth, Albert and Don all came from pro-British backgrounds but felt more Irish when they returned from the war than when they left. Jack's family produced a succession of British soldiers, but also a die-hard republican who could not believe that his brothers had fought in British uniform; Hilda's family included members of the IRA, the Black and Tans and Blueshirts; Danny considered joining the British forces, then Eoin O'Duffy's contingent to fight for Franco before joining the Irish army in 1940. But the Fianna Fáil government seemed unable – or unwilling – to process this phenomena and ex-servicemen sensed wariness from the government towards them. Cathal always felt that to fit into the Ireland to which he returned in 1948, 'you had to have a fainne, to be a Catholic and, preferably, to be a member of the Fianna Fáil party.'

Ex-servicemen were also isolated because they did not have a political voice in post-war Ireland. There was no counterpart to William Redmond's National League after 1945. Fine Gael, which evolved from Cumann na nGaedheal, carried a pro-British, or at least a pro-Common-wealth, tag for many years and may have been considered to be the natural home for Irish ex-servicemen. But its support for Irish neutrality drained away much of its distinctiveness and throughout the war Fine Gael struggled to wriggle free of Fianna Fáil's tight grip on Irish politics. Cosgrave did attempt to redefine the party's position during the

Emergency, and in July 1940 he suggested in a letter to de Valera that Fine Gael would support an Irish declaration of war.[12] However, by then neutrality was the only game in town. In 1942, when James Dillon spoke out in favour of the Allies, particularly the United States, he was forced to resign from the party.[13] By 1945, it was a beaten team and in electoral decline. Fine Gael's frustration at playing second fiddle is evident in accusations of dictatorship levelled at de Valera by Richard Mulcahy after the war, and Fianna Fáil dominance is illustrated in Gerald Boland's sardonic reply: 'Are we to take it then that dictatorships are formed as a result of an election by a majority of electors?'[14] The party's evolution away from its Cosgravite roots was completed in 1948 when the Republic was declared under the stewardship of Fine Gael Taoiseach John A. Costello.

If Fine Gael was not an acceptable option for ex-servicemen, then the Labour Party seems the next obvious choice. In 1945 British general election, which surprisingly toppled Winston Churchill, demobbed ex-servicemen voted mostly for Labour,[15] but things were different in Ireland. The labour movement was fragmented and at war with itself. The Labour Party also supported neutrality and in 1943, the party leader William Norton forcefully denied in the Dáil that he had ever donned a British uniform in the past.[16] In truth, none of the three major parties held any real attraction for returning servicemen.

At the same time, Irish ex-servicemen were not about to form their own political party or pressure groups. There was no tradition of ex-service political activism for Irish veterans to follow after 1945. The largest veteran's association, the British Legion, remained committed to a non-political stance, although it did occasionally consult the government on ex-service matters. Ireland's brief flirtation with ex-service militancy, the Army Comrades Association, had collapsed in chaos in the mid-1930s. It could be argued that the Irish political arena was stony ground upon which a dedicated ex-servicemen's party would struggle to grow, but the simple fact was that there was no impulse from Irish ex-servicemen to establish one. As we have already seen, there were multiple reasons why Irish men and women left the country to join the

British forces, and in most cases, each individual had several personal motivations to join. It is not a viable argument that Irish veterans could have formed a coherent voting bloc after the war. All that held them together was their time in British uniform and after they returned, their family backgrounds, economic circumstances, religion and personal opinions pulled them away in other directions to various political parties. Jack, for instance, went on to represent Labour in the Seanad, while Frank was (and remains) a staunch Fianna Fáil supporter. Their war service brought them together in their clubs, their associations and their commemorative ceremonies; but it not a strong enough centrifugal force to bind them together politically.

However, we must also acknowledge that, despite the government's wary attitude towards ex-servicemen, there was no concerted campaign against them. Research in the government archives revealed no evidence of government-inspired discrimination. The paths of ex-servicemen and the government rarely crossed. True, Dublin placed restrictions on commemoration ceremonies, stopped Irish veterans wearing their uniforms and punished Irish deserters, but these measures were largely inspired by maintaining the public face of neutrality or by Fianna Fáil realpolitik. On no occasion did de Valera indicate, or even hint, that he was motivated by a sense of vindictiveness towards Irish ex-servicemen. The worst charge that can be levelled against de Valera and his ministers is that they were largely indifferent to Irish ex-servicemen. But if we are going to condemn de Valera for this, then we must also condemn the Irish public after the war as well. De Valera mostly followed the same path W.T. Cosgrave had walked before him: he kept Irish veterans, their associations and their ceremonies at arm's length, but was not hostile towards them.

In recent years, matters have changed a great deal. The success of the peace process in Northern Ireland undoubtedly has a great deal to do with the improved relations between ex-servicemen and the Irish state, as does Ireland's increasing self-confidence. Commentators such as Ronald Ingelhart and Christian Welzel have theorised that societies become more open and tolerant once they pass through the 'survival' phase of their development. Once the population stop thinking in terms of day-to-day economic survival and take stability and continuity for granted, then group concerns shift towards issues such as political activism, minority rights and self-expression.[17] Since the foundation of the State in 1922, Ireland has undergone a series of crises: civil war, political instability, paramilitary threats, the situation in Northern Ireland and a series of economic recessions. By contrast, the 1990s and 2000s have seen both the sustained economic success of the so-called Celtic Tiger and the implementation of the Good Friday Agreement in Northern Ireland. Despite the current economic problems, the Republic has become far more self-confident and at peace with itself. This means we are far more willing to accept the more controversial aspects of our past.

Irish recruitment into the British forces has also continued over the years. During the 1991 Gulf War, the journalist Robert Fisk noted that 35 per cent of the Royal Irish Hussars were from the Republic and many of their tanks were named after Irish towns.[18] The *Irish Independent* reported in 2008 that the British forces were taking advantage of Irish military cutbacks by increasing their recruitment in the Republic.[19] After years of ambivalence and silence, the Republic of Ireland seems increasingly ready to embrace its veterans of the British forces. The war memorial park in Islandbridge was rescued from neglect in the 1990s, and was officially opened by the Taoiseach of the time, John Bruton. Following on from the work of people like Kevin Myers, authors such as John Horne, Myles Dungan, Jarlath Dunford and Richard Doherty have uncovered more and more veteran's stories, and books on Irish war experiences have become increasingly popular. Commemorations are now inclusive affairs in July and November, where veterans of British forces stand alongside survivors from Irish UN service. This is all commendable and welcome, but some veteran's stories are still tinged with regret, despite the advances of recent years. One described his feelings poignantly: in England, 'all the streets were decorated, "Welcome home Pat, Welcome home Johnny, George".'[20] But there was no 'Welcome Home Paddy' in Ireland.

Epilogue

As this book goes to print, the issue of deserters during the Second World War has become a topic of heated debate, burning up many column inches in newspaper opinion pages, after Justice Minister Alan Shatter raised the possibility of a pardon for deserters. Currently, the discussion has polarised between two extremes: those who argue that the men deserve a pardon because they fought against Nazism, and those who feel that deserters fled the country in a time of national emergency, putting the nation in danger regardless of where they ended up. It is a topic which has become obscured by emotion. Families of deserters are, understandably, eager to clear their relative's names, while advocates of the Defence Forces are no less passionate in their resistance to a pardon. But when the sentiment has been stripped away – and sensationalist, unhelpful hyperbole such as deserters being 'court-martialled' after death,[1] 'blacklist' and 'starvation order' are removed – we can see that the issue is far more complicated than it seems.

To begin with, the public arguments of both sides contain serious errors. Those who want a blanket pardon ignore the fact that, as Michael Kennedy has pointed out, we cannot be sure if all the deserters fought for the Allies.[2] Some men may have found jobs in British factories, or settled in Northern Ireland, or simply went home to their families. Even the Irish Soldiers' Pardon Campaign (WW2), which bases its argument in favour of a pardon on the fact that deserters were denied the right to defend themselves at a court-martial, assume that all of them subsequently joined the British forces. This viewpoint also suggests that the men deserted for moral reasons, while recent research has shown that it was dissatisfaction with life in the Irish forces or a sense of adventure which prompted most men to desert. Indeed, many Irish veterans' testimonies show that they had no idea of the true nature of the Nazi regime until 1944-45, as we have already seen in this book.

However, the argument that deserters abandoned the country to fight for a potential invader is not wholly tenable either. The Irish government provided many facilities to the Allies during the war, and as the war went on Irish cooperation with the Allies seriously stretched the definition of neutrality. Is it then fair to condemn and punish those deserters who *did* join the British forces or the war industry, for doing openly that which the Irish government was doing secretly – aiding the Allied war effort? In a way, Dublin's two-handed approach to the war – loudly proclaiming neutrality while helping the Allies – has come home to roost sixty years later in the deserter issue.

This leads us to the conclusion that the deserter issue does not stand on its own, but that it is intimately connected to the whole question of Irish neutrality, as evidenced by the sparring between Diarmaid Ferriter and Geoffrey Roberts in the letters pages of the *Irish Times*. Issuing an unconditional pardon to the deserters will call the entire policy of neutrality in the Second World War into question. Indeed, Alan Shatter has moved some way down that road already, saying that 'in the context of the Holocaust, Irish neutrality was a principle of moral bankruptcy'.[3] He is correct in highlighting Ireland's poor record for taking in refugee Jews, that there were some Irish officials who were anti-Semitic, and that de Valera's visit to the German Legation in May 1945 was a bad decision. But viewing history backwards armed with the gift of hindsight is always a dangerous occupation. It is very easy to condemn de Valera for not participating in the war, now that we know the details of the German attempt to exterminate the Jews. But Irish policy makers in 1939 did not know that the Holocaust was going to happen, nor did Allied leaders. Should we censure the Irish government for not knowing in advance that Berlin would use the war to exterminate the Jews of Europe? History is always being re-evaluated and reinterpreted – that is a historian's job – but context is vital. Refashioning history without the proper context is pointless.

There is another viewpoint on the deserter issue: that a pardon will help to create an atmosphere of trust and reconciliation between the Republic and Northern Ireland. Kevin Myers has been a vocal campaigner for this, arguing that the 'spirit of Islandbridge' should be applied to the deserters.[4] Sinn Fein has backed the pardon campaign,[5] as has the DUP.[6] The idea that Irish volunteers in the Second World War can help along a kind of Irish *vergangenheitsbewältigung* is an intriguing one. Voluntary service in the British forces is one of the areas of common ground between north and south, and a thorough investigation of it could lead to a better understanding of a truly Irish contribution to the war.

Because it has become impossible to determine with any accuracy where each and every deserter ultimately ended up – in the British forces, in employment abroad, or at home – it is questionable whether a blanket pardon is the way forward. We simply do not know enough about why they decided to desert and where they went. It would also be very difficult to square the circle of pardoning the deserters, but not devaluing the service of thousands of men who remained in the Defence Forces throughout the war. As already noted, being 'Tadh a' dá thaobh' is what Aiken spoke out against during the war, and it is still hard to see how the present government can simultaneously applaud the men who deserted the Defence Forces while at the same time applauding those who did not. To do so would be to repeat the mistake made by the de Valera government during the war, which contributed to this problem in the first place.

Notes

Introduction

1   British National Archives, Ministry of Pensions and National Insurance [hereafter TNA PIN] 7/286, 'High Commission for Ireland Aide-Memoire Date 30 April 1945 Unemployment Insurance Relation with Eire', notes of a meeting held in the Dominions Office, 31 October 1945.

2   L. Berggren, 'Swedish Fascism: Why Bother?', *Journal of Contemporary History*, 37, 3 (July 2002), p.404.

3   C. Leitz, *Nazi Germany and Neutral Europe During the Second World War* (Manchester: Manchester University Press, 2000), p.127.

4   *Irish Times*, 29 April 1995.

5   F.S.L. Lyons, *Ireland Since the Famine* (London: Fontana, 1973), p.557.

6   Y. McEwen, 'Fian na h-Eireann: Irish Volunteers and Volunteer Deaths in Irish Regiments, 1939–1945' (MSc Thesis, University of Edinburgh, 2003), p.50.

7   TNA PIN 7/286, 'High Commission for Ireland Aide-Memoire Date 30th April 1945 Unemployment Insurance Relation with Eire', notes of a meeting held in the Dominions Office, 31 October 1945.

8   National Archives of Ireland Department of Foreign Affairs [hereafter NAI DFA] P81, 'Recruiting of Irishmen for the British Forces and Position re deserters from the Irish Army', memo by Dan Bryan to Joseph Walshe, 12 January 1944.

9   TNA Dominions Office [hereafter DO] 35/1230, File WX 132/1/24, 'Service of Eire citizens in UK Forces. Statistics of Eire and Ulster contribution in manpower to the fighting forces', letter from Machtig to Maffey, February 1945.

10 E. O'Halpin, *MI5 and Ireland, 1939–1945: The Official History* (Dublin: Irish Academic Press, 2003), p.32.

11 B. Girvin, *The Emergency: Neutral Ireland, 1939–1945* (London: Macmillan, 2006), p.275.

12 M. Wheeler, 'Episodic Memory and Autonoetic Awareness' in Endel Tulving & Fergus Craik (eds), *The Oxford Handbook of Memory* (Oxford: Oxford University Press, 2000), p.597.

13 D. Reynolds, *In Command of History: Churchill Fighting and Writing the Second World War* (London: Penguin, 2004), p.391.

Chapter One

1 T. Bartlett, 'Counter-Insurgency and rebellion' in T. Bartlett & K. Jeffery (eds), *A Military History of Ireland* (Cambridge: Cambridge University Press, 1997), p.249.

2 J. & D. Bowen, *Heroic Option: The Irish in the British Army* (Barnsley: Pen & Sword Books, 2005), p.xiv.

3 *Seanad Debates*, Vol. 8 (9 March 1927), col. 420.

4 E.M. Spiers, 'Army organisation and society in the nineteenth century' in Bartlett & Jeffery, *A Military History of Ireland*, p.336.

5 T. Denman, '"The Red Livery of Shame": The Campaign against Army Recruitment in Ireland, 1899–1914', *Irish Historical Studies*, 29, 114 (November 1994), p.209.

6 D. McCracken, *Forgotten Protest: Ireland and the Anglo-Boer War* (Belfast: Ulster Historical Foundation, 2003), p.46.

7 Denman, 'The Red Livery of Shame', p.213.

8 McCracken, *Forgotten Protest*, p.56.

9 Denman, 'The Red Livery of Shame', p.220.

10 D. Fitzpatrick, 'Militarism in Ireland, 1900–1922' in Bartlett & Jeffery, *A Military History of Ireland*, p.386.

11 D. George Boyce, *Nineteenth Century Ireland: The Search for Stability* (Dublin: Gill and MacMillan, 2005), p.284.

12 P. Karsten, 'Irish Soldiers in the British Army, 1792–1922: Suborned or Subordinate?', *Journal of Social History*, 17, 1 (Autumn, 1983), p.47.

13 T. Kenny, *Galway: Politics and Society, 1910–1923* (Dublin: Four Courts Press, 2011), p.17.

14 D. Fitzpatrick, 'Militarism in Ireland, 1900–1922' in Bartlett & Jeffery, *A Military History of Ireland*, p.397.

15 W. Laqueur (ed.), *Fascism: A Reader's Guide* (Harmondsworth: Penguin, 1979), p.92.

16 S.R. Ward, 'Intelligence Surveillance of British Ex-Servicemen, 1918–1920', *The Historical Journal*, 16, 1 (March 1973), p.183.

17 R.M. Watt, *The Kings Depart. The Tragedy of Germany: Versailles and the German Revolution* (London: Phoenix Press, 2003), p.75.

18 D. Fitzpatrick, *Politics and Irish Life, 1913–1921: Provincial Experience of War and Revolution* (Aldershot: Gregg Revivals, 1993), p.202.

19 M. O'Driscoll, *Ireland, Germany and the Nazis: Politics and Diplomacy, 1919–1939* (Dublin: Four Courts Press, 2004), p.35.

20 R. Bessel, *Germany after the First World War* (Oxford: Clarendon Press, 1995), p.81.

21 Fitzpatrick, 'Militarism in Ireland, 1900–1922', in Bartlett & Jeffery, *Military History of Ireland*, p.400.

22 NAI Department of Justice [hereafter NAI JUS] H/257/10 'British Naval, Military reservists in Saorstát Éireann Police Force' memo 19 February 1925.

23 M. Coleman, *County Longford and the Irish Revolution, 1910–1923* (Dublin: Irish Academic Press, 2006), p.140.

24 P. Hart, 'Michael Collins and the Assassination of Sir Henry Wilson', *Irish Historical Studies*, 28, 112 (1992), p.152.

25   Quoted in Tim Pat Coogan, *Michael Collins: A Biography* (London: Hutchinson, 1991), p.375.
26   Coleman, *County Longford and the Irish Revolution*, p.155.
27   R. English, *Irish Freedom: The History of Nationalism in Ireland* (London: Pan Books, 2006), p.292.
28   J. Leonard, 'Getting them at last: the IRA and Ex-Servicemen' in D. Fitzpatrick (ed.), *Revolution? Ireland 1917–1923* (Dublin: Trinity History Workshop, 1990), p.120.
29   P. Hart, *The IRA and Its Enemies: Violence and Community in Cork, 1916–1923* (Oxford: Oxford University Press, 1999), p.311.
30   Coleman, *County Longford and the Irish Revolution*, p.154.
31   Hart, p.304.
32   Leonard in Fitzpatrick, *Revolution?*, p.124.
33   T. Barry, *Guerilla Days in Ireland* (Dublin: Anvil Books, 1981), p.105.
34   Ibid., p.82.
35   Ibid., p.7.
36   Ibid., p.106.
37   Denman, 'The Red Livery of Shame', p.217.
38   P. Maume, *The Long Gestation: Irish Nationalist Life, 1891–1918*, (Dublin: Gill and Macmillan, 1999), p.209.
39   P. Hart, 'Youth Culture and the IRA' in Fitzpatrick, *Revolution?*, p.22.
40   Coleman, *County Longford and the Irish Revolution*, p.143.
41   J. Borgonovo, *Spies, Informers and the 'Anti-Sinn Féin Society': The Intelligence War in Cork City, 1920–1921* (Dublin: Irish Academic Press, 2007), p.78.
42   Fitzpatrick, 'Militarism in Ireland, 1900–1922' in Bartlett & Jeffery, *A Military History of Ireland*, p.397.
43   Leonard in Fitzpatrick, *Revolution?*, p.129.
44   Leonard, 'Getting Them at Last' in Fitzpatrick, *Revolution?* p.120.
45   C.A. Lockwood, 'From Soldier to Peasant? The Land Settlement Scheme in East Sussex, 1919–1939' in *Albion: A Quarter Journal Concerned with British Studies*, 30, 3 (Autumn, 1998), p.439.
46   British National Archives, Treasury [hereafter TNA T] T160/127, 'Irish Free State – Future administration of certain services which have been established for the benefit of ex-members of the British Military Services', unsigned letter, 15 March 1922.
47   Fitzpatrick, *Politics and Irish Life*, p.156.
48   K. Jeffery, *Ireland and the Great War* (Cambridge: Cambridge University Press, 2000), p.117.
49   J.P. Duggan, *A History of the Irish Army*, (Dublin: Gill and Macmillan, 1991), p.84.
50   J.M. Regan, *The Irish Counter-Revolution, 1921–1936: Treatyite Politics and Settlement in Independent Ireland* (Dublin: Gill and Macmillan, 2001), p.102.
51   E. O'Halpin, 'The Army in Independent Ireland' in Bartlett & Jeffery, *Military History of Ireland*, p.408.
52   Fitzpatrick, 'Militarism in Ireland' in Bartlett & Jeffery, *A Military History of Ireland*, p.399.
53   Regan, *The Irish Counter-Revolution*, p.103.

54 Ibid., p.112.
55 Karsten, 'Irish Soldiers in the British Army, 1792–1922', p.54.
56 J.M. Regan, 'The Politics of Reaction: The Dynamics of Treatyite Government and Policy, 1922–32', *Irish Historical Studies*, 30, 120 (November 1997), p.555.
57 M.G.Valiulis, 'The "Army Mutiny" of 1924 and the Assertion of Civilian Authority in Independent Ireland', *Irish Historical Studies*, 23, 92 (November 1983), p.358.
58 *Dáil Debates*, vol. 19 (22 April 1927), col. 1448.
59 Ibid., vol. 21 (16 November 1927), col. 1397.
60 Ibid., col. 1434.
61 NAI Department of the Taoiseach [hereafter TAOIS] S 5560A, 'Committee on the Claims of British Ex-Servicemen', committee report, 8 November 1928.
62 NAI TAOIS 5560B, Draft statement by Cosgrave, no date.
63 R. Fanning, M. Kennedy, D. Keogh, E. O'Halpin (eds), *Documents on Irish Foreign Policy Volume III, 1926–1932*, p.706, letter from Walshe, 21 November 1930.
64 *Dáil Debates*, vol. 61 (30 April 1936), col. 2022.

Chapter Two

1 P. Galvin, *The Raggy Boy Trilogy* (Dublin: New Island, 2002), p.283.
2 D. Power, *A Long Way from Tipperary* (Clonmel: Glen Publications, 1994), p.13.
3 J. Harte & S. Mara, *To the Limits of Endurance: One Irishman's War* (Dublin: Liberties Press, 2007), p.9.
4 R. Lambkin, *My Time in the War: An Irishwoman's Diary* (Dublin: Wolfhound Press, 1992), p.5.
5 T. Wilson, *The Myriad Faces of War: Britain and the Great War, 1914–1918* (Cambridge: Polity Books, 1988), p.50.
6 B. Novick, *Conceiving Revolution: Irish Nationalist Propaganda During the First World War* (Dublin: Four Courts Press, 2001), p.15.
7 D. Fitzpatrick, 'Militarism in Ireland, 1900–1922' in Bartlett & Jeffery (eds), *A Military History of Ireland*, p.397.
8 Harte & Mara, *To the Limits of Endurance*, p.233.
9 University College Cork Volunteers Oral Archive [hereafter UCCVOA], tape reference A7.
10 Ibid., tape reference 7S.
11 C. Kavanagh, 'Irish and British government policy towards the volunteers' in B. Girvin & G. Roberts, *Ireland and the Second World War: Politics, Society and Remembrance* (Dublin: Four Courts Press, 2000), p.81.
12 Imperial War Museum Sound Archive [hereafter IWMSA], accession no. 25513.
13 Galvin, *The Raggy Boy Trilogy*, p.243.
14 G. Cusack, *Westport Men and Women in the Second World War* (unpublished manuscript), p.1.
15 C. Wills, *That Neutral Island: A Cultural History of Ireland During the Second World War* (London: Faber & Faber, 2007), p.51.
16 National Archives of Ireland, Department of Foreign Affairs [hereafter NAI DFA] 241/65 'Attitude of the Irish Govt towards the calling up of Irish citizens for duty with the British Reserve Defence Forces', letter from Walshe 22 June 1939.

17 NAI DFA 241/76, 'Permission for Irish Civil Servants to enlist in the British Defence Forces', memo, 29 August 1939.

18 Lambkin, *My Time in the War*, p.66.

19 M. Hastings, *Armageddon: The Battle for Germany 1944–45* (London: Macmillan, 2004), p.103.

20 UCCVOA, tape reference 1L.

21 M. Dungan, *Distant Drums: Irish Soldiers in Foreign Armies* (Belfast: Appletree Press, 1993), p.123.

22 Lambkin, *My Time in the War*, p.42.

23 B. Inglis, *West Briton* (London: Faber & Faber, 1962), p.61.

24 M. Connelly, *We Can Take It! Britain and the Memory of the Second World War* (Harlow: Pearson Longman, 2004), p.55.

25 Wills, *That Neutral Island*, p.2–3.

26 Galvin, *Raggy Boy Trilogy*, p.238.

27 TNA Cabinet Papers [hereafter CAB] 129/2, 'The Irish Question in 1945' memo by Maffey to the cabinet, 21 August 1945.

28 UCCVOA, tape reference 7S.

29 UCCVOA, tape reference A14.

30 UCCVOA, tape reference 6S.

31 B. Grob-Fitzgibbon, *The Irish Experience During the Second World War: An Oral History* (Dublin: Irish Academic Press, 2004), p.179.

32 IWMSA Accession no. 19089.

33 A. Calder, *The Peoples' War: Britain, 1939–1945*, (London: Panther Books, 1969), p.478.

34 Y. McEwen, 'Fian na h-Eireann: Irish Volunteers and Volunteer Deaths in Irish Regiments, 1939–1945' (MSc Thesis, University of Edinburgh, 2003).

35 S. McAughtry, *McAughtry's War* (Belfast: Blackstaff Press, 1985), p.6.

36 Ibid., p.7.

37 UCCVOA, tape reference A 15.

38 Cusack, *Westport Men and Women*, p.1.

39 Inglis, *West Briton*, p.64.

40 Ibid., p.65.

41 Ibid., p.67.

42 NAI DFA 241/382, 'Members of the British RAF who are in training in America and are known as the "Squadron of Eire".'

43 Lambkin, *My Time in the War*, p.165.

44 McAughtry, *McAughtry's War*, p.170.

Chapter Three

1 D.Leach, *Fugitive Ireland: European Minority Nationalists and Irish Political Asylum, 1937–2008* (Dublin: Four Courts Press, 2009), p.68.

2 E.O'Halpin (ed.), *MI5 and Ireland, 1939–1945: The Official History* (Dublin: Irish Academic Press, 2003), p.28.

3 *Dáil Debates*, vol. 96 (25 April 1945), col. 2382.

4 TNA CAB 129/2, 'Relations with Eire', memo by Addison, 7 September 1945.

5   Wills, *That Neutral Island*, p.114.
6   R. Service, *Comrades: A World History of Communism* (London: Macmillan, 2007), p.126.
7   W. Churchill, *The Second World War Vol. 1: The Gathering Storm* (London: Cassell & Co. Ltd., 1949), p.382.
8   D. Keogh & A. McCarthy, *Twentieth Century Ireland: Revolution and State Building* (Dublin: Gill and MacMillan, 2005), p.119.
9   University College Dublin Archive [hereafter UCDA], de Valera papers, P150/2604, memo from David Gray to de Valera, 26 April 1941.
10   E. Keane, *An Irish Statesman and Revolutionary: The Nationalist and Internationalist Politics of Sean McBride* (London: Tauris Academic Press, 2006), p.105-106.
11   J. O'Carroll & J.A. Murphy (eds), *De Valera and His Times* (Cork: Cork University Press, 1983), p.117.
12   UCDA, de Valera papers, P150/2604, message from Roosevelt to de Valera, 26 February 1942.
13   E. O'Halpin, *MI5 and Ireland*, p.30.
14   NAI DFA 241/233, 'Release from the British armed Forces of persons required for specialist duties in the Irish Defence Forces', letter from Dulanty, 8 March 1941.
15   Ibid., letter from the British Admiralty, 9 July 1941.
16   NAI DFA 241/233, 'Release from the British armed Forces of persons required for specialist duties in Irish Defence Forces', letter to Maffey, 30 July 1943.
17   TNA CAB 66/21/37, 'Memorandum on Irish policy received from the United Kingdom Representative to Eire', 2 February 1942.
18   C. Leitz, *Nazi Germany and Neutral Europe During the Second World War* (Manchester: Manchester University Press, 2000), pp.75, 106.
19   A. Nolan, *Joseph Walshe: Irish Foreign Policy 1922–1946* (Cork: Mercier Press, 2008), p.266.
20   UCDA, de Valera papers, P150/2658, draft reply to American Note, no date.
21   NAI DFA 241/322, 'Application from Irish Persons for Permission to join American Forces', memo 4 August 1942.
22   NAI DFA 241/251, letter from John A Belton, 17 June 1941.
23   NAI DFA 241/322, 'Application from Irish Persons for Permission to join American Forces', letter from Walshe, 31 July 1943.
24   M. Gilbert, *Auschwitz and the Allies: How the Allies Responded to the News of Hitler's Final Solution* (London: Michael Joseph, 1981), p.325.
25   UCDA, de Valera papers, P150/2689, 25 May 1945, letter from an Irish Major.
26   Leach, *Fugitive Ireland*, p.73.
27   Brian Hanley, '"No English Enemy…Ever Stooped so Low": Mike Quill, de Valera's visit to the German Legation and Irish-American Attitudes during World War II', *Radharc*, 5/7, (2004–2006), pp.245–264.
28   NAI TAOIS 97/9/165, 'Picture Post: Ban on issue of 27/vii, '40.'
29   UCDA, de Valera papers, P150/2637, 'De Valera's Neutrality' by William J.M.A. Maloney.
30   Girvin, *The Emergency*, p.258.
31   TNA CAB 66/21/37, 'Memorandum on Irish policy received from the United

Kingdom Representative to Eire', 2 February 1942.

32   Girvin, *The Emergency*, p.259.

33   *Dáil Debates*, vol. 93 (25 April 1944), col. 1454.

34   TNA Dominions Office [hereafter DO] 35/1230, File WX 132/1/24, 'Service of Eire citizens in UK Forces. Statistics of Eire and Ulster contribution in manpower to the fighting forces', letter from Machtig to Maffey, February 1945.

35   R. Fisk, *In Time of War: Ireland, Ulster and the Price of Neutrality, 1939–1945* (London: Gill and Macmillan, 1985), p.285.

36   *Irish Times*, 13 May 1945.

37   T.D. Davis, *Dublin's American Policy: Irish-American Diplomatic Relations, 1945–1952* (Washington: Catholic University of America Press, 1998), p.53.

38   *Longford Leader*, August 1945.

39   *British Legion Journal*, 25, 6, Irish Supplement, June 1945, p.(i).

40   NAI TAOIS S15262, Ireland's contribution to the Second World War, *Foreign Affairs* article 'Unneutral Neutral Eire'.

41   NAI TAOIS S15262, 'Ireland's Contribution to the Second World War 1939–1945', letter from John Ward, 10 February 1952.

42   D. Henderson (ed.), *Prelude to Leadership: The European Diary of John F. Kennedy Summer 1945* (Washington: Regnery Publishing, 1995), p.25–6.

43   E. O'Halpin, 'Irish-Allied Security Relations and the "American Note" Crisis: New Evidence from British Records', *Irish Studies in International Affairs*, 11, (2000), p.73.

44   NAI DFA 341/11, 'Demobilisation and Resettlement of Irish men and women serving with the British forces', letter from Gray to Gough, 16 January 1946.

45   Girvin, *The Emergency*, p.267.

46   DFA NAI 250/14, 'British Commonwealth "Common Foreign Policy" Proposal', *Irish Press* cutting, 20 June 1946.

47   Davis, *Dublin's American Policy*, p.10.

48   TNA CAB 129/2, 'Relations with Eire', memo by Addison, 7 September 1945.

49   G. Roberts, 'Neutrality, Identity and the challenge of the Irish Volunteers' in D. Keogh & M. O'Driscoll (eds), *Ireland in World War Two: Neutrality and Survival* (Cork: Mercier Press, 2004), p.279.

50   *Irish Press*, 12 October 1945.

51   TNA PIN 7/286, 'High Commission for Ireland Aide-Memoire Date 30th April 1945 Unemployment Insurance Relation with Eire', 'U.I Relations with Eire – a few facts', undated memo.

52   Girvin, *The Emergency*, p.264.

53   M. Kennedy & V. Laing, *The Irish Defence Forces 1940–1949: The Chief of Staff's Reports* (Dublin: Irish Manuscripts Commission, 2011), p.89.

54   Wills, *That Neutral Island*, p.208.

55   J. Duggan, *A History of the Irish Army* (Dublin: Gill & Macmillan, 1991), p.208.

56   Keogh & McCarthy, *Twentieth Century Ireland*, p.126.

57   J. Bardon, 'Northern Ireland and the Irish in the British Army' in Keogh & O'Driscoll, *Ireland in World War Two*, p.266.

58   M. Dungan, *Distant Drums: Irish Soldiers in Foreign Armies* (Belfast: Appletree Press, 1993), p.149.

59   UCCVOA, tape reference L13.

60   C. Brinton, *The United States and Britain* (London: Oxford University Press, 1945), p.116.

61   Whelan, *Ireland and the Marshall Plan, 1947–1957* (Dublin: Four Courts Press, 2000), p.39.

62   Davis, *Dublin's American Policy*, p.104.

63   E. Keane, *An Irish Statesman and Revolutionary*, p.114.

Chapter Four

1   Harte & Mara, *To the Limits of Endurance*, p.113.

2   Ibid., p.113.

3   NAI DFA 341/11, 'Demobilisation and Resettlement of Irish men and women serving in the British Forces', unsigned letter, 16 January 1946.

4   B. Shepard, *A War of Nerves: Soldiers and Psychiatrists, 1914–1994* (London: Pimlico, 2002), p.317.

5   A. Allport, *Demobbed: Coming Home After World War Two* (London: Yale University Press, 2009), p.203.

6   NAI DFA 341/11, 'Demobilisation and Resettlement of Irish men and women serving in the British Forces', 5 May 1945.

7   UCCVOA, tape reference 6S.

8   Shepard, *A War of Nerves*, p.321.

9   G. Caforio, *Handbook of the Sociology of the Military* (New York: Plenum Publishers, 2003), p.215.

10   UCCVOA, tape reference A6.

11   UCCVOA, tape reference 7S.

12   I.C.B. Dear (ed.), *The Oxford Companion to World War II* (Oxford: Oxford University Press, 2001), p.97.

13   S. Friedländer, *The Years of Extermination: Nazi Germany and the Jews, 1939–1945* (London: Weidenfeld & Nicolson, 2007), p.656.

14   L. Snyder, *The Encyclopedia of the Third Reich* (New York: Paragon House, 1989), p.246.

15   UCCVOA, tape reference 3L.

16   L. James, *The Rise and Fall of the British Empire* (London: Abacus, 2007), p.548.

17   M. Hastings, *Nemesis: The Battle for Japan, 1944–45* (London: Harper Perennial, 2008), p.64.

18   Allport, *Demobbed*, p.44.

19   McAughtry, *McAughtry's War*, p.138.

20   L. Rees, *Their Darkest Hour* (London: Ebury Press, 2008), p.8.

21   R. Doherty, *Irish Volunteers in the Second World War* (Dublin: Four Courts Press, 2000), p.196.

22   L. O'Flaherty, *Return of the Brute* (Dublin: Merlin Publishing, 1998), p.135–6.

23   J. Bourke, 'Effeminacy, Ethnicity and the End of Trauma: The Sufferings of "Shell-Shocked" Men in Great Britain and Ireland, 1914–1939', *Journal of Contemporary History*, 35, 1, Special Issue: Shell-Shock (January 2000), p.68.

24   S.E. Ambrose, *Band of Brothers: E Company, 506th Regiment, 101st Airborne from Normandy to Hitler's Eagle Nest* (New York: Touchstone, 2001), p.203.

25   B.H. Chermol, 'Wounds Without Scars: Treatment of Battle Fatigue in the US Armed Forces in the Second World War', *Military Affairs*, 49, 1 (January 1985), p.9.

26   Allport, *Demobbed*, p.209.

27   HSE Ballinasloe, 2 May 1946, letter from Acting Chief Clerk to Galway County Manager.

28   HSE Ballinasloe, Hospital Admission Book, 'Register of Patients from County Roscommon in Ballinasloe District Lunatic Asylum.'

29   J. Bourke, *An Intimate History of Killing: Face-to-Face Killing in Twentieth Century Warfare* (London: Granta Books, 2000), p.257.

30   J. Robins, *Fools and Mad: A History of the Insane in Ireland* (Dublin: Institute of Public Administration, 1986), p.197.

31   Allport, *Demobbed*, p.195.

32   *British Legion Journal*, 27, 7, Irish Supplement, July 1947, p.(i).

33   Shepard, *War of Nerves*, p.169.

34   Chermol, 'Wounds Without Scars', p.10.

35   UCCVOA, tape reference A17.

36   Doherty, *Irish Volunteers in the Second World War*, p.311.

37   Harte & Mara, *To the Limits of Endurance*, p.160.

38   Ibid., p.156.

39   UCCVOA, tape reference S11.

40   UCCVOA, tape reference A10.

41   P. Cunningham, 'War Hero', in *The Dublin Review*, 31 (Summer, 2008), p.103.

42   *British Legion Journal*, 25, 11, Irish Supplement, November 1945, p.(i).

Chapter Five

1   D. Ferriter, *The Transformation of Ireland 1900–2000* (Dublin: Profile Books, 2004), p.375.

2   R. Fanning, *The Irish Department of Finance, 1922–1958* (Dublin: Institute of Public Administration, 1978), p.395.

3   C. Ó Gráda & J.Neary, 'Protection, Economic War and Structural Change: The 1930s in Ireland', *Irish Historical Studies*, 27, 107 (May, 1991), p.262.

4   E. O'Connor, *A Labour History of Ireland 1824–1960* (Dublin: Gill & Macmillan, 1992), p.137.

5   NAI TAOIS, 3/230, undated memo from Industry and Commerce.

6   UCDA, Aiken Papers, P104/3697, 'Utilisation of our labour reserves at present listed in the Employment Exchanges or going to England' letter to de Valera, 24 February 1942.

7   IWMSA, accession no. 20299.

8   G. FitzGerald, *All in a Life: An Autobiography* (Dublin: Gill & Macmillan, 1991), p.26.

9   C. Ó Gráda, *A Rocky Road: The Irish Economy since the 1920s* (Manchester: Manchester University Press, 1977), p.8.

10   *Irish Press*, 26 May 1945.

11   *Irish Times*, 31 January 1947.

12   Kennedy & Laing, *The Irish Defence Forces*, p.xxi.

13   D. Murphy, *The Irish Brigades, 1685–2006* (Dublin: Four Courts Press, 2007), p.279.

14   Kennedy & Laing, *Irish Defence Forces*, p.365.

15   Ibid., p.xxxiii.

16   Ibid., p.xliv.

17   Department of Defence, Military Archives, [hereafter DDMA] 'General Commentary History of Emergency Period Part I: General Commentary', p.25.

18   DDMA, 'General Commentary History of Emergency Period Part I: General Commentary', p.73.

19   UCDA, de Valera papers, P150/2694.

20   DDMA, 'General Commentary History of Emergency Period part I: General Commentary', p.74.

21   DDMA, 94263 'GRO Demobilisation and Resettlement', unsigned memo, 29 September 1945.

22   NAI, Department of Industry and Commerce [hereafter IND/E], IND/E 13/1/28 'State Sponsored Bodies: Employment Concessions for Ex-Servicemen recruited after 1st January 1951', 'Concessions as regard employment in the Civil Service for persons who have had service in the Defence Forces and Auxiliary Defence Forces', 15 December 1948.

23   DDMA, 'General Commentary History of Emergency Period Part I: General Commentary', p.76.

24   Ibid.

25   Ibid.

26   Ibid.

27   NAI Government Information Service [hereafter GIS] 2/15, 9 August 1945.

28   *Dáil Debates*, vol. 129, (February 1952), col. 469-470.

29   See note 22.

30   NAI TAOIS CAB 2/8, Cabinet Minutes 18 June 1946.

31   DDMA 94263, 'G.R.O. Demobilisation and Resettlement', unsigned memo 19 January 1953.

32   NAI IND/E 13/1/28, 'State Sponsored Bodies: Employment Concessions for Ex-Servicemen recruited after 1st January 1951'.

33   DDMA, 2/94 947, letter from MacMahon, 14 April 1948.

34   Ibid., memo from J Noone, 25 July 1948.

35   R.J. Evans, *The Coming of the Third Reich* (London: Penguin, 2004), p.9.

36   W. H. Wandel, 'Unemployment Insurance and the Returning Serviceman' *Annals of the American Academy of Political and Social Science*, 227 (May 1943), p.136.

37   C.L. Jamison, 'Re-Employment of Ex-Servicemen in Public Positions' in *Annals of the American Academy of Political and Social Science*, 227 (May 1943), p.107.

38   R. England, 'Canada's Program to Aid Its Veterans' *Annals of the American Academy of Political and Social Science*, 238, March 1945, p.95.

39   UCDA, de Valera papers, P150/2694.

40   Ibid., P150/2506.

41   McAughtry, *McAughtry's War*, p.168.

42   *Ministry of Labour & National Service Report for the Years 1939–1946* [Cmd.7225] HC 1947, 147.

43   A. Calder, *The Peoples' War: Britain, 1939–1945* (London: Panther, 1969), p.658.

44   Ibid.

45   Girvin, *The Emergency*, p.271.
46   Guinness Archives [hereafter GA], GDB PE01.0050, letter to the board, 22 December 1900.
47   GA, GDB PE01.0049, letter, 3 September 1915.
48   R. Dennison, & Oliver MacDonagh, *Guinness 1886–1939: From Incorporation to the Second World War* (Cork: Cork University Press, 1998), p.231.
49   GA, GDB PE01.0049, memo from AHC Barker, 2 September 1919.
50   GA, GDB/CO04.06/0090.
51   Ibid., Draft Board Order, 5 September 1939.
52   GA, GDB CO04.06/0106, table 'Number Serving with the Forces, 30 June 1945.'
53   GA, GDB CO04.09 0001.02, Brewery Annals.
54   GA, GDB/CO04.06/0039.19, 'Extract of a letter written by Mr. Carlyle stating the position in future with regard to ex-service candidates competing at the examination', 10 January 1950.
55   GA, GDB/CO04.06/0039.19, List of successful candidates, 2 December 1949.
56   N. Meehan, 'Shorthand for Protestants: Sectarian Advertising in the *Irish Times*', *History Ireland*, 17, 5, p.46.
57   T. Garvin, 'The Anatomy of a Nationalist Revolution: 1858–1928', *Comparative Studies in Society and History*, 28, 3 (July 1986), p.499.
58   *Dáil Debates*, vol. 21 (16 November 1927), col. 1399.
59   E. Delaney, '"Almost a Class of Helots in an Alien Land": The British State and Irish Immigration, 1921–45' in D. MacRaild (ed.), *The Great Famine and Beyond: Irish Migrants in Britain in the Nineteenth and Twentieth Centuries* (Dublin: Irish Academic Press, 2000), p.255.
60   J. Wolf, '"Withholding their Due": The Dispute Between Ireland and Great Britain Over Unemployment Insurance Payments To Conditionally Landed Irish Wartime Volunteer Workers', *Saothar*, xxi (1996), p.39.
61   NAI DFA 241/199, 'Recruitment of men in Ireland for British munitions works', 1 November 1940.
62   NAI TAOIS S6091A, 'Assistance being offered to Irish citizens to enlist in the British Army', 7 May 1941.
63   NAI DFA 328/11, 'Unemployment Insurance of Irish Workers in Gt Britain and Northern Ireland', memo by Boland, 20 June 1945.
64   J.J. Lee, *Ireland 1912–1985: Politics and Society* (Cambridge: Cambridge University Press, 1990), p.227.
65   Allport, *Demobbed*, p.28.
66   Ibid., p.173.
67   Fisk, *In Time of War*, p.468.
68   Ibid., p.526.
69   *Hansard, series 5 (Commons)*, vol. 434 (12 March 1947) col. 1326.
70   W. Cohen, 'The Federal Government's Program for Ex-Servicemen', *Annals of the American Academy of Political and Social Science*, 238, 'Post-war Jobs for Veterans', (March 1945), p.64.
71   B. Girvin & G. Roberts, 'The Forgotten Volunteers of World War II', *History Ireland*, 6, 1 (Spring, 1998), pp.46–51.
72   UCDA, de Valera papers, P150/2646, *Irish Press*, 9 October 1942.

73   NAI TAOIS, s12900, 'Planning for the Post War Situation'.
74   Girvin, *The Emergency*, p.258.
75   NAI TAOIS S6091B, 'British Armed Forces: Enlistment of Irish Citizens', letter from the British Legion, 18 September 1945.
76   *British Legion Journal*, 27, 10, Irish Supplement, October 1947, p.(i).
77   NAI TAOIS S6091B, 'British Armed Forces: Enlistment of Irish Citizens', letter from Lemass to Moynihan, 17 October 1945.
78   NAI TAOIS S 13065 A, memo from Lemass.
79   C. Kavanagh, 'Irish and British government policy towards the volunteers' in Girvin & Roberts, *Ireland and the Second World War*, p.88.
80   R. McNamara, 'Blueprints from Britain: Irish Responses to Post-War Plans' in D. Keogh & M. O'Driscoll (eds), *Ireland in World War Two: Neutrality and Survival* (Cork: Mercier Press, 2004), p.253.
81   *Dáil Debates*, vol. 98 (7 November 1945), col. 745.
82   Ibid., col. 745.
83   TNA CAB 129/8, Cabinet Conclusions, 13 March 1946.
84   NAI TAOIS S 13065 A, letter from Bevin to Dulanty, 11 February 1943.
85   NAI DFA 328/11, letter from Walshe to Dulanty, 21 April 1945.
86   Allport, *Demobbed*, p.23.
87   Ibid., p.26.
88   TNA Ministry of Pensions [hereafter PIN] 7/286, 'High Commission for Ireland Aide-Memoire date 30th April 1945: Unemployment Insurance Relations with Eire', unsigned memo 'Unemployment Insurance Relations with Eire', 14 May 1945.
89   TNA DO 35/1230, WX 132/59, 'Unemployment Insurance Benefits for Eire Volunteers and Workers', letter from Hugh Dalton to Christopher Addison, 19 February 1946.
90   TNA PIN 7/286, letter from the Treasury to the Ministry of National Insurance, 6 December 1945.
91   TNA DO 35/1230, WX 132/59, 'Unemployment Benefit for Southern Irishmen. Note of a meeting held at the Dominions Office on the 5th October, 1945.'
92   DDMA 2/64848, 'Harbour Defences Pay and Allowances of British Military Cadre English Ratings Etc', letter from External Affairs to Defence, 12 December 1938.
93   TNA CAB 195/4, Cabinet conclusions, account of Dulanty's visit, 26 June 1946.
94   TNA PIN 7/286, Treasury memo to Ministry of National Insurance, 6 December 1945.
95   NAI TAOIS S6091A, Petition sent to Atlee, November 1945.
96   TNA Cabinet discussions, [hereafter CAB] 195/4, 21 March 1946.
97   NAI GIS 2/15, undated government press release.
98   TNA CAB 128/5, Cabinet Conclusions, 21 March 1946.
99   TNA PIN 7/287, 'Instructions to legal division', 14 October 1946.
100   *Hansard, series 5 (Commons)* vol. 427, (15 October 1946), col. 861.
101   Ibid., col. 862.
102   Ibid., col. 866.
103   Ibid., col. 864.

104 *Dáil Debates*, vol. 103 (28 November 1946), col. 1680.

105 Ibid., col. 1691.

106 TNA PIN 7/287, 'Instructions to Legal Division', 'Legislation to Implement an Arrangement with the Government of Eire for the Payment of unemployment benefit in Eire to Men and Women discharged from H.M. (United Kingdom) Forces, undated memo.

107 NAI Office of the Secretary of the President [hereafter PRES] /1/P2932 'Unemployment Insurance Act 1946'.

108 *Hansard, series 5 (Lords)*, vol. 148 (18 June 1947), col. 933.

109 *Hansard, series 5 (Lords)*, vol. 152 (26 November 1947), col. 936.

110 TNA PIN 7/287, 'Instructions to Legal Division', 'Details of Payments of Special benefit under the Unemployment Insurance (Eire Volunteers) Act, 1946', undated list.

111 TNA PIN 7/347, 'Payment made under NI Act 1946 for continuance of payment of benefit to Eire Volunteers after 5-7-8', 'Memo on the payment of Special Benefit in Eire Unemployment Insurance (Eire Volunteers) Act, 1946.', memo by J.F. Danielli, 5 April 1949.

112 NAI Department of Social Welfare [hereafter SW] 1A/93/53, 'Social Welfare Reciprocal Arrangements Act 1948 Bill File', note dated Meitheamh (June) 1948.

113 TNA CAB 129/8, 'Joint Memorandum by the Secretary of State for Dominion Affairs and the Minister of National Insurance', 13 March 1946.

114 TNA PIN 7/347, 'Regulations made under NI Act 1946 for continuance of Payment of Benefit to Eire Volunteers after 5-7-48', memo from Danielli, 5 April 1949.

115 NAI DFA 341/11, 'Demobilisation and Resettlement of Irish men and women serving in the British Forces', unsigned letter, 16 January 1946.

116 *Ministry of Labour & National Service Report for the Years 1939–1946* [Cmd.7225] HC 1947, 189.

117 NAI DFA P81, 'Recruiting of Irishmen for the British Forces and Position re: deserters from the Irish Army', memo from Walshe, 3 December 1945.

118 Ibid.

119 NAI DFA 328/11/A, 'Unemployment Insurance for Irish Workers in Great Britain and Northern Ireland', memo by Lemass, 3 September 1946.

120 Ó Gráda, *A Rocky Road*, p.21.

Chapter Six

1 A. Dolan, *Commemorating the Irish Civil War: History and Memory, 1923–2000* (Cambridge: Cambridge University Press, 2003), p.3.

2 Jeffery, *Ireland and the Great War*, p.93.

3 J. Leonard, 'The Twinge of Memory', in English, *Unionism in Modern Ireland*, p.102.

4 Ibid.

5 NAI JUS 8/684, Commissioner's Office report, 26 November 1929.

6 *Irish Times*, 12 November 1930.

7 *Irish Times*, 11 November 1932.

8 UCDA, Aiken Papers P104/3712, 'Confidential: Office of the Minister for Justice Departmental Notes on Events, from 1st January to 31st December 1940.'

9   B. Hanley, *The IRA, 1926–1936* (Dublin: Four Courts Press, 2002), p.73.

10   K. Jeffery, p.131.

11   B. Sexton, *Ireland and the Crown, 1922–1936: Governor-Generalship of the Irish Free State* (Dublin: Irish Academic Press, 1989), p.100.

12   D. Fitzpatrick, 'Commemoration in the Irish Free State: a chronicle of embarrassment' in I. McBride (ed.), *History and Memory in Modern Ireland* (Cambridge: Cambridge University Press, 2001), p.193.

13   Ibid., p.191.

14   D. Keogh & G. Doherty (eds), *De Valera's Irelands* (Cork: Mercier Press, 2003), p.140.

15   R. Dunphy, *The Making of Fianna Fáil Power in Ireland, 1923–1948* (Oxford: Clarendon Press, 1995), p.64.

16   Sexton, *Ireland and the Crown*, p.119.

17   D. Ó Drisceoil, *Censorship in Ireland 1939–1945: Neutrality, Politics and Society* (Cork: Cork University Press, 1996), p.37.

18   NAI JUS 8/684, 'Armistice Celebrations Poppy Day 1928–1936', Garda report, 12 November 1928.

19   Ibid., letter to Justice, 8 November 1928.

20   NAI TAOIS S3370D, list of government attendance at Armistice/Remembrance ceremonies, 22 May 1948.

21   NAI TAOIS S 4156B, 'Opening of Irish National War Memorial', memo of 15 December 1938.

22   NAI PRES 1/P1820, 'President—Pro-British Incidents', 'Armistice Day Celebrations 1938' memo by McDunphy, 11 November 1938.

23   *British Legion Journal*, 26, 12, Irish Supplement, December 1946.

24   NAI PRES 1/P2102, 'Armistice Day Celebrations 1939', clipping from the *Evening Mail* 'Poppy Fund Appeal', 31 October 1939.

25   NAI TAOIS S3370D, memo of 23 September 1948.

26   Ó Drisceoil, *Censorship in Ireland*, p.109.

27   NAI TAOIS S3370D, 'Summary of restrictions on parades', 23 October 1948.

28   Ó Drisceoil, *Censorship in Ireland*, p.109.

29   *Irish Times*, 12 November 1940.

30   NAI TAOIS S 11409, 'Easter Week – 1916 Twenty-Fifth Anniversary Commemorations 1941', letter from Defence, 6 May 1940.

31   Ibid., letter from de Valera, 9 August 1940.

32   Ibid., 25 October 1940.

33   Ibid., letter from Beary, 19 December 1940.

34   Ibid., letter from de Valera, 11 January 1941.

35   *Irish Independent*, 14 April 1941.

36   *Irish Times*, 14 April 1941.

37   *Irish Press*, 14 April 1941.

38   D. Peifer, 'Commemoration of Mutiny, Rebellion and Resistance in Postwar Germany: Public Memory, History and the Formation of "Memory Beacons"', *The Journal of Military History*, 65, 4 (October 2001), p.1016.

39   D. Ferriter, *Judging Dev: A Reassessment of the Life and Legacy of Eamon de Valera* (Dublin: Royal Irish Academy, 2007), p.13.

40   NAI PRES/1/P2085, 'Armistice Day Celebrations 1941'.

41   NAI PRES/1/P2085, 'Armistice Day 1941' *Irish Independent* clipping, 12 November 1941.
42   M. Mazower, *Hitler's Empire: Nazi Rule in Occupied Europe* (London: Penguin Books, 2009), p.448.
43   B. Inglis, *West Briton*, p.64.
44   NAI JUS 8/978, 'Victory Day celebrations, Flying of Flags, etc 1949–1954', instructions to Gardaí, 24 April 1945.
45   Ibid., memo from Stephen Roche to the Garda Commissioner, 5 May 1945.
46   *Irish Press*, 8 May 1945.
47   Ibid.
48   *Irish Press*, 9 May 1945.
49   NAI JUS 8/978, 'Victory Day celebrations, Flying of Flags, etc 1949–1954.', Garda reports.
50   NAI TAOIS S9950A, 10 May 1945.
51   *Evening Mail*, 21 August 1945.
52   F.R. De Meneses, 'Investigating Portugal, Salazar and the New State: The Work of the Irish Legation in Lisbon, 1942–1945', *Contemporary European History*, 11, 3 (August 2002), p.405.
53   B. Barton, *The Blitz: Belfast in the War Years* (Belfast: Blackstaff Press, 1999), p.295.
54   *Dáil Debates*, vol. 98 (15 November 1945), col. 1242.
55   Ibid., col. 1244.
56   Ibid., col. 1247.
57   *British Legion Journal*, 27, 4, Irish Supplement, April 1946, p.(i).
58   *British Legion Journal*, 26, 12, Irish Supplement, December 1945.
59   *Irish Times*, 12 November 1945.
60   NAI TAOIS S3370D, list of restrictions, 23 October 1948.
61   Ibid.
62   NAI TAOIS S3370D, letter from Humphries to JA Costello, 1 October 1948.
63   Jane Leonard, 'The Twinge of Memory: Armistice Day and Remembrance Sunday in Dublin since 1919' in R. English & G. Walker (eds), *Unionism in Modern Ireland: New Perspectives on Politics and Culture* (London: Macmillan Press, 1996), p.108.
64   NAI DFA P81, 'Recruiting of Irishmen for the British Forces and Position re deserters from the Irish Army', memo from Dan Bryan, 16 October 1943.
65   NAI PRES/1/P1220, 'National War Memorial Unauthorised Reference to President', 22 February 1939.
66   NAI PRES/1/P1820, 'President—Pro-British Incidents', 19 February 1939.
67   Ibid., 'The President and British Incidents', 4 October 1940.
68   NAI PRES/1/P1820, 'President—Pro-British Incidents', 'Design of the crest of the Irish Red Cross Society', 18 September 1939.
69   NAI PRES/1/P3007, 'Armistice Day 1942'.
70   *Dáil Debates*, vol. 95 (9 November 1944), col. 797.
71   NAI DFA 365/30, 'The British Legion', letter from Lt.-Col. John Lucy, 4 August 1945.
72   Ibid., 4 September 1946.
73   Ibid., letter from Belton to Walshe, undated.
74   Grob-Fitzgibbon, *The Irish Experience During the Second World War*, p.179.

75   *Irish Times*, 7 February 1946.

76   *Dáil Debates* Vol. 101 (25 June 1946), col. 2399.

77   Ibid., col. 2398.

78   Ibid., col. 2402.

79   *British Legion Journal*, 26, 8, Irish Supplement, August 1946, p.(i).

80   NAI DT TAOIS 97/9/574, 'The Royal Air Force (Comrades) Association: Proposed Establishment in Ireland', note 4 May 1945. 'The Secretary of the E/A Department told me yesterday that he would rather if this story was killed—time will settle it!'

81   NAI DFA 241/419, 'The "Men of Eire" Association', letter from Walshe, 27 February 1945.

82   NAI DFA 341/11, 'Demobilisation and Resettlement of Irish men and women serving in the British forces', memo by Walshe, 22 March 1945.

83   TNA DO 35/1230, File WX132/46, 'Resettlement of ex-service personnel in Eire', letter from Maffey to Machtig, 19 March 1945.

84   *British Legion Journal*, 25, 2, Irish Supplement, January – February 1945, p.(i).

85   DFA PRES 1/P5002, 'World Veterans Federation', memo by Michael Rynne, 14 October 1953.

86   NAI TAOIS 97/9/746, memo of 8 March 1947.

87   NAI DFA, 'Demobilisation and Resettlement of Irish men and women serving in the British Forces', letter from the Irish Commonwealth Association, no date.

88   TNA DO 35/1230, File WX 134/46, 'Resettlement of ex-service personnel in Eire', letter from Maffey to Eric Machtig, 19 March 1945.

89   *Irish Times*, 26 October 1983.

90   NAI TAOIS 2000/6/263, memo from Defence, 28 March 1969.

91   Ibid., letter from Lynch, 28 March 1969.

Chapter Seven

1   D. Fitzpatrick, 'Unofficial Emissaries: British Army Boxers in the Irish Free State, 1926', *Irish Historical Studies*, 30, 118 (November 1996), p.213.

2   NAI DFA 241/95, 'Wearing of Foreign Uniforms in Ireland', letter from Department of Justice, 24 April 1928.

3   NAI JUS 8/684, 'Armistice Celebrations Poppy Day 1928–1936', letter from Brun to Garda Commissioner, 19 October 1933.

4   NAI DFA 241/95, 'Wearing of Foreign Uniforms in Ireland', letter from Old IRA Men's Association (Cork No. 1 Brigade), 26 September 1939.

5   Ibid., 23 September 1936, letter from Walshe to Dulanty.

6   Ibid., 14 October, memo by Roche.

7   NAI JUS 8/472, 'German Police Boxing Team Visiting Saorstát Eireann (1937)', memo from Roche, 12 May 1937.

8   NAI DFA 241/95, 'Wearing of Foreign Uniforms in Ireland', 14 October, memo by Roche.

9   Ibid.

10   NAI JUS 8/383, 'Members of army, navy and police of other countries appearing in uniform in the Saorstát', Garda reports from 29 November onwards.

11   NAI DFA 241/95, 'Wearing of Foreign Uniforms in Ireland', Report from DMP Chief Superintendent, 13 October 1936.

12   Ibid., Garda report, 12 December 1936.

13   Ibid., Garda report, 19 October 1936.

14   Ibid., letter from Batterbee, 3 March 1937.

15   Ibid., memo by Walshe, 11 December 1934.

16   G. Mullins, *Dublin Nazi No. 1: The Life of Adolf Mahr* (Dublin: Liberties Press, 2007), p.56.

17   NAI DFA 241/95, 'Wearing of Foreign Uniforms in Ireland', letter from General de Brantes, 29 November 1934.

18   NAI JUS 8/383, 'Members of army, navy and police of other countries appearing in uniform in the Saorstát', memo from Aiken to Boland, 15 September 1939.

19   NAI DFA 241/95, 'Wearing of Foreign Uniforms in Ireland', letter from Old IRA Men's Association (Cork No. 1 Brigade), 26 September 1939 & Boland's reply, 6 October 1939.

20   Ibid., memo from Stephen Roche, 16 November 1939.

21   Ibid., memo from Roche, 16 November 1939.

22   Ibid., memo from Boland, 2 November 1939.

23   Ibid., Copy of draft Bill, November 1939.

24   DFA 241/354, 'Wearing of uniforms by Military, Naval and Air Attachés', letter from Frederick Boland to Liam Archer, 6 January 1943.

25   DFA 241/307, 'Uniforms, Insignia etc of Foreign armies', letter from Irish Legation in Washington, 25 January 1943.

26   NAI JUS 8/383, Garda report, 30 March 1940.

27   Interview with Don.

28   NAI JUS 8/383, Garda report, 26 June 1940.

29   'Dublin, Eire', *History Ireland*, 12, 2, (Summer 2004), p.46.

30   *Connacht Tribune*, 2 June 1945.

31   NAI DFA 366/7, 'American Troops Visiting Ireland 1945–1946.'

32   NAI GIS 2/14, 26 May 1945.

33   *Dáil Debates*, vol. 97 (4 July 1945), col. 1786.

34   Roberts, 'Neutrality, Identity and the challenge of the Irish Volunteers' in Keogh & O'Driscoll, *Ireland in World War Two*, p.5.

35   NAI DFA 241/95, 'Wearing of Foreign Uniforms in Ireland', memo from Roche, 16 November 1939.

36   NAI TAOIS S 1741 B, 'British Army: Wearing of Uniforms and Carrying Arms in Ireland', letter of 4 May 1953.

37   Ibid., letter of 26 November 1953.

38   *Longford Leader*, 5 January 1946.

Chapter Eight

1   R. Doherty, *Irish Men and Women in the Second World War* (Dublin: Four Courts Press, 1999), p.41.

2   NAI TAOIS S/3644, letter to T.M. Healy, 29 February 1924.

3   TNA Home Office [hereafter HO] HO 45/16964, 'Return of Deserters from

the United Kingdom to the Dominions', memo from L.S. Brass, 25 January 1923.

4   Ibid., memo by Brass, 5 February 1925.

5   NAI JUS H1665/5, letter from Mulcahy to O'Higgins, 1 May 1923.

6   NAI TAOIS S/3644, 'Governor-General: Deserters from the British Army'.

7   NAI Attorney-General's Office [hereafter AGO] 89/26, 'Arrest of deserters from British forces in Saorstát Eireann', opinion by Costello, 8 October 1926.

8   C. Kavanagh, 'Irish and British government policy towards the volunteers' in Roberts & Girvin (eds), *Ireland and the Second World War*, p.84.

9   NAI TAOIS S6091A, 'British Armed Forces: Enlistment of Irish Citizens', memo s/297, 5 September 1941.

10   Kennedy & Laing, *Irish Defence Forces*, p.69.

11   Wills, *That Neutral Island*, p.108.

12   NAI DFA 241/50, 'Enlistment of Six County Residents in the Irish Defence Forces', undated draft reply by MacMahon.

13   Kennedy & Laing, *Irish Defence Forces*, p.325.

14   Ibid., p.155.

15   NAI DFA P81, 'Recruiting of Irishmen from the British Forces and Position re: deserters from the Irish Army', memo by Dan Bryan, 16 October 1943.

16   Ibid., memo by Dan Bryan to Joseph Walshe, 12 January 1944.

17   Wills, *That Neutral Island*, p.227.

18   Kennedy & Laing, *Irish Defence Forces*, p.184.

19   Ibid., p.227.

20   Interview with Danny.

21   Kennedy & Laing, *Irish Defence Forces*, p.245.

22   IWMSA, Accession 25513.

23   O'Halpin, *MI5 and Ireland*, p.27.

24   NAI DFA P81, 'Recruiting of Irishmen for the British Forces and Position re: deserters from the Irish Army', memo from Dan Bryan to Joseph Walshe, 12 January 1944.

25   P. Young, 'The Irish State Preparedness and Planning for War: Defence and the New Irish State' in Keogh & O'Driscoll, *Ireland in World War Two*, p.31.

26   DDMA, 'General Commentary History of Emergency Period Part I: General Commentary', p.16.

27   Fanning, *The Irish Department of Finance*, p.313.

28   Kennedy & Laing, *Irish Defence Forces*, p.184.

29   Ibid., p.336.

30   Ibid., p.193.

31   *Dáil Debates*, vol. 94 (27 June 1944), col. 1212.

32   NAI DFA 202/1680, 'Issue of Travel Permits to Deserters', draft from Sean McMoráin, 13 April 1943.

33   NAI JUS/8/877, 'Claim for Expenses incurred by the Garda Siochana in the Case of Sergeant John Roberts, RAF Squadron Topcliff Yorkshire – deserter'.

34   NAI DFA 241/95, Wearing of Foreign Uniforms in Ireland', 18 April 1940.

35   Allport, *Demobbed*, p.183.

36   Ibid., p.184.

37   NAI DFA 241/130/1, 'Desertion from the British Army', memo of 20 July 1944.

38   *Daily Express*, 13 June 1945.

39   *Longford Leader*, 7 July 1945.

40   *Daily Express*, 13 June 1945.

41   TNA DO 35/1230, WX 132/50, 'Military Personnel: Position of men who had deserted from Eire army to enlist in the British forces', letter from H.E. Smith, War Office, to R.B. Pugh at Dominions, 30 July 1945.

42   *Dáil Debates*, vol. 97 (17 May 1945), col. 570.

43   *Dáil Debates*, vol. 98 (18 October 1945), col. 400.

44   Ibid., col. 398.

45   Ibid., col. 399.

46   Ibid., col. 442.

47   Ibid., col. 425.

48   Ibid., col. 427.

49   Ibid., col. 406.

50   Ibid., col. 407.

51   TNA CAB 129/2, 'Relations with Eire', memo by Addison, 7 September 1945.

52   TNA CAB 129/2, 'The Irish Question in 1945', memo by Maffey, 21 August 1945.

53   TNA DO 35/1230, WX 132/50, "Unemployment Insurance. Special Arrangements for Ex-servicemen and Industrial workers from Eire', paper presented to the cabinet, 13 March 1946.

54   *Dáil Debates*, vol. 98 (18 October 1945), col. 428.

55   F. Gaffen, *Cross-Border Warriors: Canadians in American Forces, Americans in Canadian Forces* (Toronto: Dundurn Press, 1995), p.47.

56   *Dáil Debates*, vol. 97 (17 May 1945), col. 570.

57   Canny, 'Pariah Dogs', p.234.

58   NAI DFA P81, 'Recruiting of Irishmen for the British Forces and Position re: deserters from the Irish Army', mail check, April-May 1945.

59   Allport, *Demobbed*, p.32.

60   NAI DFA 241/215, letter from Defence to External Affairs, 16 November 1945.

Conclusion

1   *Dáil Debates*, vol. 19, No. 5 (29 March 1927), col. 400.

2   Ibid., col. 403.

3   Ibid.

4   *Connacht Tribune*, 16 November 1946.

5   C. Molohan, *Germany and Ireland, 1945–1955: Two Nation's Friendship* (Dublin: Irish Academic Press, 1999), p.42.

6   UCCVOA, tape reference S13.

7   M. Clarke, 'On the Concept of "Sub-Culture"', *The British Journal of Sociology*, 25, 4 (December 1974), p.433.

8   B. Anderson, *Imagined Communities: Reflections on the Origins and Spread of Nationalism* (London: Verso, 1998), p.7.

9   Lambkin, *My Time in the War*, p.39.

10   'Memorandum by Joseph P. Walshe on Irish neutrality for Eamon de Valera', 25 August 1939, in *Documents on Irish Foreign Policy Volume V*, p.495.

11   UCDA, de Valera papers, P150/2626, Speech, 5 October 1941.

12   UCDA P150/2597, letter from Cosgrave to de Valera, 16 July 1940.

13   M. Manning, *James Dillon: A Biography* (Dublin: Wolfhound Press, 1999), p.176.

14   *Irish Press*, 7 May 1945.

15   Allport, *Demobbed*, p.28.

16   *Dáil Debates*, vol. 91 (1 July 1943), cols. 61–2.

17   R. Ingelhart & C. Welzel, 'How Development Leads to Democracy', *Foreign Affairs*, 88, 2 (March/April 2009), p.40.

18   R. Fisk, *The Great War for Civilisation: The Conquest of the Middle East* (London: Harper Perennial, 2006), p.745.

19   *Irish Independent*, 10 October 2008.

20   UCCVOA, tape reference L15.

Epilogue

1   R. Widders, *Spitting on a Soldier's Grave: Court Martialled after Death, the Story of the Forgotten Irish and British Soldiers* (Leicester: Matador, 2012), p. 75.

2   'Wrong to Assume all Irish Deserters were Allied Veterans', *Irish Times*, 15 February 2012.

3   'Shatter Stirs Things Up on Neutrality', *Irish Times*, 5 February 2012.

4   'Apply Spirit of Islandbridge to WW2 Heroes', *Irish Independent*, 24 May 2011.

5   'Sinn Fein to Back Pardon for War Deserters', *The Times*, 4 January 2012.

6   'Pardon Call for Irish WWII Soldiers', *British Forces News* website http://www.bfbs.com/news/northern-ireland/pardon-call-irish-wwii-soldiers-54357.html, accessed 21 February 2012.

Bibliography

Interviews:

Albert left Dublin in 1941 and joined the RAF in Belfast. He landed in Normandy shortly after D-Day as part of the RAF ground crew, and was attached to Canadian forces as they pushed their way through France, Belgium and Holland. The aerodromes at which he was based were usually temporary ones and he witnessed several Luftwaffe air raids, although they gradually faded away as the war drew to a close and the Allies dominated the skies more and more. Remarkably, he visited Belsen soon after its liberation and saw harrowing sights which haunted him for the rest of his life. He saw out the war in Denmark, where he remained as part of the occupation force. After returning to Ireland, he emigrated to England, where he joined the police force. Albert now lives in Belfast with his wife.

Hilda joined the Army Nursing Service in 1941, leaving Dublin behind in search of adventure, and served in the Far East, all over India and Burma. Her abiding memory of her time in uniform was her encounter with former POWs who had suffered terribly in Japanese camps. She returned to Ireland in December 1945 on board a ship full of POWs, who were both mentally and physically destroyed, and their condition and behaviour left a deep impression on her. Hilda passed away in 2011.

Cathal joined the RAF as a 16 year-old, just as the war was ending and was posted to the Far East, where he remained until 1948 when he returned to Britain to be demobbed. Cathal did not see much action, as he joined so late in 1945, but still felt that the war changed him completely. He returned to Ireland to a career as a journalist and broadcaster. Cathal passed away in 2011.

Irving, also from Dublin, was a young man when he enlisted. He joined the British forces much earlier than Cathal, enlisting in the Royal Artillery in 1940, and trained to be an anti-aircraft gunner. He was present when the Luftwaffe attacked Belfast in April 1941 and saw the city in flames, as well as the destruction in the streets the next day. After that, he was shipped out to Egypt and fought through the North African campaign, before volunteering for an infantry unit and transferring to Italy. When the war ended he was with the British occupation forces in Austria. Subsequently, Irving returned to his job in the Royal Bank and remains in Dublin.

Kenneth also joined the Royal Artillery, in his case leaving Dublin in 1942, and was stationed in Dover, where his anti-aircraft crew was frequently attacked by German cross-channel aircraft. He even witnessed German long-range guns shelling England from bases in France. In 1944 his unit was sent to East Africa – on the way the convoy survived a U-Boat attack – and was attached to a contingent of African soldiers, before being shipped to India. He remained there until the end of the war, and witnessed some terrible violence as post-war India was wracked with civil unrest. He returned to Ireland via a stint in Allied-occupied Italy. Kenneth still lives in Dublin and is an avid collector of militaria.

Joe was another young Dubliner who left to join the RAF in 1941. He initially trained to be a glider pilot and was poised to be at the spearhead of the Allied attack on the Rhine in 1945, but was transferred to the Far East before it took place, although he later heard that his comrades had suffered heavy casualties. In Asia, Joe flew DC-3 Dakotas and B-24 Liberators, mostly doing supply runs, but had an eventful time; sometimes the temporary airstrips they used were recaptured by the Japanese and he had to be careful not to land on an enemy-occupied runway. After the Japanese surrendered, he helped to fly former POWs to transit camps before returning to Europe on a troopship in 1946. His brother was also in the RAF and was a bomb-aimer, who was shot down and killed over Germany. Joe still lives in county Dublin.

Jack was another veteran who saw a remarkable amount of action. He ran away from home in Dublin in 1937 to join the British infantry and served in the Mediterranean and Palestine before the war broke out. He later joined the elite Special Boat Service (SBS) and participated in the British attack on the Dodecanese Islands in 1943. Following some fierce fighting, he was captured by the Germans and spent the rest of the war in a POW camp in Germany, suffering severe health problems as a result. He returned to Ireland after a lengthy recuperation in Britain in 1945. Jack went to work for Guinness, became a Senator and still lives in Dublin.

John, who left his native Kilkenny to join the Irish Guards, also saw his fair share of combat. He was part of the British force which was sent to Norway in 1940 to counter the German invasion, but his troopship was sunk by a Stuka and he was rescued from the sea by a Royal Navy destroyer. His unit later took part in the North African campaign and journeyed on to Italy. John was in the first wave ashore at Anzio in January 1944 and was very badly wounded; his injuries ended his war and he was invalided back to Britain shortly afterwards. John passed away in 2009.

By contrast, **Geoffrey** had a relatively quiet war in the RAF. Leaving Dublin to join in 1941, he became a Leading Aircraft Man and spent much of his time servicing and repairing aircraft. He travelled a great deal around the UK, spending long periods in Scotland and in Northern Ireland, before being transferred to Iceland. He came back to Ireland after the war and became heavily involved in the British Legion, eventually earning an MBE for his work with charity. He still lives in County Dublin.

Frank, an Irishman who was living in England, was conscripted into the Grenadier Guards in 1944. He landed in Europe late in the war and his armoured unit travelled throughout Germany as the war ended. His abiding memories of the war were rounding up Nazi suspects for questioning and the terrible scenes he witnessed at Belsen and the lesser-known concentration camp, Neuengamme. This was so traumatic that he refused to go into details during his interview in 2009. Frank was demobilised in 1947. Although he was conscripted, he too had a military heritage: his cousins served in the Connaught Rangers during the First World War. He came back to Ireland and worked with the OPW. He lives in Roscommon.

Don was an engineering student at Trinity College when war broke out in 1939. He enlisted in the Royal Engineers along with a group of his friends and spent his war in Italy and the Middle East. When he returned to Ireland, he joined Guinness and became a leading figure in the British Legion. He still lives in Dublin.

Thomas joined the Local Security Force and the Local Defence Force during the Emergency, and did a short stint of duty at the internment camp at the Curragh. Thomas went to work for Guinness after the war and came across many ex-servicemen during his time there. He was, and is, involved in many different ventures and lives in Meath with his wife.

Archival Sources:

National Archives of Ireland
Department of the Taoiseach (DT)
Department of Foreign Affairs (DFA)
Department of Justice (JUS)
Department of Industry and Commerce (IND/E)
Department of Social Welfare (SW)
Office of the Secretary of the President (PRES)

Department of Defence, Military Archives (DDMA)

Guinness Archives (GA)

UCD Archives (UCDA)
De Valera Papers
Frank Aiken Papers
John A. Costello Papers

HSE Archives, St. Bridget's Hospital, Ballinasloe
Hospital Record Books
Records of correspondence

University College Cork Volunteers Project (UCCVP)
Tape References: A7
                   6S
                   1L
                   7S
                   S14
                   L15

British National Archives
Ministry of Pensions (PIN)
Ministry of Labour (LAB)
Dominions Office (DO)

Imperial War Museum Sound Archive (IWMSA)
Accession Numbers: 30391
                       25513
                       20299
                       20007
                       19089
                       13262

Manuscripts:

Jones, George Edward, *Life in the RAF 1940–1946*, unpublished manuscript in the possession of the author.

Cusack, Gerardine, *Westport Men and Women in the Second World War*, unpublished manuscript in the possession of the author.

Cusack, Gerardine, *Love and War*, unpublished poetry collection in the possession of the author.

Theses:

Drumm, Alan, 'Forgotten Voices / Concealed Heritages: Three Case Studies of Irishmen, Who Served in the British Army, The Irish in the British Forces 1943–1978', BA Thesis, GMIT, 2006.

McEwen, Yvonne, 'Irish Volunteers and Volunteer Deaths in Irish Regiments, 1939–1945', MSc thesis, University of Edinburgh, 2003.

Published Sources:

Newspapers:
The British Legion Journal
The Catholic Bulletin
The Connacht Tribune
The Daily Telegraph
The Evening Herald
The Evening Mail

The Galway Advertiser
The Irish Independent
The Irish Press
The Irish Times
The Longford Leader
The Sunday Business Post
The Times
The Western People

Magazines:
BBC History
History Ireland
Military Illustrated

Magazine Articles:
Girvin, Brian & Roberts, Geoffrey, 'The Forgotten Volunteers of World War II', *History Ireland*, Vol. 6, No. 1 (Spring, 1998), pp.46–51.
Meehan, Niall, 'Shorthand for Protestants: Sectarian Advertising in the *Irish Times*', *History Ireland*, Vol. 17, No. 5, pp.46–9.
Strachan, Hew, 'What can history teach us about the treatment of returning soldiers?' *BBC History*, Vol. 10, No. 6 (June, 2009), pp.16–17.

Journal Articles:
Akenson, D.H., 'Was De Valera a Republican?', *The Review of Politics*, Vol. 33, No. 2 (April, 1971), pp.233–253.
Bell, J.B., 'Ireland and the Spanish Civil War, 1936–1939', *Studia Hibernica*, No. 9 (1969), pp.137–163.
Berggren, L., 'Swedish Fascism: Why Bother?' in *Journal of Contemporary History*, Vol. 37, No. 3 (July, 2002), pp.395–417.
Bourke, J., 'Effeminacy, Ethnicity and the End of Trauma: The Sufferings of "Shell-Shocked" Men in Great Britain and Ireland, 1914–1939', *Journal of Contemporary History*, Vol. 35, No.1 Special Issue: Shell-Shock (January, 2000), pp.57–69.
Burke, T., '"Poppy Day" in the Irish Free State', *Studies: An Irish Quarterly Review*, Vol. 92, No. 368 (Winter, 2003), pp.349–358.
Canny, L., 'Pariah Dogs: Deserters from the Irish Defence Forces who joined the British Armed Forces during "the Emergency"', *Studia Hibernica*, No. 30, (1998-99), pp.231–250.
Carr, C., W.A. Leitch, R.D. Farrant & A.D. Pringle, 'British Isles', *Journal of Comparative Legislation and International Law*, Third Series, Vol. 30, No. 1/2, (1948), pp.1–24.
Chermol, B.H., 'Wounds Without Scars: Treatment of Battle Fatigue in the U.S. Armed Forces in the Second World War', *Military Affairs*, Vol. 49, No.1, (January, 1985), pp.9–12.
Cohen, W., 'The Federal Government's Program for Ex-Servicemen', *Annals of the American Academy of Political and Social Science*, Vol. 238, 'Post-War Jobs for Veterans' (March, 1945), pp.63–70.
Clarke, M., 'On the Concept of "Sub-Culture"', *The British Journal of Sociology*, Vol. 25, No. 4 (December, 1974), pp.428–441.

Cook, J., 'The Obelisks of Greater Dublin', *Dublin Historical Record*, Vol. 56, No. 2 (Autumn, 2003), pp.146–160.

Cunningham, P., 'War Hero', *The Dublin Review*, No. 31 (Summer, 2008), pp.84–111.

Denman, T., '"The Red Livery of Shame": The Campaign against Army Recruitment in Ireland, 1899–1914', *Irish Historical Studies*, Vol. 29, No. 114 (November, 1994), pp.208–233.

De Meneses, F.R., 'Investigating Portugal, Salazar and the New State: The Work of the Irish Legation in Lisbon, 1942–1945', *Contemporary European History*, Vol. 11, No. 3 (August, 2002), pp.391–408.

Doherty, G., 'National Identity and the Study of Irish History', *The English Historical Review*, Vol. 111, No. 441 (April, 1996), pp.324–349.

England, R. 'Canada's Program to Aid Its Veterans', *Annals of the American Academy of Political and Social Science*, Vol. 238, 'Post-War Jobs for Veterans' (March, 1945), pp.95–102.

Fanning, R., 'Irish Neutrality: An Historical Review', *Irish Studies in International Affairs*, Vol. 1, No. 3 (1982), pp.27–38.

Fitzpatrick, D., 'The Logic of Collective Sacrifice: Ireland and the British Army, 1914–1918', *The Historical Journal*, Vol. 38, No. 4 (December, 1995), pp.1017–1030.

Fitzpatrick, D., 'Unofficial Emissaries: British Army Boxers in the Irish Free State, 1926', *Irish Historical Studies*, Vol. 30, No. 118 (November, 1996), pp.206–232.

Garvin, T., 'The Anatomy of a Nationalist Revolution: 1858–1928', *Comparative Studies in Society and History*, 28, 3 (Jul. 1986), p.499.

Gordon, M.M., 'The Concept of the Sub-Culture and Its Application', *Social Forces*, Vol. 26, No. 1 (October, 1947), pp.40–42.

Hanley, B., '"No English Enemy…Ever Stooped so Low": Mike Quill, de Valera's visit to the German Legation and Irish-American Attitudes during World War II', *Radharc*, Vol. 5/7, (2004–2006), pp.245–264.

Hart, P., 'Michael Collins and the Assassination of Sir Henry Wilson', *Irish Historical Studies*, 28, 112 (1992), p.152.

Ingelhart, R. & C. Welzel, 'How Development Leads to Democracy', *Foreign Affairs*, 88, 2 (March/April 2009), p.40.

Jamison, C.L., 'Re-Employment of Ex-Servicemen in Public Positions', *Annals of the American Academy of Political and Social Science*, Vol. 227, 'Our Servicemen and Economic Security' (May, 1943), pp.104–110.

Jeffrey, K., 'The British Army and Internal Security, 1919–1939', *The Historical Journal*, Vol. 24, No. 2 (June, 1981), pp.377–397.

Karsten, P., 'Irish Soldiers in the British Army, 1792–1922: Suborned or Subordinate?', *Journal of Social History*, Vol. 17, No. 1 (Autumn, 1983), pp.31–64.

Lee, R.A., 'The Army "Mutiny" of 1946', *The Journal of American History*, Vol. 53, No. 3 (December, 1966), pp.555–571.

Leese, P., 'Problems Returning Home: The British Psychological Casualties of the Great War', *The Historical Journal*, Vol. 40, No. 4 (December, 1997), pp.1055–1067.

Lockwood, C.A., 'From Soldier to Peasant? The Land Settlement Scheme in East Sussex, 1919–1939' in *Albion: A Quarter Journal Concerned with British Studies*, 30, 3 (Autumn, 1998), p.439.

Mayo, J., 'War Memorials as Political Memory', *Geographical Review*, Vol. 78, No.1, (January, 1988), pp.62–75.

Meyer, H.J. & E.O. Smigel, 'Job-Seeking and the Readjustment Allowance for Veterans', *The American Journal of Sociology*, Vol. 56, No. 4 (January, 1951), pp.341–347.

Morris, E., '"God Save the King" Versus "The Soldier's Song": The 1929 Trinity College National Anthem Dispute and the Politics of the Irish Free State', *Irish Historical Studies*, Vol. 31, No. 121 (May, 1998), pp.72–90.

Niven, B., 'War memorials at the intersection of politics, culture and memory', *Journal of War and Culture Studies*, Vol. 1, No. 1 (no date), pp.39–45.

Ó Gráda, C. & J.P. Neary, 'Protection, Economic War and Structural Change: The 1930s in Ireland', *Irish Historical Studies*, Vol. 27, No. 107 (May, 1991), pp.250–266.

O'Halpin, E., 'Irish-Allied Security Relations and the "American Note" crisis: New Evidence from British Records', *Irish Studies in International Affairs*, Vol. 11 (2000), pp.71–83.

O'Rourke, K., 'Burn Everything British but Their Coal: The Anglo-Irish Economic War of the 1930s', *The Journal of Economic History*, Vol. 51, No. 2 (June, 1991), pp.357–366.

Ordway, S.H., 'The Veteran in the Civil Service', *Annals of the American Academy of Political and Social Science*, Vol. 238, Post-War Jobs for Veterans (March, 1945), pp.133–139.

Peifer, D., 'Commemoration of Mutiny, Rebellion and Resistance in Postwar Germany: Public Memory, History and the Formation of "Memory Beacons"', *The Journal of Military History*, Vol. 65, No. 4 (October, 2001), pp.1013–1052.

Pope, R., 'British Demobilisation after the Second World War', *Journal of Contemporary History*, Vol. 30, No. 1 (January, 1995), pp.65–81.

Regan, J.M., 'The Politics of Reaction: The Dynamics of Treatyite Government and Policy, 1922–32', *Irish Historical Studies*, 30, 120 (November, 1997), p.555.

Richardson, C., 'Transforming Anglo-Ireland: R.M. Smyllie and the *Irish Times*', *Iris Eireannach Nua*, Vol. 11, No. 4 (Winter, 2007), pp.16–36.

Rosenberg, J.L., 'The 1941 Mission of Frank Aiken to the United States: An American Perspective', *Irish Historical Studies*, Vol. 22, No. 86 (September, 1980), pp.162–177.

Scott, C.-G., 'The Swedish Left's Memory of the International Brigades and the Creation of an Anti-Fascist Post-War Identity', in *European History Quarterly*, Vol. 39 (2009), pp.217–240.

Sorensen, N.A., 'Commemorating the Great War in Ireland and the Trentino: An Essay in Comparative History', *Nordic Irish Studies*, Vol. 2 (2003), pp.121–139.

Stavisky, S., 'Where Does the Veteran Stand Today?' *Annals of the American Academy of Political and Social Science*, Vol. 259, Parties and Politics: 1948 (September, 1948), pp.128–135.

Turpin, J., 'Monumental Commemoration of the Fallen in Ireland, North and South, 1920-60', *Iris Eireannach Nua*, Vol. 11, No. 4 (Winter, 2007), pp.106–119.

Valiulis, M.G., "'The Army Mutiny" of 1924 and the Assertion of Civilian Authority in Independent Ireland', *Irish Historical Studies*, Vol. 23, No. 92 (November, 1983), pp.354–366.

Wandel, W.H., 'Unemployment Insurance and the Returning Serviceman', *Annals of the American Academy of Political and Social Science*, Vol. 227, (May, 1943), pp.136–142.

Ward, S.R., 'Intelligence Surveillance of British Ex-Servicemen, 1918–1920', *The Historical Journal*, 16, 1 (March, 1973), p.183.

Wilson, R.R., 'Neutrality of Eire', *The American Journal of International Law*, Vol.34, No. 1 (January, 1940), pp.125–127.

Wolf, J., "'Withholding their Due": The Dispute Between Ireland and Great Britain Over Unemployment Insurance Payments To Conditionally Landed Irish Wartime Volunteer Workers', *Saothar*, xxi (1996).

Books:

Allport, A., *Demobbed: Coming Home After World War Two* (London: Yale University Press, 2009).

Ambrose, S.E., *Band of Brothers: E Company, 506th Regiment, 101ˢᵗ Airborne from Normandy to Hitler's Eagle Nest* (New York: Touchstone, 2001).

Anderson, B., *Imagined Communities: Reflections on the Origin and Spread of Nationalism* (London: Verso, 1998).

Augusteijn, J. (ed.), *Ireland in the 1930s: New Perspectives* (Dublin: Four Courts Press, 1999).

Barry, T., *Guerilla Days in Ireland* (Dublin: Anvil Books, 1981).

Bartlett, T. and K. Jeffery (eds), *A Military History of Ireland* (Cambridge: Cambridge University Press, 1997).

Barton, B., *The Blitz: Belfast in the War Years* (Belfast: Blackstaff Press, 1999).

Bessel, R., *Germany after the First World War* (Oxford: Clarendon Press, 1995).

Bew, P., *Ireland: The Politics of Enmity, 1789–2006* (Oxford: Oxford University Press, 2007).

Borgonovo, J., *Spies, Informers and the 'Anti-Sinn Féin Society': The Intelligence War in Cork City, 1920–1921* (Dublin: Irish Academic Press, 2007).

Bort, E. (ed.), *Commemorating Ireland: History, Politics, Culture* (Dublin: Irish Academic Press, 2004).

Bourke, J., *An Intimate History of Killing: Face-to-Face Killing in Twentieth Century Warfare* (London: Granta Books, 2000).

Bowen, E., *The Mulberry Tree: The Writings of Elizabeth Bowen*. Edited by Hermione Lee. (London: Virago Press, 1986).

Bowen, J. & D., *Heroic Option: The Irish in the British Army* (Barnsley: Pen & Sword Books, 2005).

Bowen, K., *Protestants in a Catholic State: Ireland's Privileged Minority* (Kingston and Montreal: McGill-Queens University Press, 1983).

Boyce, D.G., *Nineteenth Century Ireland: The Search for Stability* (Dublin: Gill and Macmillan, 2005).

Brinton, C., *The United States and Britain* (London: Oxford University Press, 1945).

Brown, T., *Ireland: A Social and Cultural History 1922–1985* (London: Fontana Press, 1990).

Butler, H., *Escape from the Anthill* (Mullingar: Lilliput Press, 1986).

Caforio, G., *Handbook of the Sociology of the Military* (New York: Plenum Publishers, 2003).

Calder, A., *The People's War: Britain 1939–1945* (London: Panther Books, 1969).

Carroll, J.T., *Ireland in the War Years* (Devon: David & Charles (Holdings), 1975).

Carson, W.A., *Ulster and the Irish Republic* (London: William Cleland Ltd., no date).

Carver, Field Marshal Lord, *Britain's Army in the Twentieth Century* (London: Pan Grand Strategy Series, Pan Books, 1999).

Churchill, W.S., *The Second World War Vol. I: The Gathering Storm* (London: Cassell & Co. Ltd., 1949).

Coleman, M., *County Longford and the Irish Revolution, 1910–1923* (Dublin: Irish Academic Press, 2006).

Connelly, M., *We Can Take It! Britain and the Memory of the Second World War* (Harlow: Pearson Longman, 2004).

Coogan, T.P., *Michael Collins: A Biography* (London: Hutchinson, 1991).

Cronin, M. & J.M. Regan (eds), *Ireland: The Politics of Independence, 1922–49* (London: Macmillan Press, 2000).

Crowe, C., et al (eds), *Documents on Irish Foreign Policy* (5 Vols, Dublin: Royal Irish Academy, 1998–2006).

Davies, N., *Europe at War, 1939–1945: No Simple Victory* (London: Pan Books, 2006).

Davis, T.D., *Dublin's American Policy: Irish-American Diplomatic Relations, 1945–1952* (Washington: Catholic University of America Press, 1998).

Dear, I.C.B. (ed.), *The Oxford Companion to World War II* (Oxford: Oxford University Press, 2001).

Dennison, S.R. & O. MacDonagh, *Guinness 1886–1939: From Incorporation to the Second World War* (Cork: Cork University Press, 1998).

De Valera, E., *Ireland's Stand: Being a Selection of the Speeches of Eamon de Valera During the War (1939–1945)* (Dublin: Gill & Son, 1946).

Diehl, J.M., *The Thanks of the Fatherland: German Veterans after the Second World War* (Chapel Hill & London: University of North Carolina Press, 1993).

Doherty, R., *Irish Men and Women in the Second World War* (Dublin: Four Courts Press, 1999).

Doherty, R., *Irish Volunteers in the Second World War* (Dublin: Four Courts Press, 2000).

Dolan, A., *Commemorating the Irish Civil War: History and Memory, 1923–2000* (Cambridge: Cambridge University Press, 2003).

Douglas, R.M., *Architects of the Resurrection: Ailtirí na hAiséirghe and the fascist 'new order' in Ireland* (Manchester: Manchester University Press, 2009).

Duggan, J.P., *A History of the Irish Army* (Dublin: Gill & Macmillan, 1991).

Dungan, M., *Distant Drums: Irish Soldiers in Foreign Armies* (Belfast: Appletree Press, 1993).

Dungan, M., *Irish Voices from the Great War* (Dublin: Irish Academic Press, 1995).

Dunphy, R., *The Making of Fianna Fáil Power in Ireland, 1923–1948* (Oxford: Clarendon Press, 1995).

Dwyer, R.T., *De Valera's Finest Hour: In Search of National Independence, 1932–1959* (Cork: Mercier Press, 1982).

English, R., *Irish Freedom: The History of Nationalism in Ireland* (London: Pan Books, 2006.

English, R. & G. Walker (eds), *Unionism in Modern Ireland: New Perspectives on Politics and Culture* (London: Macmillan Press, 1996).

Evans, M. & K. Lunn (eds), *War and Memory in the Twentieth Century* (Oxford: Berg, 1997).

Evans, R.J., *The Coming of the Third Reich* (London: Penguin, 2004).

Fanning, R., *The Irish Department of Finance, 1922–1958* (Dublin: Institute of Public Administration, 1978).

Ferriter, D., *Judging Dev: A Reassessment of the Life and Legacy of Eamon de Valera* (Dublin: Royal Irish Academy, 2007).

Ferriter, D., *The Transformation of Ireland, 1900–2000* (London: Profile Books, 2004).

Fisk, R., *In Time of War: Ireland, Ulster and the Price of Neutrality, 1939–1945* (Dublin: Gill & Macmillan, 1985).

Fisk, R., *The Great War for Civilisation: The Conquest of the Middle East* (London: Harper Perennial, 2006).

FitzGerald, G., *All in a Life: An Autobiography* (Dublin: Gill & Macmillan, 1991).

Fitzpatrick, D., *Politics and Irish Life, 1913–1921: Provincial Experience of War and Revolution* (Aldershot: Gregg Revivals, 1993).

Fitzpatrick, D. (ed.), *Revolution? Ireland 1917–1923* (Dublin: Trinity History Workshop, 1990).

Friedländer, S., *The Years of Extermination: Nazi Germany and the Jews, 1939–1945* (London: Weidenfeld & Nicolson, 2007).

Gaffen, F., *Cross-Border Warriors: Canadians in American Forces, Americans in Canadian Forces* (Toronto: Dundurn Press, 1995).

Galvin, P., *The Raggy Boy Trilogy* (Dublin: New Island, 2002).

Gilbert, M., *Auschwitz and the Allies: How the Allies Responded to the News of Hitler's Final Solution* (London: Michael Joseph, 1981).

Girvin, B., *Between Two Worlds: Politics and Economy in Independent Ireland* (Savage: Barnes & Noble Books, 1989).

Girvin, B., *The Emergency: Neutral Ireland, 1939–1945* (London: Macmillan, 2006).

Girvin, B. & G. Roberts (eds), *Ireland and the Second World War: Politics, Society and Remembrance* (Dublin: Four Courts Press, 2000).

Gray, T., *Mr Smyllie, Sir* (Dublin: Gill & MacMillan, 1991).

Gregory, A., *The Silence of Memory: Armistice Day, 1919–1946* (Oxford: Berg, 1994).

Grob-Fitzgibbon, B., *The Irish Experience During the Second World War: An Oral History* (Dublin: Irish Academic Press, 2004).

Hanley, B., *A Guide to Irish Military Heritage* (Dublin: Four Courts Press, 2004).

Hanley, B., *The IRA, 1926–1936* (Dublin: Four Courts Press, 2002).

Harkness, D., *Ireland in the Twentieth Century: Divided Island* (London: MacMillan, 1996.

Harris, R.G., *The Irish Regiments: A Pictorial History, 1683–1987* (Kent: The Nutshell Publishing Company Ltd.,1989).

Hart, P., *The IRA and Its Enemies: Violence and Community in Cork, 1916–1923* (Oxford: Oxford University Press, 1999).

Harte, J. & S. Mara, *To the Limits of Endurance: One Irishman's War* (Dublin: Liberties Press, 2007).

Hastings, M., *Armageddon: The Battle for Germany, 1944–45* (London: Macmillan, 2004).

Hastings, M., *Nemesis: The Battle for Japan, 1944–45* (London: Harper Perennial, 2008).

Hecter, M., *Internal Colonialism: The Celtic Fringe in British National Development, 1536–1966* (London: Routledge & Kegan Paul, 1975).

Henderson, D. (ed.), *Prelude to Leadership: The European Diary of John F. Kennedy Summer 1945* (Washington: Regnery Publishing, 1995).

Holmes, R., *Redcoat: The British Soldier in the Age of Horse and Musket* (London: Harper-Collins, 2002).

Horne, J. (ed.), *Our War: Ireland and the Great War* (Dublin: Royal Irish Academy, 2008).

Hull, M.M., *Irish Secrets: German Espionage in Ireland, 1939–1945* (Dublin: Irish Academic Press, 2003).

Inglis, B., *West Briton* (London: Faber & Faber, 1962).

Jackson, A., *The British Empire and the Second World War* (London: Hambledon Continuum, 2006).

James, L., *The Rise and Fall of the British Empire* (London: Abacus, 2007).

Jeffery, K., *Ireland and the Great War* (Cambridge: Cambridge University Press, 2000).

Keane, E., *An Irish Statesman and Revolutionary: The Nationalist and Internationalist Politics of Sean McBride* (London: Tauris Academic Press, 2006).

Kennedy, M., *Ireland and the League of Nations, 1919–1946: International Relations, Diplomacy and Politics* (Dublin: Irish Academic Press, 1996).

Kennedy, M., *Guarding Neutral Ireland: The Coast Watching Service and Military Intelligence, 1939–1945* (Dublin: Four Courts Press, 2008).

Kennedy, M. & V. Laing (eds), *The Irish Defence Forces 1940–1949: The Chief of Staff's Reports* (Dublin: Irish Manuscripts Commission, 2011).

Kenny, T., *Galway: Politics and Society, 1910–1923* (Dublin: Four Courts Press, 2011).

Keogh, D. & G. Doherty (eds), *De Valera's Irelands* (Cork: Mercier Press, 2003).

Keogh, D., F. O' Shea & C. Quinlan (eds), *The Lost Decade: Ireland in the 1950s* (Cork: Mercier Press, 2004).

Keogh, D. & M. O'Driscoll (eds), *Ireland in World War Two: Neutrality and Survival* (Cork: Mercier Press, 2004).

Keogh D. & A. McCarthy, *Twentieth Century Ireland: Revolution and State Building* (Dublin: Gill and MacMillan, 2005).

Lambkin, R., *My Time in the War: An Irishwoman's Diary* (Dublin: Wolfhound Press, 1992).

Laqueur, W., *Fascism: A Reader's Guide* (Harmondsworth: Penguin, 1979).

Leach, D., *Fugitive Ireland: European Minority Nationalists and Irish Political Asylum, 1937–2008* (Dublin: Four Courts Press, 2009).

Lee, J.J., *Ireland 1912–1985: Politics and Society* (Cambridge: Cambridge University Press, 1990).

Lee, J.J. (ed.), *Ireland 1945–70* (Dublin: Gill & MacMillan, 1979).

Leitz, C., *Nazi Germany and Neutral Europe During the Second World War* (Manchester: Manchester University Press, 2000).

Lyons, F.S.L., *Ireland Since the Famine* (London: Fontana Press, 1973).

MacCarron, D., *Step Together! The story of Ireland's Emergency Army as told by its veterans* (Dublin: Irish Academic Press, 1999).

MacRaild, D. (ed.), *The Great Famine and Beyond: Irish Migrants in Britain in the Nineteenth and Twentieth Centuries* (Dublin: Irish Academic Press, 2000).

Manning, M., *Irish Political Parties: An Introduction*. Studies in Irish Political Culture 3 (Dublin: Gill & Macmillan, 1972).

Manning, M., *James Dillon: A Biography* (Dublin: Wolfhound Press, 1999).

Mansergh, N., *Britain and Ireland* (New York: Longmans, Green & Co. Ltd., 1942).

Maume, P., *The Long Gestation: Irish Nationalist Life, 1891–1918* (Dublin: Gill & Macmillan, 1999).

Maye, B., *Fine Gael 1923–1987: A General History with Biographical Sketches of Leading Members* (Dublin: Blackwater Press, 1993).

Mazower, M., *Hitler's Empire: Nazi Rule in Occupied Europe* (London: Penguin Books, 2009).

McAughtry, S., *McAughtry's War* (Belfast: The Blackstaff Press, 1985).

McBride, I. (ed.), *History and Memory in Modern Ireland* (Cambridge: Cambridge University Press, 2001).

McCabe, I., *A Diplomatic History of Ireland 1948–49: The Republic, The Commonwealth and NATO* (Dublin: Irish Academic Press, 1991).

McCracken, D., *Forgotten Protest: Ireland and the Anglo-Boer War* (Belfast: Ulster Historical Foundation, 2003).

McDaniel, D., *Enniskillen: The Remembrance Sunday Bombing* (Dublin: Wolfhound Press, 1997).

McGlinchey, C., *The Last of the Name* (Cork: Collins Press, 2007).

Mitchell, A. and P. Ó Snodaigh (eds), *Irish Political Documents, 1916–1949* (Dublin: Irish Academic Press, 1985).

Molohan, C., *Germany and Ireland, 1945–1955: Two Nation's Friendship* (Dublin: Irish Academic Press, 1999).

Moynihan, M. (ed.), *Speeches and Statements by Eamon de Valera, 1917–73* (Dublin: Gill & Macmillan, 1980).

Muldowney, M., *The Second World War and Irish Women: An Oral History* (Dublin: Irish Academic Press, 2007).

Mullins, G., *Dublin Nazi No. 1: The life of Adolf Mahr* (Dublin: Liberties Press, 2007).

Murphy, D., *The Irish Brigades, 1685–2006* (Dublin: Four Courts Press, 2007).

Nolan, A., *Joseph Walshe: Irish Foreign Policy 1922–1946* (Cork: Mercier Press, 2008).

Novick, B., *Conceiving Revolution: Irish Nationalist Propaganda During the First World War* (Dublin: Four Courts Press, 2001).

Nowlan, K. & T.D. Williams (eds), *Ireland in the War Years and After, 1939–1951* (Dublin: Gill & Macmillan, 1969).

O'Carroll, J. & J.A. Murphy (eds), *De Valera and His Times* (Cork: Cork University Press, 1983).

O'Connor, E., *A Labour History of Ireland 1824–1960* (Dublin: Gill & Macmillan, 1992).

Ó Drisceoil, D., *Censorship in Ireland, 1939–1945: Neutrality, Politics and Society* (Cork: Cork University Press, 1996).

O'Driscoll, M., *Ireland, Germany and the Nazis: Politics and Diplomacy, 1919–1939* (Dublin: Four Courts Press, 2004).

O'Flaherty, L., *Return of the Brute* (Dublin: Merlin Publishing, 1998).

Ó Gráda, C., *A Rocky Road: The Irish Economy since the 1920s* (Manchester: Manchester University Press, 1977).

O'Halpin, E. (ed.), *MI5 and Ireland, 1939–1945: The Official History* (Dublin: Irish Academic Press, 2003).

O'Halpin, E., *Spying on Ireland: British Intelligence and Irish Neutrality During the Second World War* (Oxford: Oxford University Press, 2008).

O'Reilly, T., *Hitler's Irishmen* (Dublin: Mercier Press, 2008).

Patterson, H., *Ireland since 1939: The Persistence of Conflict* (Dublin: Penguin, 2006).

Perks, R. & A. Thomson (eds), *The Oral History Reader*, 2nd edn., (Oxford: Routledge, 2006).

Power, D., *A Long Way from Tipperary* (Clonmel: Glen Publications, 1994).

Rees, L., *Their Darkest Hour* (London: Ebury Press, 2008).

Rees, L., *World War Two Behind Closed Doors: Stalin, the Nazis and the West* (London: BBC Books, 2009).

Regan, J. M., *The Irish Counter-Revolution, 1921–1936: Treatyite Politics and Settlement in Independent Ireland* (Dublin: Gill & Macmillan, 2001).

Reynolds, D., *In Command of History: Churchill Fighting and Writing the Second World War* (London: Penguin, 2004).

Robertson, D., *Deeds Not Words* (Westmeath: self published, 1998).

Robins, J., *Fools and Mad: A History of the Insane in Ireland* (Dublin: Institute of Public Administration, 1986).

Salmon, T.C., *Unneutral Ireland: An Ambivalent and Unique Security Policy* (Oxford: Clarendon Press, 1989).

Service, R., *Comrades: A World History of Communism* (London: Macmillan, 2007).

Sexton, B., *Ireland and the Crown, 1922–1936: Governor-Generalship of the Irish Free State* (Dublin: Irish Academic Press, 1989).

Share, B., *The Emergency: Neutral Ireland, 1939–1945* (Dublin: Gill & Macmillan, 1978).

Shinwell, E., *When the Men Come Home* (London: Victor Gollancz, 1944).

Shepard, B., *A War of Nerves: Soldiers and Psychiatrists, 1914–1994* (London: Pimlico, 2002).

Sloan, G.R., *The Geopolitics of Anglo-Irish Relations in the Twentieth Century* (London: Leicester University Press, 1997).

Snyder, L.L., *Encyclopedia of the Third Reich* (New York: Paragon House, 1989).

Strachan, H., *The Politics of the British Army* (Oxford: Clarendon Press, 1997).

Streets, H., *Martial Races: The Military, Race and Masculinity in British Imperial Culture, 1857–1914* (Manchester: Manchester University Press, 2004).

Suleiman, S.R., *Crises of Memory and the Second World War* (Cambridge: Harvard University Press, 2008).

Tulving, E. & C. Fergus Craik (eds), *The Oxford Handbook of Memory* (Oxford: Oxford University Press, 2000).

Watt, R.M., *The Kings Depart. The Tragedy of Germany: Versailles and the German Revolution* (London: Phoenix Press, 2003).

Whelan, B., *Ireland and the Marshall Plan, 1947–1957* (Dublin: Four Courts Press, 2000).

Whyte, J.H., *Church & State in Modern Ireland, 1923–1979* (Dublin: Gill & Macmillan, 1984).

Widders, R., *Spitting on a Soldier's Grave: Court Martialled after Death, the Story of the Forgotten Irish and British Soldiers* (Leicester: Matador, 2012).

Wills, C., *That Neutral Island: A Cultural History of Ireland During the Second World War* (London: Faber & Faber, 2007).

Wilson, T., *The Myriad Faces of War: Britain and the Great War, 1914–1918* (Cambridge: Polity Books, 1988).

Wood, I., *Ireland During the Second World War* (London: Caxton Editions, 2002).

Wootton, G., *The Politics of Influence: British Ex-Servicemen, Cabinet Decision and Cultural Change (1917–1957)* (London: Routledge & Kegan Paul, 1963).

Wylie, P., *Ireland and the Cold War: Diplomacy and Recognition, 1949–63* (Dublin: Irish Academic Press, 2006).

Index